ISLAM

ISLAM
THE STRAIGHT PATH

Expanded Edition

John L. Esposito

New York   Oxford
OXFORD UNIVERSITY PRESS
1991

Oxford University Press

Oxford   New York   Toronto
Delhi   Bombay   Calcutta   Madras   Karachi
Petaling Jaya   Singapore   Hong Kong   Tokyo
Nairobi   Dar es Salaam   Cape Town
Melbourne   Auckland

and associated companies in
Berlin   Ibadan

Published by Oxford University Press, Inc.,
200 Madison Avenue, New York, New York 10016

Oxford is a registered trademark of Oxford University Press

Library of Congress Cataloging-in-Publication Data
Esposito, John L.
Islam : the straight path / by John L. Esposito.—Expanded ed.
p. cm.   Includes bibliographical references.
ISBN 0-19-506225-6
1. Islam.   I. Title.
BP161.2.E85   1991
297—dc20   90-30148

2 4 6 8 9 7 5 3

Printed in the United States of America
on acid-free paper

For Jeanette P. Esposito

PREFACE

The reception of *Islam: The Straight Path* by colleagues as well as by non-Muslim and Muslim audiences and its widespread use in academic and ecumenical contexts motivated Oxford University Press to publish an expanded edition for both text and trade use. This has provided me with an opportunity to include brief country case studies that exemplify the themes and issues embodied in the contemporary Muslim experience. The goal of the volume remains essentially the same—to enable readers to understand the faith and practice of Muslims. Because this edition will incorporate a broader nonacademic audience, the use of Arabic has been limited. However, most important technical terms have been retained and indicated in Arabic the first time they appear in the text. The select bibliography has been updated and expanded, as has the glossary.

I continue to be indebted to many colleagues and friends who have been supportive of my work and have taken time out of their busy schedules to discuss matters of mutual interest as well as to critically read portions of my work. Although I cannot mention all of them, three in particular stand out: Yvonne Y. Haddad, James P. Piscatori, and John O. Voll. I remain indebted to Mary Boliver for her secretarial support. Finally, Cynthia A. Read has been the quintessential editor, working with me on all of my Oxford books. Her comments and encouragement have made the process that much more enjoyable.

Wayland, Mass.   J.L.E.
March 1990

PREFACE TO
THE FIRST EDITION

For a number of years, I have taught a variety of courses that require an introductory text on Islam. While there are a number available, none have fully suited my needs. Some, while quite good, are now dated. Others are too long for contexts that require more limited coverage. Most devote a minimum of time to the modern period. After finding that many of my colleagues experienced the same problem, I determined to write an introductory volume that had multiple uses—one that could be used as one of several texts in world religion courses as well as in those courses in Middle East history, politics, and anthropology that require brief background coverage of Islam.

The goal of this volume is to enable readers to understand and appreciate what Muslims believe and practice. Although Muslims maintain that there is one divinely revealed and mandated Islam, there have been and continue to be many Muslim interpretations of Islam. I have tried to select, describe, and analyze those beliefs, practices, issues, developments, and movements that provide some appreciation of that faith which has inspired and informed the lives of a major portion of the world community. Where feasible I have incorporated brief examples from primary texts such as the Quran and traditions of the Prophet for those who might otherwise have no exposure to these formative sources and to motivate further investigation.

As with any introduction, more is omitted than included. This is an inevitable frustration for both the author and the reader. Therefore, a select bibliography is included. Some will be surprised that diacritical marks are not used at all. Full diacriticals are confusing for the beginner and tend to underscore the "foreignness" of materials. Modified use of diacriticals is often of little use in pronunciation.

I am indebted to many colleagues, friends, and students who have both informed my understanding and challenged my presuppositions about the nature of religion, the meaning(s) of Islam, and the vitality of religion in Muslim life. In particular, I have been fortunate to see and experience Islam as a "lived" religion in classes, seminars, and conversations, and in working and living with Muslim colleagues and friends both here and overseas. I owe an enormous debt of gratitude to Ismail and Lois al-Faruqi and to my Muslim fellow graduate students. Statements and teachings about the centrality of God and the Quran, the place of Muhammad, and the function of Prophetic traditions in Muslim life and piety took on a life, vitality, and relevance that was immediately and concretely evident. They brought a dimension of understanding to my study of Islam that has been reinforced and expanded by my work in Muslim societies from the Sudan to Malaysia, where I came to appreciate the unity in diversity that characterizes Islam as it does all of the world's great religions.

I am particularly grateful to several colleagues: professors Yvonne Y. Haddad, James P. Piscatori, Abdulaziz A. Sachedina, and John O. Voll, who read and commented on my manuscript. Although I have benefited greatly from their comments, I alone bear responsibility for the contents. In addition, Mary Boliver has been patient and helpful in typing the bibliography and making last-minute changes.

As in all my work, my parents, my brothers, and particularly my wife, Jean, have provided a context in which to live and learn that has enabled me to be sensitive to issues of faith, identity, and values and that motivates, inspires, and sustains my work.

Wayland, Mass.   J.L.E.

CONTENTS

Illustrations follow page 98.

INTRODUCTION

The Arab oil embargo, the Iranian revolution, the assassination of Anwar Sadat, the threatening pronouncements and acts of Muammar Qaddafi and the Ayatollah Khomeini, American hostages in Lebanon, the
Iran–Iraq war, the Rushdie affair—events in the Muslim world have
captured headlines and made the terms Islam and Muslim common to
many in the West. However, too often it has simply been a knowledge
of stereotypes and distortions, the picture of a monolithic reality dubbed
Islamic fundamentalism, a term often signifying militant radicalism
and violence. Thus Islam, a rich and dynamic religious tradition of almost one billion people, the second largest world religion, has been
buried by menacing headlines and slogans, images of hostage takers and
gun-toting mullahs.

For more than fourteen centuries, Islam has grown and spread from
the seventh-century Arabia of the Prophet Muhammad to a world religion whose followers may be found across the globe. It spawned and
informed Islamic empires and states as well as a great world civilization
that stretched from North Africa to Southeast Asia. In the process, a
great monotheistic tradition, sharing common roots with Judaism and
Christianity, has guided and transformed the lives of millions of believers down through the ages. Characterized by an uncompromising belief
in the one, true God—His revelation and Prophet—Islam developed a
spiritual path whose law, ethics, theology, and mysticism have made it
one of the fastest growing religions both in the past and today. Media
images of Islam have often obscured the fact that Muslims, Jews, and
Christians share much in common; they are indeed all children of Abraham. Like Jews and Christians, Muslims worship the God of Abraham
and Moses, believe in God's revelation and prophets, place a strong
emphasis on moral responsibility and accountability. The vast majority
of Muslims, like most members of other religious traditions, are pious,
hardworking women and men, family and community oriented, who
wish to live in peace and harmony rather than in warfare.

In an increasingly globally interdependent world, mutual under-standing is both important and necessary. Understanding the religion of Islam as well as its reemergence in Muslim politics and society is not only religiously fruitful, but also, as events in recent decades have dem-onstrated, politically important. This volume seeks to explain the faith, the belief, and the doctrines of Islam. It provides a guide to understand-ing how Islam has developed, spread, and informed the faith and lives of Muslims throughout the ages.

Islam: The Straight Path addresses a variety of questions that un-derscore the strength, vitality, and diversity of Islam as well as its role in Muslim history: What is Islam? What do Muslims believe? How does one explain the lure and spread of Islam throughout the world? Have Muslims, like religious believers throughout the world, wrestled with issues of change and reform to assure the continued relevance of Islam to modern Muslim life? What is the Islamic resurgence? How has Islam informed the faith and politics of Muslim life? The answers to these questions are the concerns of all.

The foundation of Islamic belief and practice is the Quran, for Mus-lims the revealed literal word of God, and the example and teachings of the Prophet Muhammad. Chapter 1, "Muhammad and the Quran: Mes-senger and Message," describes the emergence of Islam, focusing in particular on the life and role of the Prophet and the teachings of the Quran regarding God, prophecy and revelation, the purpose and goal of human life, morality, and the afterlife. Where relevant, comparisons are drawn between Muslim, Jewish, and Christian teachings.

The Muslim community has been the central vehicle for the spread and actualization of Islam's universal message and mission. Chapter 2, "The Muslim Community in History," discusses the formation and development of the Muslim community, the phenomenal expansion of Islam, the creation of Islamic empires and states, the emergence of the Sunni and Shii branches of the Islamic community, and the florescence of Islam as a world civilization that made major contributions to the history of philosophy, theology, the sciences, literature, mathematics, astronomy, and medicine.

Muslim faith and practice are rooted in revelation but expressed in a variety of beliefs, attitudes, rituals, laws, and values. Chapter 3, "Reli-gious Life: Belief and Practice," analyzes the development of Islamic theology, philosophy, law, and mysticism. In particular, it discusses the Five Pillars of Islam, those fundamental acts that provide the unity underlying the rich cultural diversity of Muslim life, as well as Muslim family law. As the Five Pillars are the core of a Muslim's duty to worship God, family law is central to social life, providing guidelines for marriage, divorce, and inheritance.

Like all great world religions, Islam has passed through many stages in its development. Throughout its long history, the community has had to respond to internal and external threats to its continued life and vitality. As a result, Islam has a long tradition of religious renewal and reform, extending from its earliest history to the present. The eighteenth century proved to be a turning point in Islamic history. The power, prosperity, and dynamic expansionism of imperial Islam went into decline. A previously ascendant and expanding community and civilization has had to struggle for its survival in the face of indigenous forces and the political and religio-cultural threat of European colonialism. Chapter 4, "Modern Interpretations of Islam," chronicles the rise of Islamic activist ("fundamentalist") movements, bent upon the restoration of Islam, which sprang up across much of the Islamic world—the Wahhabi in Saudi Arabia, the Mahdi in the Sudan, the Sanusi in Libya—and which served as forerunners to twentieth-century revivalism. Most importantly, this chapter analyzes key individuals, movements, and organizations, such as the Islamic modernist movement, the Muslim Brotherhood, and the Jamaat-i-Islami, who have had a profound effect upon twentieth-century Islam, its faith, intellectual, and community life.

Although the Iranian revolution drew the attention of many to Islam and the Islamic resurgence, contemporary Islamic revivalism has had an impact on the personal and public lives of Muslims for the past two decades. Chapter 5, "Contemporary Islam: Religion and Politics," reviews the causes, worldview, and manifestations of Islamic revivalism. A series of case studies of Saudi Arabia, Libya, Iran, Lebanon, and Egypt is briefly presented to demonstrate the diversity of ways in which Islam has been used by governments and by opposition groups and the issues that the process has raised.

Muslims today, like believers the world over, continue to grapple with the continued relevance of their faith to the realities of contemporary society. The adaptability of a religious tradition, its relevance to life in the twentieth century, raises as many questions as it offers potential answers. The history of modern Islam has challenged many presuppositions and expectations, in particular, the notion that modernization results in the secularization of societies. Islamic revival and reform, the attempt to apply Islam to modern or postmodern life, have generated many questions and issues that are examined in Chapter 6, "Islam and Change: Issues of Authority and Interpretation": What are the parameters and direction of Islamic reform? Should it be a restoration of the past or a process of reinterpretation and reconstruction? Is the future of Islam to be left in the hands of traditional religious leaders *(ulama)*, Muslim rulers, the laity? If change is to occur, how much is necessary or possible? What are the implications of a greater Islamization of society for women and minorities?

Islam in the last decade of the twentieth century has ceased to be solely of interest to those who are concerned with "foreign" religions or cultures. As we are only slowly realizing, Islam is truly a world religion, increasingly visible in Europe and the United States as well as Asia, Africa, and the Middle East. Muslims are very much part of the mosaic of Western societies, no longer foreign visitors but fellow citizens and colleagues. Thus, to understand the world in which we live requires a knowledge of the straight path of Islam as a prerequisite for an appreciation of our theologically interconnected and historically intertwined Judaeo-Christian-Islamic heritage.

ISLAM

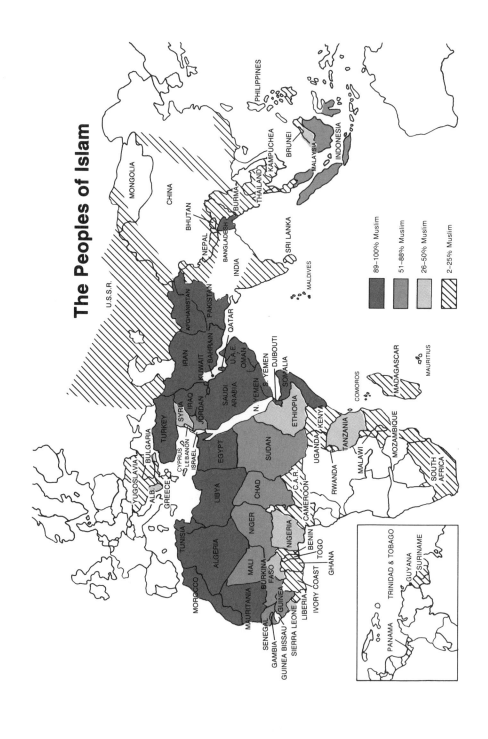

The Peoples of Islam

89–100% Muslim

51–88% Muslim

26–50% Muslim

2–25% Muslim

U.S.S.R.

MONGOLIA

CHINA

BHUTAN

NEPAL

BANGLADESH

INDIA

SRI LANKA

MALDIVES

BURMA

THAILAND

KAMPUCHEA

BRUNEI

MALAYSIA

INDONESIA

PHILIPPINES

AFGHANISTAN

PAKISTAN

QATAR

BAHRAIN

U.A.E.

OMAN

IRAN

KUWAIT

SAUDI ARABIA

N. YEMEN

YEMEN

DJIBOUTI

SOMALIA

ETHIOPIA

COMOROS

MADAGASCAR

MAURITIUS

KENYA

UGANDA

TANZANIA

MOZAMBIQUE

RWANDA

MALAWI

SOUTH AFRICA

TURKEY

SYRIA

IRAQ

JORDAN

CYPRUS

LEBANON

ISRAEL

EGYPT

SUDAN

C.A.R.

CAMEROON

YUGOSLAVIA

ALB.

BULGARIA

GREECE

LIBYA

CHAD

NIGER

NIGERIA

BENIN

TOGO

GHANA

IVORY COAST

TUNISIA

ALGERIA

MALI

BURKINA FASO

MOROCCO

MAURITANIA

SENEGAL

GAMBIA

GUINEA BISSAU

GUINEA

SIERRA LEONE

LIBERIA

PANAMA

TRINIDAD & TOBAGO

GUYANA

SURINAME

1

Muhammad and the Quran: Messenger and Message

In the name of God, the Merciful and Compassionate: praise belongs to God, the Lord of the Worlds, the Merciful, the Compassionate; Master of the Day of Judgment, You do we worship and You do we call on for help; guide us on the Straight Path, the path of those whom You have blessed, not of those who earn your anger nor those who go astray. (Quran 1:1–7)

Five times each day, hundreds of millions of Muslims face Mecca to pray. They are part of an Islamic community that spans the globe, numbers perhaps 900 million adherents, and continues to spread its message successfully throughout Europe, Asia, Africa, and North America. While the more than forty-four Muslim countries extend from Senegal to Indonesia, the message of Islam and significant Muslim populations may be found in such diverse environments as the Soviet Union, China, India, England, and the United States. Islam, the second largest of the world's religions, is indeed a world presence and force. If much of the Western world had missed that fact, events since the Arab oil embargo have rectified this oversight. However, Muslim politics, from the Iranian revolution to terrorist outbursts, have often obscured or, at the very least, raised more questions than provided answers regarding the faith of Islam to which Muslims appeal as the source of their inspiration and guidance.

Islam stands in a long line of Semitic, prophetic religious traditions that share an uncompromising monotheism, and belief in God's revelation, His prophets, ethical responsibility and accountability, and the Day of Judgment. Indeed, Muslims, like Christians and Jews, are the Children of Abraham, since all trace their communities back to him. Islam's historic religious and political relationship to Christendom and Judaism has remained strong throughout history. This interaction has

3

been the source of mutual benefit and borrowing as well as misunderstanding and conflict.

Although the followers of Islam belong to a single community of believers, there are two major historic divisions: Sunni and Shii. Sunni Muslims constitute 85 percent of the world's Muslims; Shii about 15 percent. While this volume focuses on the common faith and belief epitomized by the Five Pillars of Islam, attention will also be given to differences in Muslim belief and practice. For while, as we shall see, all Muslims enjoy a unity of faith in Allah, the Quran, and the teachings of Muhammad, the interpretations and applications of Islam have varied in different cultural contexts and eras. Despite this recognition of diversity, the focus of this volume will be the core of beliefs, practices, and institutions that unite and are integral to Muslim life, whatever the differences may be.

Muhammad and the Muslim Community

The Near East spawned and nurtured a rich variety of religious traditions: ancient Egyptian and Mesopotamian religions, Zoroastrianism, Judaism, Christianity. However, given the nature of tribal society in seventh-century Arabia and the presence of the Roman (Byzantine) and Persian (Sasanid) empires as buffer states of the Arabian Peninsula, the rise of a new religious movement and the inauguration of a new stage in world history would have seemed unthinkable. Yet, this occurred with the revelation of the Quran and under the leadership of the Prophet Muhammad. Islamic religion and the activity of the Muslim community produced a new empire and a rich civilization which came to dominate much of Europe, the Middle East, Asia, and Africa. Because Islam developed in central Arabia, its religious and social milieu provide the context for understanding Muhammad's reformist message and mission.

Arabia

Arabian religion and society reflected the tribal realities of the Peninsula. Arabia's 1 million square miles (nearly one-third the size of the United States or Europe) was dominated by desert and steppe areas. Bedouin tribes pursuing a pastoral and nomadic lifestyle traveled from one area to another, seeking water and pasture for their flocks of sheep and camels. The landscape was dotted with oasis towns and cities. Among the more prominent were Mecca, a center of trade and commerce, and Yathrib (Medina), an important agricultural settlement. The principal sources of livelihood were herding, agriculture, trade, and raiding. Intertribal warfare was a long-established activity governed by clear guidelines and rules. For example, raiding was illegal during the four sacred months of pilgrimage. Its object was to capture livestock from enemy Bedouin tribes with a minimum of casualties. Its ultimate goal was to weaken and eventually absorb other tribes by reducing them to a dependent or "client" status.

Whether nomadic or sedentary, the peoples of Arabia lived in a Bedouin tribal society and culture. Social organization and identity were rooted in membership in an extended family. A grouping of several related families comprised a clan. A cluster of several clans constituted a tribe. Tribes were led by a chief (*shaykh*) who was selected by a consensus of his peers—that is, the heads of leading clans or families. These tribal elders formed an advisory council within which the tribal chief exercised his leadership and authority as the first among equals. Muhammad belonged to the Banu Hashim (sons of Hashim), a lesser clan of the powerful Quraysh tribe which dominated Meccan society.

The Arabs placed great emphasis on tribal ties, group loyalty or solidarity as the source of power for a clan or tribe. The celebrated rugged individualism of the Bedouin Arab ethos was counterbalanced by subordination to tribal authority and tribal customs, the unwritten oral law of society. Tribal affiliation and law were the basis not only for identity but also for protection. The threat of family or group vendetta, the law of retaliation, was of vital importance in a society lacking a central political authority or law.

The religion of Arabia reflected its tribal nature and social structure. Gods and goddesses served as protectors of individual tribes, and their spirits were associated with sacred objects—trees, stones, springs, and wells. Local tribal deities were feared and respected rather than loved, the objects of cultic rituals (sacrifice, pilgrimage, prayer) and of supplication and propitiation celebrated at local shrines. Mecca possessed a central shrine of the gods, the Kaba, a cube-shaped building that housed the 360 idols of tribal patron deities, and was the site of a great annual pilgrimage and fair. While these deities were primary religious actors and objects of worship, beyond this tribal polytheism was a shared belief in Allah ("the god"). Allah, the supreme high god, was the creator and sustainer of life but remote from everyday concerns and thus not the object of cult or ritual. Associated with Allah were three goddesses who were the daughters of Allah: al-Lat, Manat, and al-Uzza.

The value system or ethical code of Arabia has been aptly termed a "tribal humanism," a way of life whose origins were not ascribed to God but were the product of tribal experience or tradition.[1] It was epitomized by its key virtue, manliness, which emphasized bravery in battle, loyalty to family and protection of its members, hospitality, patience, and persistence—in sum, the preservation of tribal and family honor. This was accompanied by a fatalism that saw no meaning or accountability beyond this life—no resurrection of the body, divine judgment, or eternal punishment or reward. Justice was guaranteed and administered not by God, but by the threat of group vengeance or retaliation. Thus, Arabian religion had little sense of cosmic moral purpose or of individual or communal moral responsibility.

Although it is common to speak of Islam's origins in seventh-century Arabia, such a notion is historically inaccurate and, from a Muslim perspective, theologically false. Islam was not an isolated, totally new monotheistic religion. The monotheistic message of the Quran and the preaching of Muhammad did not occur in a vacuum. Monotheism had been flourishing in Semitic and Iranian cultures for centuries preceding Muhammad's ministry. The Scriptures and prophets of Judaism, Christianity, and Zoroastrianism had a long-established presence and roots in Irano-Semitic societies. Beyond their distinctive differences, all three religious traditions shared a monotheistic faith (the conviction that God is one), prophets, Scriptures, beliefs in angels and devils, and a moral universe encompassing individual and communal accountability and responsibility. All were the product of primarily urban, not rural or desert, experiences, and were institutionalized in commercial centers by scholarly elites, often supported by state patronage, who interpreted the early preaching of their prophets and apostles. Among their common themes were community, fidelity/infidelity, individual moral decision making, social justice, final judgment, and reward and punishment. In contrast to Indian religious notions of cyclical history, rebirth, and personal perfection, the Judaeo-Christian and Zoroastrian traditions affirmed a sacred history with a beginning and an end within which believers were to follow God's will and realize their eternal destiny in the next life. To differing degrees, all had become associated with political power, that is, had become an official state religion: Judaism in the kingdoms of Judaea and Israel, Christianity in the Roman (Byzantine) empire, Zoroastrianism in the Persian (Sasanid) empire.

Forms of monotheism did exist in Arabia alongside pre-Islamic tribal polytheism. Both Jewish and Christian Arab communities had been present in Arabia before Muhammad. Jewish communities in Khaybar, Tayma, and Yathrib (later called Medina) were successful in agriculture and trade. While some Christians were settled in Mecca, most of the Christian communities were on the periphery of central Arabia (the

Hijaz), along caravan routes in North and South Arabia. Particular contact with monotheism resulted from the caravan trade that brought Zoroastrian, Jewish, and Christian merchants to Mecca, a thriving commercial center, as well as from the travels of Meccan traders far and wide throughout the Middle East. Finally, in addition to biblical monotheism, native or pre-Islamic Arab monotheists, called *hanifs*, seem to have existed. The Quran (3:95) and Muslim tradition portray them as descendants of Abraham and his son Ismail.

Arabian tribal society, with its Bedouin, polytheistic ethos, provided the context for the rise of Islam. Of equal importance, this period was marked by the tensions and questioning that accompany change in a transitional society, for this was a period when cities like Mecca and Medina were prospering and attracting many from a nomadic to a more sedentary life. The emergence of Mecca as a major mercantile center precipitated the beginnings of a new political, social, and economic order. New wealth, the rise of a new commercial oligarchy from within the Quraysh tribe, greater division between social classes, and a growing disparity between rich and poor strained the traditional system of Arab tribal values and social security—its way of life. This was the time and social milieu in which Muhammad was born.

Muhammad: Prophet of God

History, legend, and Muslim belief portray Muhammad as a remarkable man and prophet. While we know a good deal about Muhammad's life after his "call" to be God's messenger, historical records tell us little about Muhammad's early years prior to becoming a prophet at the age of forty in 610 c.e. The Quran has served as a major source for information regarding the life of the Prophet. In addition, Prophetic traditions (reports about what Muhammad said and did) and biographies give us a picture of his meaning and significance in early Islam as do Islamic calligraphy and art, where the names of Allah and Muhammad often occur side by side—God and His Prophet. Muhammad serves both as God's human instrument in bearing His revelation and as the model or ideal whom all believers should emulate. Thus, understanding Muhammad and his role in the early Islamic community is crucial for an appreciation of the development of early Islam as well as the dynamics of contemporary Muslim belief and practice.

Muhammad ibn Abdullah (the son of Abd Allah) was born in 570 c.e. Tradition tells us that he was orphaned at a young age. His father was a trader who died before Muhammad was born; his mother, Amina, died when he was only six years old. As a young man, Muhammad was employed in Mecca's thriving caravan trade. The city was at the cross-roads of trade routes between the Indian Ocean and the Mediterranean. Central Arabia was emerging as a major commercial power, sitting astride important trade routes that extended from Africa across the Middle East to China and Malaysia. Muhammad became a steward or business manager for the caravans of a wealthy widow, Khadija, whom he subsequently married. Tradition tells us that at the time, Muhammad was twenty-five years old and Khadija was forty. During their fifteen years of marriage, they enjoyed a very close relationship and had three sons (who died in infancy) and four daughters. The most famous of Muhammad's surviving children was Fatima, who would marry Ali, the revered fourth caliph of Sunni Islam and the first legitimate *Imam* (leader) of Shii Islam.

Mecca was a prosperous center of trade and commerce. Yet it was a society in which traditional tribal ways were strained by Mecca's transition from a semi-Bedouin to a commercial, urban society. This process was accompanied by serious economic and social cleavages. Muhammad, who had become a successful member of Meccan society, was apparently profoundly affected by these changes. He enjoyed great respect for his judgment and trustworthiness, as was reflected by his nickname al-Amin, the trusted one. This rectitude was complemented by a reflective nature that led him to retreat regularly to a cave on Mt. Hira, a few miles north of Mecca. Here, in long periods of solitude, he contemplated his life and the ills of his society, seeking greater meaning and insight. Here, at the age of forty during the month of Ramadan, Muhammad the caravan leader became Muhammad the messenger of God. On the night Muslims call "The Night of Power and Excellence," he received the first of many revelations from God. A heavenly intermediary, later identified by tradition as the angel Gabriel, commanded, "Recite." Muhammad responded that he had nothing to recite. Twice the angel repeated the command, and each time a frightened and bewildered Muhammad pleaded that he did not know what to say. Finally, the words came to him:

> Recite in the name of your Lord who has created, Created man out of a germ-cell. Recite for your Lord is the Most Generous One Who has taught by the pen, Taught man what he did not know!

With this revelation, Muhammad joined that group of individuals whom Semitic faiths acknowledge as divinely inspired messengers or prophets of God. Muhammad continued to receive divine revelations over a period of twenty-two years (610–632). These messages were finally collected and written down in the Quran ("The Recitation"), Islam's sacred scripture.

Muslim tradition reports that Muhammad reacted to his "call" in much the same way as the Hebrew prophets. He was both frightened and reluctant. Frightened by the unknown—for surely he did not expect such an experience. Reluctant, at first, because he feared he was possessed and that others would dismiss his claims as inspired by spirits, or *jinns*. Despondent and confused, Muhammad resolved to kill himself but was stopped when he again heard the voice say, "O Muhammad! You are the messenger of God and I am Gabriel." This message was reinforced by his wife, Khadija, who reassured him that he was neither mad nor possessed; the messenger was from God and not a demon. Interestingly, according to Muslim tradition a Christian played an important role as well. One of those to whom Khadija and Muhammad turned for advice was her Christian cousin, Waraqa ibn Qusayy. When he heard of Muhammad's experience, Waraqa reassured him:

> Surely, by Him in whose hand is Waraqa's soul, thou art the prophet of this people. There hath come unto thee the greatest Namus (angel or Gabriel) who came unto Moses. Like the Hebrew prophets, Thou wilt be called a liar, and they will use thee despitefully and cast thee out and fight against thee.[2]

For just such reasons, Muhammad, like many of the prophets before him, was initially reluctant to preach God's message. His fears were well-founded.

The first ten years of Muhammad's preaching were difficult, marked by Meccan resistance and rejection. While there was a trickle of converts, opposition to Muhammad was formidable. For the powerful and prosperous Meccan oligarchy, the monotheistic message of this would-be reformer, with its condemnation of the socioeconomic inequities of Meccan life, constituted a direct challenge not only to traditional polytheistic religion but also to the power and prestige of the establishment, threatening their economic, social, and political interests. The Prophet denounced false contracts, usury, and the neglect and exploitation of orphans and widows. He defended the rights of the poor and the oppressed, asserting that the rich had an obligation to the poor and dispossessed. This sense of social commitment and responsibility was institutionalized in the form of religious tithes or taxes on wealth and agricultural lands. Like Amos and Jeremiah before him, Muhammad was a "warner" from God who admonished his hearers to repent and obey God, for the final judgment was near:

Say: "O men, I am only for you a warner." Those who believe, and do deeds of righteousness—theirs shall be forgiveness and generous provision. And those who strive against Our signs to avoid them—they shall be inhabitants of Hell. (Quran 22:49–50)

Muhammad's rejection of polytheism undermined the religious prestige of the Meccans (in particular, the Umayyad clan) as keepers of the Kaba, the religious shrine that housed the tribal idols. It threatened the considerable revenues that accrued from the annual pilgrimage and festival to this central sanctuary of Arabian tribal religion. This potential economic loss was coupled with the undermining of Meccan tribal political authority by Muhammad's claim to prophetic authority and leadership and his insistence that all true believers belonged to a single universal community (*umma*) that transcended tribal bonds.

Creation of the Islamic Community

For almost ten years, Muhammad struggled in Mecca, preaching God's message and gathering a small band of faithful followers. Among the early converts were Ali, his cousin and son-in-law, and Abu Bakr, his future father-in-law and the first caliph, or successor of the Prophet. The deaths of Khadija and of his uncle and protector, Abu Talib, in 619 C.E. made life even more difficult. Meccan opposition escalated from derision and verbal attacks to active persecution. The core of the opposition came from the Umayyad clan of the Quraysh tribe. As we shall see, their descendants, even after their later conversion to Islam, would continue to challenge the family of the Prophet. As conditions deteriorated in Mecca, Muhammad sent some of his followers to other areas, such as Christian Abyssinia, for safety. The situation changed significantly in 620. Muhammad was invited by a delegation from Yathrib (later called Medina), a city two hundred miles north of Mecca, to serve as a chief arbitrator or judge in a bitter feud between its Arab tribes. Muhammad and two hundred of his followers quietly emigrated, from July to September 622, to Medina. This migration (*hijra*) marked a turning point in Muhammad's fortunes and a new stage in the history of the Islamic movement. Islam took on political form with the establishment of an Islamic community-state at Medina. The importance of the *hijra* is reflected in its adoption as the beginning of the Islamic calendar. Muslims chose to date their history from neither Muhammad's birth nor his reception of the first revelation in 610, but from the creation of the Islamic community (*umma*). The community, as much as the individual, was to be the vehicle for realizing God's will on earth.

Muhammad at Medina

At Medina, Muhammad had the opportunity to implement God's governance and message, for he was now the prophet-head of a religiopolitical community. He did this by establishing his leadership in Medina, subduing Mecca, and consolidating Muslim rule over the remainder of Arabia through diplomatic and military means.

Muhammad had come to Medina as the arbiter or judge for the entire community, Muslim and non-Muslim alike. In addition, he was the leader of all the Muslims, the commander of the faithful, both those who had emigrated from Mecca and those raised in Medina. While the majority of the Arab tribes came to embrace Islam, the Jewish tribes (that is, those Arabs who had previously converted to Judaism) remained an important minority. Muhammad promulgated a charter, sometimes called the constitution of Medina, that set out the rights and duties of all citizens and the relationship of the Muslim community to other communities. Muslims constituted a community whose primary identity and bond were no longer to be tribal ties but a common religious faith and commitment. Jews were recognized as a separate community allied to the Muslim *umma*, but with religious and cultural autonomy.

As the Medinan state was taking shape, Muhammad turned his attention to Mecca. Mecca was the religious, political, economic, and intellectual center of Arabia. Its importance was not diminished by its hostility to Muhammad's preaching. If anything, further revelations to Muhammad, which designated Mecca as the direction (*qibla*) for prayer and the site for Muslim pilgrimage (*hajj*), increased its religious significance. Muslim religious fervor was matched by the power of Meccan tribal mores that branded the Muslims as secessionists and traitors. All the ingredients were there for a formidable battle. Muhammad initiated a series of raids against Meccan caravans, threatening both the political authority and the economic power of the Quraysh. Several important battles ensued. In 624 at Badr, near Medina, Muslim forces, though greatly outnumbered, defeated the Meccan army. For Muslims, then and now, the Battle of Badr has special significance. It was the first and a most decisive victory for the forces of monotheism over those of polytheism, for the army of God over the followers of ignorance and unbelief. God had sanctioned and assisted His soldiers (Quran 3:123, 8:42ff) in victory. Quranic witness to divine guidance and intervention made Badr a sacred symbol, and it has been used throughout Muslim history, as evidenced most recently in the 1973 Egyptian-Israeli war, whose Egyptian code name was "Operation Badr."

The elation after Badr was dissipated when Muslims were defeated by the Meccans in the Battle of Uhud in 625, in which Muhammad himself was wounded. Finally, in 627, frustrated by the growing strength of Muhammad, the Meccans mounted an all-out seige of Medina in order to crush their opposition once and for all. At the Battle of the "Ditch" (so named because the Muslims dug a trench to neutralize the Meccan cavalry), the Muslims held out so successfully against a coalition of Meccans and mercenary Bedouins that the coalition disintegrated. The Meccans withdrew. The failure of the Quraysh enhanced Muhammad's prestige and leadership among the tribes of Arabia, placing him in the ascendant position. He had consolidated his leadership in Medina, extended his influence over other tribal areas in the Hijaz, and asserted his independence of the dominant tribe in central Arabia. The balance of power had shifted. Muhammad would now initiate, and Mecca would respond.

The final phase in the struggle between Medina and Mecca highlights the method and political genius of Muhammad. He employed both military and diplomatic means, often preferring the latter. Instead of seeking to rout his Meccan opponents, Muhammad sought to gain submission to God and His messenger by incorporating them within the Islamic community-state. A truce was struck in 628 at Hudaybiyah to permit the Muslims to make their pilgrimage to Mecca the following year. In 629, Muhammad established Muslim control over the Hijaz and led the pilgrimage to Mecca, as had been scheduled. Then in 630, Muhammad accused the Quraysh of breaking the treaty, and the Muslims marched on Mecca, ten thousand strong. The Meccans capitulated. Eschewing vengeance and the plunder of conquest, the Prophet instead accepted a settlement, granting amnesty rather than wielding the sword toward his former enemies. For their part, the Meccans converted to Islam, accepted Muhammad's leadership, and were incorporated within the *umma*.

During the next two years, Muhammad established his authority over much of Arabia. The Bedouin who resisted were defeated militarily. At the same time, so many tribes in Arabia sent delegations to come to terms with the successor to the Quraysh that Muslim history remembers this period as the year of deputations. Alliances were forged. While many converted to Islam, others did not. Representatives were sent from Medina to teach the Quran and the duties and rituals of Islam, and to collect the taxes due Medina. In the spring of 632, Muhammad led the pilgrimage to Mecca, where the sixty-two-year-old leader preached his farewell sermon, exhorting his followers:

> Know ye that every Moslem is a brother unto every other Moslem, and that ye are now one brotherhood. It is not legitimate for any one of you, therefore, to appropriate unto himself anything that belongs to his brother unless it is willingly given him by that brother.[3]

These words summarize both the nature of the Islamic community and the accomplishment of the Prophet Muhammad. When he died three months later in June 632, all Arabia was united under the banner of Islam.

Muhammad: Exemplar of Muslim Life and Piety

Muhammad was among those great religious figures, prophets and founders of religions, whose remarkable character and personality inspired uncommon confidence and commitment. His phenomenal success in attracting followers and creating a community-state that dominated Arabia could be attributed not only to the fact that he was a shrewd military strategist but also to the fact that he was an unusual man who elicited steadfast loyalty despite persecution and oppression. Muhammad's followers found him righteous, trustworthy, pious, compassionate, honest. He was revered from earliest times: Muslims remembered and recounted what he said and did. Both during his lifetime and throughout the following centuries, Muhammad has served as the ideal model for Muslim life, providing the pattern that all believers are to emulate. He is, as some Muslims say, the "living Quran"—the witness whose behavior and words reveal God's will. Thus the practices of the Prophet became a material source of Islamic law alongside the Quran.

Muslims look to Muhammad's example for guidance in all aspects of life: how to treat friends as well as enemies, what to eat and drink, how to make love and war. Nowhere is this seen more clearly than in the growth of Prophetic traditions. For the tribes of Arabia, the ideals and norms of their way of life had been contained and preserved in their practices (*sunna*, trodden path), the customs or oral laws handed down from previous generations by word and example. As Prophet and leader of the community, Muhammad reformed these practices. Old ways were modified, eliminated, or replaced by new regulations. His impact on Muslim life cannot be overestimated, since he served as both religious and political head of Medina: prophet of God, ruler, military commander, chief judge, lawgiver. As a result, the practice of the Prophet, his *Sunna* or example, became the norm for community life. Muslims observed and remembered stories about what the Prophet said and did. These reports or traditions (*hadith*) were preserved and passed on in oral and written form. The corpus of *hadith* literature reveals the comprehensive scope of Muhammad's example; he is the ideal religiopolitical leader as well as the exemplary husband and father. Thus when many Muslims pray five times each day or make the pilgrimage to Mecca, they seek to pray as the Prophet prayed, without adding or subtracting from the way Muhammad is reported to have worshipped. Traditions of the Prophet provide guidance for personal hygiene, dress, eating, marriage, treatment of wives, diplomacy, and warfare.

Reformer

Muhammad was not the founder of Islam; he did not start a new religion. Like his prophetic predecessors, he came as a religious reformer. Muhammad maintained that he did not bring a new message from a new God but called people back to the one, true God and to a way of life that most of his contemporaries had forgotten or deviated from. Worship of Allah was not the evolutionary emergence of monotheism from polytheism but a return to a forgotten past, to the faith of the first monotheist, Abraham. The Prophet brought a revolution in Arabian life, a reformation that sought to purify and redefine its way of life. False, superstitious practices such as polytheism and idolatry were suppressed. Such beliefs were viewed as the worst forms of ingratitude or unbelief, for they contradicted and denied the unity or oneness (*tawhid*) of God. Polytheism, or association (*shirk*) of anything with Allah, was denounced as the worst of sins, idolatry. For Muhammad, the majority of Arabs lived in ignorance (*jahiliyya*) of Allah and His will as revealed to the prophets Adam, Abraham, Moses, and Jesus. Moreover, he believed that both the Jewish and the Christian communities had distorted God's original revelation to Moses and later to Jesus. Thus, Islam brought a reformation; it was the call once again to total surrender or submission (*islam*) to Allah and the implementation of His will as revealed in its complete form one final time to Muhammad, the last, or "seal," of the prophets. For Muhammad, Islam was not a new faith but the restoration of the true faith (*iman*), a process that required the reformation of an ignorant, deviant society, Repentance, or the heeding of God's warning, required turning away from the path of unbelief and turning toward or returning to the straight path (*sharia*) or law of God. This conversion required both individual and group submission to God. Muslims were not only individuals but also a community or brotherhood of believers. They were bound by a common faith and committed to the creation of a socially just society through the implementation of God's will—the establishment of the rule or kingdom of God on earth.

The example of the Prophet offers a paradigm and the basis for an ideology for the fusion of religion and state in Muslim experience. The early Islamic worldview provides a model both for the formation of a state and for protest and revolution. The world is seen as divided between the believers or the friends of God, who represent the forces of good, and the unbelievers (*kafirs*) and hypocrites, who are the allies of evil, the followers of Satan:

> God is the Protector of the believers; He brings them forth from darkness to the light. And the unbelievers—their protectors are the idols, that bring them forth from the light into the shadows; those are the inhabitants of the Fire, therein dwelling forever. (Quran 2:257–59)

> The believers fight in the way of God, and the unbelievers fight in the idols' way. Fight you therefore against the friends of Satan. (4:76)

The Muslims in Mecca were the oppressed and disinherited, struggling in an unbelieving society. The Quran compares their plight with that of Moses and the Israelites before them (Quran 28:4–5). Muslims were reminded that God is their refuge and helper:

> And remember when you were few and abased in the land, and were fearful that the people would snatch you away; but He gave you refuge, and confirmed you with His help. (8:26)

Faced with persecution, Muslims, like Muhammad at Mecca, had two choices: emigration (*hijra*) and armed resistance (*jihad*). First, the true believers were expected to leave a godless society and establish a community of believers under God and His Prophet. Second, Muslims were permitted, indeed exhorted, to struggle against the forces of evil and unbelief, and if necessary sacrifice their lives, in order to establish God's rule:

> So let them fight in the way of God who sell the present life for the world to come; and whosoever fights in the way of God and is slain, or conquers, We shall bring him a mighty wage. (4:74)

God's preference is made even clearer a few verses later: "God has preferred in rank those who struggle with their possessions and their selves over the ones who sit at home" (4:95).

Those who wage war (*jihad*) for God engage in a religiopolitical act, a holy war. The God who commands this struggle against oppression and unbelief will assist His Muslim holy warriors as He did at the Battle of Badr, where, the Quran states, an unseen army of angels aided the

Muslim army. These holy warriors (*mujahidin*) will be rewarded in this life with victory and the spoils of war. Those who fall in battle will be rewarded with eternal life as martyrs (*shahid*, witness) for the faith. The Arabic term for martyr comes from the same root ("witness") as the word for the confession or profession of faith, indicating that willingness to sacrifice all, even life itself, is the ultimate profession or eternal witness of faith. In this way, early Islamic history provides Muslims with a model and ideology for protest, resistance, and revolutionary change.

The reformist spirit of Islam affected religious ritual as well as politics and society. This process of adaptation or Islamization would characterize much of the development of Islam. While Islam rejected some beliefs and institutions and introduced others, the more common method was to reformulate or adapt existing practices to Islamic norms and values. Rituals such as the annual pilgrimage (*hajj*) and prayer (*salat*) were reinterpreted. The Kaba remained the sacred center, but it was no longer associated with the tribal idols which had been destroyed when Muhammad conquered Mecca. Instead, he rededicated it to Allah, for whom, Muslims believe, Abraham and Ismail had originally built the Kaba. Similarly, Arab pagan and Jewish prayer practices were adapted rather than totally replaced. Muslims, too, were to pray at fixed times each day. However, they would pray to Allah, facing Mecca and reciting the Quran. Initially, Muslims, like the Jews of Arabia, faced Jerusalem to pray. However, when the Jews did not accept Muhammad's prophetic claims, a new revelation directed Muhammad to shift the center of prayer to Mecca.

Muhammad introduced a new moral order in which the origin and end of all actions was not self or tribal interest but God's will. Belief in the Day of Judgment and resurrection of the body added a dimension of human responsibility and accountability that had been absent in Arabian religion. Tribal vengeance and retaliation were subordinated to a belief in a just and merciful creator and judge. A society based on tribal affiliation and man-made tribal law or custom was replaced by a religiously bonded community (*umma*) governed by God's law.

Muhammad and the West

Talk of Islam's new moral order and the normative nature that Muhammad's life had for Muslims seems to clash with Western perceptions of Islam. If Muslim tradition tended to mythify the Prophet, Western tradition too often has denigrated and vilified his memory. Two issues in particular—Muhammad's treatment of the Jews and his (polygynous) marriages—have proven popular stumbling blocks, or perhaps more accurately whipping posts, for Western critics and polemics.

In his early preaching, Muhammad had looked to the Jews and Christians of Arabia as natural allies whose faiths had much in common with Islam. He anticipated their acceptance and approval. When the Islamic community was established at Medina, Muslims, like the Jews, had faced Jerusalem to pray. However, the Jewish tribes, which had long lived in Medina and had political ties with the Quraysh, tended to resist both religious and political cooperation with the Muslims. They denied Muhammad's prophethood and message and cooperated with his Meccan enemies. While the constitution of Medina had granted them autonomy in internal religious affairs, political loyalty and allegiance were expected. Yet the Quran accuses the Jewish tribes of regularly breaking such pacts: "Why is it that whenever they make pacts, a group among them casts it aside unilaterally?" (2:100).

After each major battle, one of the Jewish tribes was accused and punished for such acts. Muslim perception of distrust, intrigue, and rejection on the part of the Jews led first to exile and later to warfare. After Badr, the Banu Qainuqa tribe and after the Battle of Uhud, the Banu Nadir, with their families and possessions, were expelled from Medina. After the Battle of the Ditch in 627, the Jews of the Banu Qurayza were denounced as traitors who had consorted with the Meccans. As was common in Arab (and, indeed, Semitic) practice, the men were massacred; the women and children were spared but enslaved. However, it is important to note that the motivation for such actions was political rather than racial or theological. Although the Banu Qurayza had remained neutral, they had also negotiated with the Quraysh. Moreover, the exiled Jewish clans had actively supported the Meccans. Muhammad moved decisively to crush the Jews who remained in Medina, viewing them as a continued political threat to the consolidation of Muslim dominance and rule in Arabia.

One final point should be made. Muhammad's use of warfare in general was alien neither to Arab custom nor to that of the Hebrew prophets. Both believed that God had sanctioned battle with the enemies of the Lord. Biblical stories about the exploits of kings and prophets such as Moses, Joshua, Elijah, Samuel, Jehu, Saul, and David recount the struggles of a community called by God and the permissibility, indeed requirement, to take up arms when necessary against those who had defied God, and to fight "in the name of the Lord of hosts, the God of the armies of Israel."[4] Similarly, in speaking of the Israelite conquests,

Moses recalls: "And I commanded you at that time, saying, 'The Lord your God has given you this land to possess. . . . You shall not fear them; for it is the Lord your God who fights for you'" (Deuteronomy 3:18–22).

Muhammad's marriages have long provided another source of Western criticism of the moral character of the Prophet. A noted British author has observed:

> No great religious leader has been so maligned as Muhammad. Attacked in the past as a heretic, an imposter, or a sensualist, it is still possible to find him referred to as a "the false prophet." A modern German writer accuses Muhammad of sensuality, surrounding himself with young women. This man was not married until he was twenty-five years of age, then he and his wife lived in happiness and fidelity for twenty-four years, until her death when he was forty-nine. Only between the age of fifty and his death at sixty-two did Muhammad take other wives, only one of whom was a virgin, and most of them were taken for dynastic and political reasons. Certainly the Prophet's record was better than that head of the Church of England, Henry VIII.[5]

In addressing the issue of Muhammad's polygynous marriages, it is important to remember several points. First, Semitic culture in general and Arab practice in particular permitted polygyny. It was common practice in Arabian society, especially among nobles and leaders. Though less common, polygyny was also permitted in biblical and even in postbiblical Judaism. From Abraham, David, and Solomon down to the reformation period, polygyny was practiced by some Jews. While Jewish law changed after the Middle Ages due to the influence of Christian rule, for Jews under Islamic rule, polygyny remained licit, though it was not extensively practiced.[6] Second, during the prime of his life, Muhammad remained married to one woman, Khadija. Third, it was only after her death that he took a number of wives. Fourth, Muhammad's use of the special dispensation from God to exceed the limit of four wives imposed by the Quran, occurred only after the death of Khadija. Moreover, most of the eleven marriages had political and social motives. As was customary for Arab chiefs, many were political marriages to cement alliances. Others were marriages to the widows of his companions who had fallen in combat and were in need of protection. Remarriage was difficult in a society that emphasized virgin marriages. Aisha was the only virgin that Muhammad married and the wife with whom he had the closest relationship. Fifth, as we shall see later, Muhammad's teachings and actions, as well as the Quranic message, improved the status of all women—wives, daughters, mothers, widows, and orphans.

Talk of the political and social motives behind many of the Prophet's marriages should not obscure the fact that Muhammad was attracted to women and enjoyed his wives. To deny this would contradict the Islamic outlook on marriage and sexuality, found in both revelation and Prophetic traditions, which emphasizes the importance of family and views sex as a gift from God to be enjoyed within the bonds of marriage. The many stories about Muhammad's concern and care for his wives reflect these values.

The Quran: The Word of God

For Muslims, the Quran is the Book of God. It is the eternal, uncreated, literal word of God sent down from heaven, revealed one final time to the Prophet Muhammad as a guide for humankind (2:185). The Quran consists of 114 chapters of 6,000 verses, originally revealed to Muhammad over a period of twenty-two years. It is approximately four-fifths the size of the New Testament, and its chapters are arranged according to length, not chronology. The longer chapters, representing the later Medinan revelations, precede the shorter, earlier Meccan revelations to Muhammad.

Islam teaches that God's revelation has occurred in several forms: in nature, history, and Scripture. God's existence can be known through creation; nature contains pointers or "signs" of God, its creator and sustainer (3:26–27). The history of the rise and fall of nations, victory and defeat, provides clear signs and lessons of God's sovereignty and intervention in history (30:2–9). In addition, God in His mercy determined to reveal His will for humankind through a series of messengers: "Indeed, We sent forth among every nation a Messenger, saying: 'Serve your God, and shun false gods'" (16:36) (see also 13:7, 15:10, 35:24). The verses of revelation are also called signs of God. Thus, throughout history, human beings could not only know that there is a God but also know what God desires and commands for His creatures.

If Scripture is a sign from God sent to previous generations, what can be said about these Scriptures and prophets? Why was the Quran subsequently revealed, and what is the relationship of the Quran and Muhammad to previous revelations?

Although God had revealed His will to Moses and the Hebrew prophets and later to Jesus, Muslims believe that the Scriptures of the Jewish community (Torah) and that of the Christian church (the Evangel or Gospel) were corrupted. The current texts of the Torah and the New Testament are regarded as a composite of human fabrications mixed with divine revelation. Of God's revelation to the Jews, the Quran declares:

> Surely We sent down the Torah, wherein is guidance and light; thereby
> the Prophets who had surrendered themselves gave judgment for those
> of Jewry, as did the masters and rabbis, following that portion of God's
> book as they were given to keep and were witness to. (5:47)

Muslims believe that after the deaths of the prophets, extraneous, nonbiblical beliefs infiltrated the texts and thus altered and distorted the original, pure revelation. The Jews, and later the Christians, are portrayed as having distorted their mission to witness into a doctrine of their divine election as a chosen people:

> And the Jews and Christians say, "We are the sons of God, and His
> beloved ones." Say: "Why then does He chastise you for your sins? No
> you are mortals, of His creating; He forgives whom He will, and He
> chastises whom He will." (5:20)

The Quran teaches that a similar degeneration or perversion of Scripture occurred in Christianity. God sent Jesus as a prophet: "He [God] will teach him [Jesus] the Book, the Wisdom, the Torah, the Gospel, to be a messenger to the Children of Israel" (3:48–49). Yet, the Quran declares that after his death, Jesus' meaning and message were soon altered by those who made him into a god:

> The Christians say, "The Messiah is the Son of God." . . . God assail
> them! How they are perverted! . . . They were commanded to serve but
> One God; There is no God but He. (9:30–31)

After the falsification of the revelation given to the Jews and the Christians, Muslims believe that God in His mercy sent down His word one final time. The Quran does not abrogate or nullify, but rather corrects, the versions of Scripture preserved by the Jewish and Christian communities: "People of the Book, now there has come to you Our messenger making clear to you many things you have been concealing of the Book, and effacing many things" (5:16).

Thus, Islam is not a new religion with a new Scripture. Instead of being the youngest of the major monotheistic world religions, from a Muslim viewpoint it is the oldest. Islam represents the "original" as well as the final revelation of the God of Abraham, Moses, Jesus, and Muhammad. The Quran, like the Torah and the Evangel, is based on a preexisting heavenly tablet, the source or mother of Scripture. It is a book written in Arabic that exists in heaven with God; from it, the discourses or teachings of the three Scriptures are revealed at different stages in history: "Every term has a book . . . and with Him is the essence of the Book" (13:38–39).

Since Muslims believe that the Quran's Arabic language and character are revealed (26:195; 41:44), all Muslims, regardless of their national language, memorize and recite the Quran in Arabic whether they fully understand it or not. Arabic is the sacred language of Islam because, in a very real sense, it is the language of God. In contrast to Judaism and Christianity, whose Scriptures were not only translated into Greek and Latin at an early date but also disseminated in vernacular languages, in Islam Arabic has remained the language of the Quran and of religious learning. Until modern times, the Quran was printed only in Arabic; it could not be translated in Muslim countries. Even now, translations are often accompanied by the Arabic text.

Since the Quran is God's book, the text of the Quran, like its author, is regarded as perfect, eternal, and unchangeable. This belief is the basis for the doctrine of the miracle of inimitability of the Quran, which asserts that the ideas, language, and style of the Quran cannot be reproduced. The Quran proclaims that even the combined efforts of human beings and jinns could not produce a comparable text (17:88). The Quran is regarded as the only miracle brought by the Prophet. Muslim tradition is replete with stories of those who converted to Islam on hearing its inimitable message and of those pagan poets who failed the Quranic challenge (10:37–38) to create verses comparable with those contained in the Quran. Indeed, throughout history, many Arab Christians as well have regarded it as the perfection of Arabic language and literature.

In addition to its place as a religious text, the Quran was central to the development of Arabic linguistics and provided the basis for the development of Arabic grammar, vocabulary, and syntax. As Philip K. Hitti observed:

> In length the Koran is no more than four-fifths that of the New Testament, but in use it far exceeds it. Not only is it the basis of the religion, the canon of ethical and moral life, but also the textbook in which the Moslem begins his study of language, science, theology, and jurisprudence. Its literary influence has been incalculable and enduring. The first prose book in Arabic, it set the style for future products. It kept the language uniform. So that whereas today a Moroccan uses a dialect different from that used by an Arabian or an Iraqi, all write in the same style.[7]

Today, crowds fill stadiums and auditoriums throughout the Islamic world for public Quran recitation contests. Chanting of the Quran is an art form. Reciters or chanters are held in an esteem comparable with that of opera stars in the West. Memorization of the entire Quran brings great prestige as well as merit. Recordings of the Quran are enjoyed for their aesthetic as well as their religious value.

Revelation and Prophecy

While sharing a belief in revelation and prophecy, Islam's doctrine of prophecy is broader than that of Judaism and Christianity. In addition to prophets, there are messengers from God. Both are divinely inspired, sinless recipients of God's revelation. However, messengers are given a message for a community in book form and, unlike prophets, are assured success by God. While all messengers are prophets, all prophets are not messengers. The word "prophet" is applied far more inclusively in Islam than in the Judaeo-Christian traditions. It is applied to Abraham, Noah, Joseph, and John the Baptist as well as nonbiblical prophets of Arabia like Hud and Salih. "Messenger" is limited to men like Abraham, Moses, Jesus, and Muhammad who are both prophets and messengers.

The Quran, like the Bible, is a history of prophecy and God's revelation but with fundamental differences. Muslims trace their heritage back to Abraham, or Ibrahim. Thus, Jews, Christians, and Muslims are not only "People of the Book," but also Children of Abraham. However, they belong to different branches of the same family. While Jews and Christians are descendants of Abraham and his wife Sarah through their son Isaac, Muslims trace their lineage back to Ismail, Abraham's first-born son by his Egyptian bondswoman, Hagar. Islamic tradition teaches that Abraham, pressured by Sarah who feared that Ismail, as first born, would overshadow Isaac, took Hagar and Ismail to the vicinity of Mecca, where he left them on their own. Ismail became the progenitor of the Arabs in northern Arabia. When Abraham later returned, Ismail helped his father build the Kaba as the first shrine to the one true God. Muslim tradition also holds that it was here at the Kaba that Abraham was to sacrifice his son. In contrast to the biblical tradition (Genesis 22), Islam designates Ismail rather than Isaac as the intended victim, spared by divine intervention.

Islam's doctrine of revelation (wahy) also contrasts with that of modern biblical criticism. Both the form and the content, as well as the message and the actual words, of revelation are attributed to an external source, God. Muhammad is merely an instrument or a conduit. He is neither author nor editor of the Quran, but God's intermediary. Traditional teachings, emphasizing that the Prophet was illiterate, that he received the revelation from God through the angel Gabriel, and that even the order of the chapters of the Quran was revealed, may be seen as underscoring the belief that in every sense the Quran is the literal word of God with no input from Muhammad.

In Islam, God does not reveal Himself, for God is transcendent, but rather His will or guidance. Revelation occurs through the direct inspiration of prophets or through angelic intercession:

> God speaks to no human except through revelation wahy or from behind a veil or He sends a messenger [angel] and reveals whatever he wills . . . a straight path, the path of God. (42:51–53)

The Quran was initially preserved in oral and written form during the lifetime of the Prophet. Portions of the revelation were committed to memory by companions of the Prophet as they were received, or were written down by his secretaries. The entire text of the Quran was finally collected in an official, authorized version during the rule of the third caliph, Uthman ibn Affan (reigned 644–56). The Quran was collected, not edited or organized thematically. This format has long proved frustrating to many non-Muslims who find the text disjointed or disorganized from their point of view, since the topic or theme often changes from one paragraph to the next. However, many Muslims believe that the ordering of the chapters and verses was itself divinely inspired. Moreover, this format enables a believer, however brief one's schedule, to simply open the text at random and start reciting at the beginning of any paragraph, since each bears a truth to be learned and remembered.

Major Teachings of the Quran

While the Muslim sees but one divine source for the Quran, the non-Muslim will search out human sources and explanations. This is particularly true where parallels exist between Quranic and biblical stories. Christian and Jewish communities did exist in Arabia. Moreover, Muhammad's travels as a caravan trader brought him into contact with other People of the Book. He would have known and been aware of these forms of monotheism. However, determining the movement from social and mercantile contacts to religious influences and causal connections is difficult. Muslims offer a simple and direct solution. Similarities in revelation and practice are due to their common divine source; differences occur where Judaism and Christianity departed from their original revelation.

If there is a statement of the core doctrines of Islam, it occurs in the fourth chapter of the Quran:

> O believers, believe in God and His Messenger and the Book He has sent down on His Messenger and the Book which He sent down before. Whoever disbelieves in God and His angels and His Books, and His messengers, and the Last Day, has surely gone astray into far error. (4:136)

Allah

At the center and foundation of Islam is Allah, the God, whose name appears more than 2,500 times in the Quran. In a polytheistic, pagan society Muhammad declared the sole existence of Allah, the transcendent, all-powerful and all-knowing Creator, Sustainer, Ordainer, and

Judge of the universe. While God is concerned about mankind, knows people intimately, and can act in history, He is and remains transcendent: "No vision can grasp Him, but His grasp is over all vision. He is above all comprehension, yet is acquainted with all things" (6:103). Thus, people cannot know God directly. The Quran does not reveal God, but God's will or law for all creation.

The transcendent God is the one God, and He is the only God: "And your God is One God. There is no god but He" (2:163). God is not a Trinity (5:76); He has no begotten son (2:116) nor daughters nor consorts (6:100–01); and finally, unlike the religion of pre-Islamic Arabia, God has no partners or associate deities (6:22–24).

When Muslims worship five times each day, they declare Islam's absolute or radical monotheism: "I witness that there is no god but the God (Allah)." Throughout the Quran, God reminds His people that He alone exists and is to be worshipped. This radical monotheism and the consequent iconoclasm of Islam were vividly demonstrated when Muhammad entered the Kaba on his triumphant return to Mecca and destroyed the tribal idols. Its central theological significance is underscored by the Quran's condemnation of associationism or idolatry (associating or allowing anything to usurp God's place) as the great sin (31:13). Indeed it is the one unforgivable sin: "God forgives not that aught should be associated with Him . . . Whoso associates with God anything, has indeed forged a mighty sin" (4:48).

Culturally, this concern not to compromise the unity and transcendence of God led to an absolute ban on any image or representation of God or Muhammad. Many Arab Muslims extended this ban to any representation in art of the human form for fear that such statues and paintings might lead to idol worship. This attitude resulted in the use of calligraphy (Arabic script) and arabesque (geometric and floral design) as dominant forms in Islamic art.

The absolute monotheism of Islam is preserved in the doctrine of the unity and sovereignty of God which dominates Islamic belief and practice. Allah is the one, true God. As God is one, His rule and will or law are comprehensive, extending to all creatures and to all aspects of life. As we shall see, this belief affected early Muslim conceptions and institutions so that religion was viewed as integral to state, law, and society.

The overwhelming sense of God's sovereignty and power is epitomized in the declaration "God is Most Great" (*Allahu Akbar*), which has served as a preface to the call to prayer and as the traditional battle cry of God's fighters or holy warriors throughout Islamic history, from

Muhammad's early battles to contemporary struggles in Iran and Afghanistan.

If God is the Lord, then the Muslim is His servant before whom submission (*islam*) or obedience is the most natural and appropriate response. The term "Muslim" means "one who submits" or surrenders to God; it includes everyone who follows His guidance and performs His will. All the great monotheistic prophets are regarded as true Muslims. Thus, Abraham is not a Jew or a Christian but a follower of the true religion, one who submitted (*muslim*) to God (3:67). Is this submission that of a slave before a powerful and fearsome master? Many non-Muslim commentators portray Allah in this way. A careful reading of the Quran and a look at Muslim practice indicate otherwise.

While the Quran, like the Bible, underscores the awesome power and majesty of God and the Day of Judgment, the verses of the Quran reveal a merciful and just judge. Opening the Quran to its initial chapter, one reads, "In the name of God, the Merciful and Compassionate." Each of its chapters begins with this appellation, keeping before the believer a reminder of the nature of the God of this revelation. The terms "merciful" and "compassionate" are intensive forms of the same root, *rahmat*. This quality or attribute includes the idea not only of forgiveness, but also of a bounteous mercy that sustains, protects, and rewards people. "Mercy" includes such meanings as the beneficence, compassion, and graciousness of God.

God's mercy permeates the entire life and milieu of the believer. It is reflected in nature, which serves as the theater for the human realization of God's will in history and creation, and reaches its zenith in God's merciful gift to humankind, His revelation.

The Quran declares that everyone experiences the signs of God's mercy in the activities of nature:

> It is He who sends the winds like heralds of glad tidings, going before His Mercy: when they have carried the heavy-laden clouds, We drive them to a land that is dead, make rain to descend thereon, and produce every kind of harvest therewith. (7:57)

The Quran teems with references to the many wonders of nature that God's mercy provides: "Night and Day that you may rest therein" (28:73); the "sun and moon follow courses [exactly] computed" (55:5); God provides animals such as cattle and "from them you derive warmth, and numerous benefits, and of them ye eat . . . for your Lord is indeed Most Kind, Most Merciful" (16:5–7); and God created man and made all the earth subject to him (22:65).

While creation and God's dealings with His creatures reflect His Mercy, His beneficence is supremely manifest in His revelation to humankind through the prophets, culminating in the final revelation of the Quran. Its author is the Most Merciful (36:5), in it is mercy (29:51), and its motivation is the mercy of God: "We sent it down during a blessed night for We (ever) wish to warn (against evil) . . . . For We (ever) send (revelation) as a Mercy from your Lord: for He hears and knows (all things)" (44:3–6). Similarly, the sending of Muhammad was a sign of God's mercy: "We sent you not, but as a Mercy for all creatures" (21:107).

The lesson of God's mercy proclaimed by the Quran has been institutionalized and reinforced by the Muslim practice of beginning important matters such as a letter, public speech, lecture, article, or book with the phrase, "In the name of God, the Merciful and Compassionate." No wonder that Muslims take exception to those who describe Muslim faith as primarily based upon fear of a terrible God.

Strong emphasis on God's mercy should not conjure up a permissive deity. God's mercy exists in dialectical tension with His justice. The Quran gives the sobering warning, "Your Lord is quick in retribution, but He is also oft forgiving, Most Merciful" (7:167). Even here, justice is tempered by mercy toward the repentent sinner. However, sinners, such as those who fall away from the faith, can expect "the curse of Allah and the angels and of men combined" (3:86–87). The absolute justice of God and the sinner's inability to escape His retribution (save for repentance) are declared time and again:

> As to those who reject faith, if they had everything on earth, and twice repeated, to give as ransom for the penalty of the Day of Judgment, it would never be accepted of them. Theirs will be to get out therefrom: Their penalty will be one that endures. (5:39–40)

Yet, if the sinner repents of wrongdoing, the Quran assures that "Allah is Forgiving and Merciful" (5:42).

God's justice is based on the belief that He knows and sees all and that individuals are responsible for each and every action. Reward and punishment follow from individual, ethical responsibility and accountability before an all-knowing and just judge. Thus, Islamic ethics follow from mankind's special status and responsibility on earth.

THE QURANIC UNIVERSE

The Quranic universe consists of three realms: heaven, earth, and hell. Governed by its creator-judge, the world is inhabited by human beings and spirits (angels, jinns, and devils) who are called to obedience to the one, true Allah, the Lord of the Universe. Angels serve as the link between God and human beings. Created out of light, immortal and sexless, they function as guardians, recorders, and messengers from God. They are transmitters of God's message, communicating divine revelation to the prophets. Thus, Gabriel (Jibril) brought down the Quran from heaven to Muhammad. Among the more prominent angels are Michael and Israfel. Somewhere between angels and humans are the invisible, intelligent spirits called jinn. In contrast to human beings, the jinn were created from fire instead of earth (7:12, 55:14–15). They have the ability to assume visible form and, like humans, can be good or bad, sin as well as be saved (46:29–31). They will be judged on the Last Day and consigned to paradise or hell. Folk tales such as *The Thousand and One Nights* ascribe magical powers to the jinn, who became known in the West as genies. Finally, at the opposite end of the spectrum from God, the principle of good, is Satan (*shaytan*, adversary), the principle of evil. The origin of Satan goes back to the Garden, where, as will be discussed, one of the angels (Iblis or Satan, the devil) refused to pay homage to Adam. Satan is the leader of other fallen angels and jinn, disobedient servants of God who tempt human beings in their earthly moral struggle on earth. It was Iblis who tempted Adam and Eve (20:116–22). Although permitted by God to engage in their evil ways, Iblis and his followers will be consigned to hell on Judgment Day.

Of all creation, man enjoys a unique relationship with God, for after creating Adam, God breathed into him His spirit (15:29). Moreover, the Quran declares that God created human beings in "the best of molds or stature" (95:4) to be His representatives on earth. This special selection and status led to Satan's rebellion, a story that strikingly conveys the cosmic significance of humankind.

Informed by God of mankind's special status, the angels initially protested, "Will You set therein one who will do corruption there, and shed blood, while we proclaim your praise and call You Holy?" (2:30). Adam proved the uniqueness of humankind by demonstrating a God-given knowledge of creation that the angels did not possess. However, when God commanded the angels to prostrate themselves before Adam, Satan or Iblis refused (2:34 and 7:11ff). It was Satan's refusal to accept man's unique status in the hierarchy of the universe that caused his rebellion and expulsion from heaven, and led to the Fall and to the age-long moral struggle of human beings, torn between the forces of good (God) and those of evil (Satan).

> Then the angels bowed all together, except for Iblis who refused to be among those bowing. God said: Iblis, why are you not among those who bow down on their knees? He said: I am not going to kneel before a

human being that you have made from clay, from molded mud. God said: Get out of here; you are an outcast. My curse will be on you until the Day of Judgment! He said: My Lord, let me wait until the Day of Resurrection. God said: You shall be allowed to wait until the appointed time. He said: My Lord, since you have led me astray, I shall make things on the earth attractive to them and lead them astray, except for your sincere servants. God said: This will be a straight path to me. You shall have no authority except over those who are perverse and follow you. Hell shall be their promised place. (15:30–42)

The essence of human uniqueness lies in one's vocation as God's representative on earth. God has given people the earth as a divine trust (33:72); they are thus His vicegerents or agents on earth (2:30, 35:39) to whom God has made all creation subservient (16:12–14). It is on the basis of how this vicegerency is executed, or how God's will in history is realized or actualized, that a person will be rewarded or punished:

It is He who had made you (His) agents, inheritors of the earth. He hath raised you in ranks, some above others that He may try you. For thy Lord is quick in punishment, yet He is indeed Oft Forgiving, Most Merciful. (6:165)

It is here that we see the roots of Islamic ethics. God ordains; humankind is to implement His will. Human responsibility and mission are of cosmic proportion, and people will be judged on the cosmic consequences of their acts. As God's representatives, the measure of human actions, and indeed life, is the extent to which the Muslim contributes to the realization of God's will on earth. This responsibility lies squarely on each individual's shoulders, since no one can bear another's responsibility or suffer for another:

Nor can a bearer of burdens bear another's burden. If one heavily laden should call another to (bear) his load, not the least portion of it can be carried (by the other), even though he be nearly related . . . . And whosoever purifies himself does so for the benefit of his own soul. (35:18) . . . And whatever good you do, you shall not be denied the just reward of it . . . . As for the unbelievers, their riches shall not avail them, neither their children against God; those are the inhabitants of the Fire, dwelling therein forever. (3:115–16)

Although it is not a prominent theme in the Quran, Muslim tradition did come to accept the intercession of Muhammad on behalf of individuals. However, unlike Christianity, there is no vicarious suffering or atonement for humankind. Such actions are unnecessary, since Islam has no doctrine of original sin.

The story of the Fall in the Quran differs from that in the Bible in its teaching regarding personal responsibility. It is Adam, not Eve, who is tempted by the devil. Woman is not portrayed as the cause of the Fall, as in the Judeo-Christian traditions. Moreover, the sin of Adam and Eve is just that—their own personal sin. It is an act of disobedience for which they, and they alone, are responsible. Unlike Christianity, there is no notion of an inherited "original" sin, committed by the progenitors of the human race, for which all humanity suffers. Sin is not a state of being; it is the result of an act of disobedience, failure to do or not to do what God commands or prohibits. Human beings are not sinful by nature; as they are created or finite creatures, they are naturally limited, weak, and subject to temptation. Similarly, death follows from the human condition and is not due to sin or the Fall. The consequences of sin, like human responsibility, belong solely to those who commit sin.

The biblical and Quranic stories about the consequences of the Fall reveal the basis for the divergent doctrines of Christianity and Islam. The former views the Fall as the cause of man's flawed nature and existence; the latter finds here the story of sin, God's mercy, and repentance. In the Bible, the Fall brings a life of shame, disgrace, and hardship:

> To the woman He said, "I will greatly multiply your pain in childbearing; in pain you shall bring forth children, yet your desire shall be your husband, and he shall rule over you." And to Adam He said, "Because you have listened to the voice of your wife, and have eaten of the tree of which I commanded you, you shall not eat of it, cursed is the ground because of you; in toil you shall eat of it all the days of your life; thorns and thistles it shall bring forth to you." (Genesis 3:16–18)

In sharp contrast, the Quran teaches that after Adam disobeys God but repents, God extends to Adam His mercy and guidance: "But his Lord chose him. He turned to him and gave him guidance" (20:122). Adam turned away from Satan and sin and turned back to God; Adam repented, and God forgave. This is the paradigm for sin and repentance in Islam. If the Muslim is one who is to submit to God by following His will, sin is disobedience or refusal to submit. It is the arrogance and ingratitude of creatures who forget or turn away from their creator and sustainer. Repentance is simply remembering or returning to God's path, the straight path of Islam. There is little or no emphasis on feelings of shame and disgrace or guilt. What God commands, and what His awesome character engenders, is fear of God (*taqwa*): "The most honored of you in the sight of God is the most righteous or God fearing of you" (49:13).

Taqwa means self-protection or fear of God. This attitude or disposition follows from belief in an all-powerful, omnipresent God (an ever-present God who is as near as one's jugular vein, 50:16), who has commanded submission or obedience to His will and before whom the

Muslim is morally responsible and accountable. It is the response of the believer who knows what he or she must do and who lives life ever mindful of the eternal consequences that await on the Last Day. The duties and obligations of Muslim life, as well as its rewards and punishments, fall equally on men and women:

> The believers, men and women, are guardians of one another; they enjoin good and evil, perform the prayer, give alms, and obey God and His Prophet. (9:71) . . . Whoever does a righteous deed, whether man or women, and has faith, we will give a good life; and we shall reward them according to the best of their actions. (16:97)

THE MUSLIM COMMUNITY

The Muslim mission to be servants of God and to spread God's rule is both an individual and a community obligation. The Quran emphasizes the social dimension of service to God, for it is on earth and in society that God's will is to govern and prevail. As humankind came from a single pair of parents, so too God "made you into nations and tribes" (49:13). Similarly, as God had sent His prophets and revelation to the Jews and then to the Christians, He declares in the Quran that the Muslims now constitute the new community of believers who are to be an example to other nations: "Thus We made you an *umma* justly balanced, that ye might be witness over the nations" (2:143).

Guided by the word of God and the Prophet, the Muslim community has a mission to create a moral social order: "You are the best community evolved for mankind, enjoining what is right and forbidding what is wrong" (3:110). This command has influenced Muslim practice throughout the centuries, providing a rationale for political and moral activism. Government regulations, Islamic laws, and the activities of religious police who monitor public behavior have all been justified as expressions of this moral mission to command the good and prohibit evil. Again, Muhammad and the first Muslim community are seen as exemplifying this ideal, implementing the socially just society envisioned by the Quran.

While recognizing differences in status, wealth, and tribal origin, the Quran teaches the ultimate supratribal (transnational) unity and equality of all believers before God. Common faith, not tribal or family ties, binds the community together. The Quran envisions a society based on the unity and equality of believers, a society in which moral and social justice will counterbalance oppression of the weak and economic exploitation. Belief and action are to be joined; Muslims are not only to know and believe, but also to act and implement. Worship and devotion to God embrace both private and public life, affecting not only prayer, fasting, and pilgrimage, but social behavior as well. Like his prophetic predecessors, Muhammad brought a revelation that challenged the established order. The message of the Quran was reformist, if not revolutionary. Quranic prescriptions would provide the basis for the later development of Islamic law to chart this new social order. The scope of Quranic concerns reflects the comprehensiveness of Islam. It includes rules concerning modesty, marriage, divorce, inheritance, feuding, intoxicants, gambling, diet, theft, murder, fornication, and adultery.

The socioeconomic reforms of the Quran are among its most striking features. Exploitation of the poor, weak, widows, women, orphans (4:2; 4:12), and slaves is vividly condemned:

> Those who live off orphans' property without having any right to do so will only suck up fire into their bellies, and they will roast in the fires (of hell). (4:10)

False contracts, bribery, abuse of women, hoarding of wealth to the exclusion of its subordination to higher ends, and usury are denounced. The Quran demands that Muslims pursue a path of social justice, rooted in the recognition that the earth belongs ultimately to God and that human beings are its caretakers. While wealth is seen as good, a sign of hard work and God's pleasure, its pursuit and accumulation are limited by God's law. Its rewards are subject to social responsibility toward other members of the community, in particular the poor and needy:

> The alms [zakat] are for the poor and needy, those who work to collect them, those whose hearts are to be reconciled, the ransoming of slaves and debtors, and for the cause of God, and for travellers. (9:60)

Social justice was institutionalized by Quranic decrees that required the payment of an alms tax (zakat) and a voluntary charity for the poor, stipulations of fixed shares of inheritance for women and children, and a host of regulations regarding the just treatment of debtors, widows, the poor, orphans (90:13–16), and slaves (24:33). Those who practice usury are sternly rebuked and warned that they face "war from God and His prophet" (2:279).

THE LAST DAY

While Muslims are exhorted to follow God's will out of obedience and gratitude to their creator, the specter of the Last Judgment, with its eternal reward and punishment, remains a constant reminder of the ultimate consequences of each life. It underscores the Quran's strong and repeated emphasis on the ultimate moral responsibility and accountability of each believer. At a moment known only to God, all will be called to judgment in a great cosmic cataclysmic event (81:1–14), also referred to as the Day of Decision or the Day of Reckoning. Each community will be judged by the standards brought by its prophets and Book. Humans and jinn (spirits) alike will stand before the throne of God. All are responsible for their own actions and will be judged according to the record found in the Book of Deeds (45:29–30). As discussed previously, there is no redemption, atonement, or intercession through an intermediary. Allah, who is a merciful but all-powerful judge, consigns all either to heaven or to hell as He wills (5:43). While the Quran teaches that intercession belongs to God alone (39:44; 6:54, 70), belief in Muhammad's role as a divinely designated intercessor did develop and was justified by the text, "There is no intercessor [with God] unless He gives permission" (10:3).

The Quranic vision of the afterlife is both spiritual and physical. Since the Last Day will be accompanied by bodily resurrection (41: 39–40, 49–50), the pleasures of heaven and the pain of hell will be fully experienced. The Garden of Paradise is a heavenly mansion of perpetual peace and bliss with flowing rivers, beautiful gardens, and the enjoyment of one's spouses and beautiful, dark-eyed female companions (houris). Descriptions of heavenly bliss follow from the general tenor of the Quran, which is life-affirming, emphasizing the beauty of creation and enjoyment of its pleasures within the limits set by God. This more integral, comprehensive view of life stands in sharp contrast to the Christian tendency to compartmentalize life into the sacred and the profane, body and soul, sensual and spiritual. In contrast to the "spiritual" images of a more somber, celibate Paradise predominant in Christianity, the Quran offers vivid descriptions of the delights and pleasures of Paradise, seeing no contradiction between enjoyment of both the beatific vision and the fruits of creation:

> in gardens of bliss . . . a multitude will be seated on couches set close together. . . . Immortal youths will serve them with goblets, pitchers and cups filled with water from a spring which will not upset them or dull their senses; and they may choose fruit of any kind and whatever fowl they desire and chaste companions with eyes of a beauty like pearls hidden in shells . . . . We formed them perfectly and made them spotless virgins, chastely amorous and of the same age. (56:12–37)

In sharp contrast, the damned will be banished to hell, forever separated from God. Anguish and despair will be coupled with physical torment, for they will experience

> a fire whose sheets encompass them. If they should ask for relief, then water like molten copper shall be showered upon them to scald their faces. How awful is such a drink and how evil a resting place. (18:29)

Conclusion

For Muslims throughout the centuries, the message of the Quran and the example of the Prophet Muhammad have constituted the formative and enduring foundation of faith and belief. They have served as the basic sources of Islamic law and the reference points for daily life. Muslims today, as in the past, continue to affirm that the Quran is the literal word of God, the Creator's immutable guidance for an otherwise transient world. This transhistorical significance is rooted in the belief that the Book and the Prophet provide eternal principles and norms on which Muslim life, both individual and collective, is to be patterned. The challenge for each generation of believers has been the continued formulation, appropriation, and implementation of Islam in history. Islamic history and civilization provide the record of that struggle to interpret and to follow the Straight Path.

2

The Muslim Community
in History

The history of Islam has often been linked to the existence of an Islamic state or empire. From its beginnings, Islam existed and spread as a community-state; it was both a faith and a political order. Within centuries after his death, Muhammad's local Arabian polity became a vast empire, extending from North Africa to Southeast Asia. The development of Islam and state institutions (the caliphate, law, education, the military, social services) were intertwined. Again, the Prophetic period provided the paradigm for later generations. For it was in Medina that the Quranic mandate took on form and substance under the guidance and direction of the Prophet.

The Medinan community formed a total framework for state, society, and culture. It epitomized the Quranic mandate for Muslims as individuals and as a community "to transform the world itself through action in the world."[8] This aspiration and ideal has constituted the challenge for the Islamic community throughout much of its history. It inspired Muhammad to transform a local shiekdom into a transtribal state.

Muhammad and the Medinan State

Seventh-century Arabia was dominated by two great empires: the Byzantine (Christian), or Eastern Roman, empire and the Sasanian Persian (Zoroastrian) empire. In the middle was the Arabian Peninsula, composed of apparently weak and divided tribal societies. Within one hundred years, both empires would fall before the armies of Allah as Muhammad and his successors united Arabia under the umbrella of Islam, which provided a principle of organization and motivation. In time, a vast empire and a commonwealth of Islamic states would come to dominate much of the world. Its missionaries would be soldiers, merchants, and mystics. Islam would provide the basis of community identity and the rationale or legitimacy for rulers and their policies of expansion and conquest. Thus, for example, the wars of conquest were termed *fath*, "opening or victory" of the way for Islam. As Muhammad governed a transtribal state in the name of Islam, so too the Islamic community became associated with an expansive empire. Why and how did this come to pass?

Shortly after the surrender of Mecca, Muhammad turned his attention to the extension and consolidation of his authority over Arabia. Envoys were sent and alliances forged with surrounding tribes and rulers. The fiercely independent Bedouin tribes of Arabia were united behind the Prophet of Islam through a combination of force and diplomacy. As Muhammad was both head of state and messenger of God, so too were the envoys and soldiers of the state the envoys and soldiers of Islam, its first missionaries. Along with their treaties and armies, they brought the Quran and the teachings of their faith. They spread a way of life that affected the political and social order as well as individual life and worship. Islam encompassed both a faith and a sociopolitical system. Ideally, this new order was to be a community of believers, acknowledging the ultimate sovereignty of God, living according to His law, obeying His Prophet, and dedicating their lives to spreading God's rule and law. This was the message and vision that accompanied Arab armies as they burst out of Arabia and established their supremacy throughout the Middle East.

What is most striking about the early expansion of Islam is its rapidity and success. Western scholars have marveled at it. Muslim tradition has viewed the conquests as a miraculous proof or historic validation of the truth of Islam's claims and a sign of God's guidance. Within a decade, Arab forces overran the Byzantine and Persian armies, exhausted by years of warfare, and conquered Iraq, Syria, Palestine, Persia, and Egypt. The momentum of these early victories was extended to a series of brilliant battles under great generals like Khalid ibn al-Walid and Amr ibn al-As, which extended the boundaries of the Muslim empire to Morocco and Spain in the west and across Central Asia to India in the east. Driven by the economic rewards from conquest of richer, more developed areas, united and inspired by their new faith, Muslim armies proved to be formidable conquerors and effective rulers, builders rather than destroyers. They replaced the indigenous rulers and armies of the conquered countries, but preserved much of their government, bureaucracy, and culture. For many in the conquered territories, it was no more than an exchange of masters, one that brought peace to peoples demoralized and disaffected by the casualties and heavy taxation that resulted from the years of Byzantine-Persian warfare. Local communities were free to continue to follow their own way of life in internal, domestic affairs. In many ways, local populations found Muslim rule more flexible and tolerant than that of Byzantium and Persia. Religious communities were free to practice their faith—to worship and be governed by their religious leaders and laws in such areas as marriage, divorce, and inheritance. In exchange, they were required to pay tribute, a poll tax (*jizya*) that entitled them to Muslim protection from outside aggression and exempted them from military service. They were therefore called the "protected ones" (*dhimmi*). In effect, this often meant lower taxes, greater local autonomy, rule by fellow Semites with closer linguistic and cultural ties than the hellenized, Greco-Roman elites of Byzantium, and greater religious freedom for Jews and indigenous Christians. Most of the Christian churches, such as the Nestorians, Monophysites, Jacobites, and Copts had been persecuted as heretics and schismatics by Christian orthodoxy. For these reasons, some Jewish and Christian communities aided the invading armies, regarding them as less oppressive than their imperial masters. In many ways, the conquests brought a Pax Islamica to an embattled area:

> The conquests destroyed little: what they did suppress were imperial rivalries and sectarian bloodletting among the newly subjected population. The Muslims tolerated Christianity, but they disestablished it; henceforward Christian life and liturgy, its endowments, politics and theology, would be a private and not a public affair. By an exquisite irony, Islam reduced the status of Christians to that which the Christians had earlier thrust upon the Jews, with one difference. The reduction in Christian status was merely judicial; it was unaccompanied by either systematic persecution or a blood lust, and generally, though not everywhere and at all times, unmarred by vexatious behavior.[9]

A common issue associated with the spread of Islam is the role of jihad, so-called holy war. While Westerners are quick to characterize Islam as a religion spread by the sword, modern Muslim apologists sometimes explain jihad as simply defensive in nature. In its most general sense, jihad in the Quran and in Muslim practice refers to the obligation of all Muslims to strive (*jihad*, self-exertion) or struggle to follow God's will. This includes both the struggle to lead a virtuous life and the universal mission of the Muslim community to spread God's rule and law through teaching, preaching, and, where necessary, armed struggle. Contrary to popular belief, the early conquests did not seek to spread the faith through forced conversion but to spread Muslim rule. Many early Muslims regarded Islam solely as a Arab religion. Moreover, from an economic perspective, increase in the size of the community through conversion diminished Arab Muslims' share in the spoils of conquest. As Islam penetrated new areas, people were offered three options: (1) conversion, that is, full membership in the Muslim community, with its rights and duties; (2) acceptance of Muslim rule as "protected" people and payment of a poll tax; (3) battle or the sword if neither the first nor the second option was accepted. The astonishing expansion of Islam resulted not only from armed conquest but also from these two peaceful options. In later centuries, in many areas of Africa, the Indian subcontinent, and Southeast Asia, the effective spread of Islam would be due primarily to Muslim traders and Sufi (mystic) missionaries who won converts by their example and their preaching.

The Caliphate (632–1258)

Given Muhammad's formative and pivotal role, his death (632) threatened to radically destabilize the community. Who was to lead? What was to happen to the community? The companions of the Prophet moved quickly to steady and reassure the community. Abu Bakr, an early follower of Muhammad, announced the death of the Prophet to the assembled faithful: "Muslims! If any of you has worshipped Muhammad, let me tell you that Muhammad is dead. But if you worship God, then know that God is living and will never die!" Nevertheless, the Prophet's death did plunge the Islamic community into a series of political crises revolving around leadership and authority. Issues of succession and secession were to plague the early community.

The caliphate (632–1258) has traditionally been divided into three periods: the "Rightly Guided Caliphs" (632–661), the Umayyad empire (661–750), and the Abbasid empire (750–1258). During these eras, a vast empire was created with successive capitals in Medina, Kufa, Damascus, and Baghdad. Stunning political success was complemented by a cultural florescence in law, theology, philosophy, literature, medicine, mathematics, science, and art.

The Rightly Guided Caliphs

The caliphate began in 632 with the selection of Muhammad's successor. The first four caliphs were all companions of the Prophet: Abu Bakr (reigned 632–634), Umar ibn al-Khattab (634–644), Uthman ibn Affan (644–656), and Ali ibn Abi Talib (656–661). Their rule is especially significant not only for what they actually did, but also because the period of Muhammad and the Rightly Guided Caliphs came to be regarded in Sunni Islam as the normative period. It provides the idealized past to which Muslims have looked back for inspiration and guidance, a time to be remembered and emulated.

The vast majority of Muslims (Sunni) believe that Muhammad died without designating his replacement or establishing a system for the selection of his successor. After an initial period of uncertainty, the Prophet's companions, the elders or leaders of Medina, selected or acknowledged Abu Bakr, an early convert and the Prophet's father-in-law, as caliph (*khalifa*, successor or deputy). Abu Bakr's designation as leader was symbolized by the offering of *baya* (oath), a handclasp used by the Arabs to seal a contract, in this case an oath of obedience and allegiance. Abu Bakr had been a close companion and a trusted adviser of Muhammad; he was a man respected for his sagacity and piety. Muhammad had appointed him to lead the Friday community prayer in his absence. As caliph, Abu Bakr was the political and military leader of the community. Although not a prophet, the caliph enjoyed religious prestige as head of the community of believers. This was symbolized in later history by the caliph's right to lead the Friday prayer and the inclusion of his name in its prayers.

Having resolved the question of political leadership and succession, Abu Bakr turned to the consolidation of Muslim rule in Arabia. Muhammad's death had precipitated a series of tribal rebellions. Many tribal chiefs claimed that their allegiance had been based on a political pact with Medina that ceased with the Prophet's death. Tribal independence and factionalism, long a part of Arab history, once more threatened the unity and identity of the new Islamic state. Abu Bakr countered that the unity of the community was based on the interconnectedness of faith and politics and undertook a series of battles that later Muslim historians would call the wars of apostasy. Relying on Khalid ibn al-Walid, whom Muhammad had dubbed "the sword of Allah," he crushed the tribal revolt, consolidating Muslim rule over the entire Arabian Peninsula, and thus preserved the unity and solidarity of the Islamic community-state.

Abu Bakr's successor, Umar, initiated the great period of expansion and conquest. One of the great military leaders of his time, he added the title "Commander of the Faithful" to that of "Successor" or "Deputy of the Prophet of God." He also introduced a new method for the selection of his successor. On his deathbed, Umar appointed an "election committee" to select the next caliph. After due consultation, the council of electors chose Uthman ibn Affan from the Umayyad clan, a leading Meccan family. This was accompanied by the traditional sign of allegiance, the clasping of hands. Thus, based on the practice of the first three caliphs, a pattern was established for selecting the caliph from the Quraysh tribe through a process characterized by consultation and an oath of allegiance.

Before long, tribal factionalism and the threat of rebellion resurfaced in the community. Uthman's family had been among the strongest foes of the Prophet. Many of the Medinan elite, who had been among the early supporters of Muhammad, resented Uthman's accession to power and the increased prominence and wealth of his family. Although personally pious, Uthman lacked the presence and leadership skills of his predecessors. Accusations that the caliph was weak and guilty of nepotism fueled political intrigue. In 656, Uthman was assassinated by a group of mutineers from Egypt. The caliph's murder was the first in a series of Muslim rebellions and tribal fratricides that would plague the Islamic community's political development.

THE CALIPH ALI AND THE FIRST CIVIL WARS

Ali, the cousin and son-in-law of the Prophet, succeeded Uthman as the fourth caliph. Ali was devoted to Muhammad and among the first to embrace Islam. He had married Fatima, the only surviving child of Muhammad and Khadijah, with whom he had two sons, Hasan and Husayn. Ali was a charismatic figure who inspired fierce loyalty and commitment. Many of Ali's supporters (Alids) believed that leadership of the Islamic community should remain within the family of the Prophet and that, indeed, Muhammad had designated Ali as his rightful successor and heir. For these partisans of Ali, later to be called Shii (*shiat-u-Ali*, party of Ali), the first three caliphs were interlopers who had denied Ali his rightful inheritance. However, their satisfaction and expectations were to be short-lived. Within the few short years that Ali ruled, the caliphate was racked by two civil wars. Ali's authority was challenged by two opposition movements: first, by a coalition headed by Muhammad's widow, Aisha (the daughter of Abu Bakr), and second, by the forces of Muawiyah, the governor of Syria and a relative of Uthman. Ali's failure to find and prosecute Uthman's murderers became the pretext for both revolts. In the first, Ali crushed a triumvirate led by Aisha, the youngest wife of Muhammad. The "Battle of the Camel," so named because it took place around the camel on which Aisha was mounted, marked the first time a caliph had led his army against another Muslim army.

Of greater long-range significance was Muawiyah's challenge to Ali's authority. Securely established in Damascus with a strong army, Muawiyah, the nephew of Uthman, had refused to step down and accept Ali's appointment of a replacement. In 657, at Siffin (in modern-day Syria), Ali led his army against his rebellious governor. Faced with defeat, Muawiyah's men raised Qurans on the tips of their spears and called for arbitration according to the Quran, crying out, "Let God decide." Although the arbitration proved inconclusive, it yielded two results that would have lasting effects. A splinter group of Alids, the Kharijites or "seceders," broke with Ali for having failed to subdue Muawiyah; Muawiyah walked away from Siffin and continued to govern Syria, extending his rule to Egypt as well. When Ali was murdered by Kharijites in 661, Muawiyah laid successful claim to the caliphate, moving its capital to Damascus and frustrating Alid belief that leadership of the community should be restricted to Ali's descendants. With the establishment of the Umayyad dynasty, the "golden age" of Muhammad and the Rightly Guided Caliphs came to an end and the caliphate became an absolute monarchy.

Despite the turmoil during the early caliphal years, Muslims regard the period of Muhammad and the first generation of companions or elders as normative for a variety of reasons. First, God sent down His final and complete revelation in the Quran and the last of His prophets, Muhammad. Second, the Islamic community-state was created, bonded by a common religious identity and purpose. Third, the sources of Islamic law, the Quran and the example of the Prophet, originated at this time. Fourth, this period of the early companions serves as the reference point for all Islamic revival and reform, both traditionalist and modernist. Fifth, the success and power that resulted from the near-miraculous victories and geographic expansion of Islam constitute, in the eyes of believers, historical validation of the message of Islam.

ORGANIZATION AND INSTITUTIONS

The early caliphate established the pattern for the organization and administration of the Islamic state. Islam provided the basic identity and ideology of the state, a source of unity and solidarity. The caliph's authority and leadership were rooted in his claim to be the successor of the Prophet as head of the community. Muhammad's practice provided the model for governance. The caliph exercised direct political, military, judicial, and fiscal control of the Muslim community. He was chosen through a process of consultation, nomination, and selection by a small group of electors who, after pledging their allegiance, presented the caliph to the people for acceptance by public acclamation. The caliph was the protector and defender of the faith; he was to assure the following of

God's law and spread the rule of God through expansion and conquest. The community was a brotherhood of believers, a society based on religious rather than tribal solidarity.

In general, the Arabs did not occupy conquered cities but established garrison towns nearby, such as Basra and Kufa in Iraq, Fustat (Cairo) in Egypt, and Qariwiyin in North Africa. From these towns, conquered territories were governed and expeditions launched. They were centered around a mosque, which served as the religious and public focal point of the towns. Conquered territories were divided into provinces, each of which was administered by a governor who was usually a military commander. The internal civil and religious administration remained in the hands of local officials. An agent of the caliph oversaw the collection of taxes and other administrative activities. Revenue for the state came from the captured lands and taxes.

The Islamic system of taxes took several forms: the tithe or wealth tax to benefit the poor and a land tax paid by Muslims; the poll tax and tribute, later a land tax, paid by non-Muslims. All revenue was owned, collected, and administered by the state. The distribution of revenue was managed by the registry at Medina through a system of payments and pensions based on priority in accepting Islam. The Muslims at Medina and the family of the Prophet enjoyed a special place of honor because of their closeness to Muhammad and their fidelity to God's call.

Muslim society was divided into four major social classes. The elites of society were the Arab Muslims, with special status given to the companions of the Prophet because of their early support and role in establishing the community. Next came the non-Arab converts to Islam. Although in theory all Muslims were equal before God, in fact, practice varied. Under the Umayyads, non-Arab Muslims were clearly second-class citizens. They continued to pay those taxes levied on non-Muslims even after their conversion. The *dhimmi*, or non-Muslim People of the Book (those who possessed a revealed Scripture, Jews and Christians), constituted communities within and subject to the wider Islamic community-state. In time, this protected status was extended to Hindus and Buddhists. Finally, there were the slaves. As in much of the Near East, slavery had long existed among the Arabs. Although the Quran commanded the just and humane treatment of slaves (16:71) and regarded their emancipation as a meritorious act (90:13; 58:3), the system of slavery was adopted in a modified form. Only captives in battle could be taken as slaves. Neither Muslims nor Jews and Christians could be enslaved in early Islam.

Thus, religion played an important role in the government, law, taxation, and social organization of society.

The Umayyad Empire:
Creation of an Arab Kingdom

The advent of Umayyad rule set in motion a process of continued expansion and centralization of authority that would transform the Islamic community from an Arab shaykhdom into an Islamic empire whose rulers were dependent on religion for legitimacy and the military for power and stability.

In 661, Muawiyah (reigned 661–80) laid claim to the caliphate and ushered in the Umayyad era (661–750): imperial, dynastic, and dominated by an Arab military aristocracy. The capital was moved to Damascus. This permanent shift from the less sophisticated Arabian heartland to the established, cosmopolitan Greco-Roman Byzantine city symbolized the new imperial age. From this new center, the Umayyads completed the conquest of the entire Persian and half the Roman (Byzantine) empire. When Muawiyah seized power, Islam had already spread to Egypt, Libya, the Fertile Crescent, Syria, Iraq, and Persia across Armenia to the borders of Afghanistan. Under the Umayyads, Muslims captured the Maghreb (North Africa), Spain, and Portugal, marched across Europe until they were halted in the heart of France by Charles Martel at the Battle of Tours in 732, and extended the empire's borders to the Indian subcontinent. The accomplishments of the Umayyads were indeed remarkable. Damascus became an even greater imperial capital than it had been under Byzantine rule. Umayyad rulers developed a strong centralized dynastic kingdom, an Arab empire. The more advanced government, institutions, and bureaucracy of Byzantium were adopted and adapted to Arab Muslim needs. Native civil servants and ministers were retained to guide and train their Muslim masters. In time, through a process of conversion and assimilation, language and culture, state and society were Arabized and Islamized. Arabic became the language of government as well as the lingua franca of what today constitutes North Africa and much of the Middle East. Islamic belief and values constituted the official norm and reference point for personal and public life.

Umayyad rulers relied on Islam for legitimacy and as a rationale for their conquests. Caliphs were the protectors and defenders of the faith charged with extending the rule of Islam. The basis of Umayyad unity and stability was the establishment of an Arab monarchy and reliance on Arab, in particular Syrian, warriors. Contrary to previous practice, hereditary succession, not selection or election, restricted the caliphate to the Umayyad house. This innovation, or departure from early Islamic practice, became the pretext for later Muslim historians, writing with

Abbasid patronage, to denounce Umayyad rule as kingship and thus un-Islamic. In fact, a form of hereditary succession and dynastic rule became standard practice for the remainder of the caliphal period. Centralization and militarization of the state resulted in an increasingly autocratic and absolutist government supported and protected by its military.

Umayyad society was based on the creation and perpetuation of an Arab military aristocracy that constituted a hereditary social caste. Syrian troops were the heart of the caliphs' powerful military. As the source of caliphal power and security, they were amply rewarded from the booty and tribute that poured into Damascus as a result of the conquests. Arab Muslims enjoyed special tax privileges, exempted from the more substantial taxes levied on non-Arab Muslims and non-Muslims. This preferential treatment became a source of contention, especially among non-Arab Muslims, who regarded their lesser status as a violation of Islamic egalitarianism. Their alienation contributed to the eventual downfall of the Umayyad dynasty.

DIVISIONS WITHIN THE ISLAMIC COMMUNITY

As had been done from the time of the Prophet, critics and opponents used an "Islamic yardstick" to judge or condemn the Umayyads and legitimate their own actions and aspirations. Political, social, economic, and religious grievances were viewed through the prism of an Islamic ideal relevant to all areas of life. Thus, Umayyad practice incurred an opposition that ranged from Kharijites, Alids (Shii), and disgruntled non-Arab Muslims to the early legal scholars and mystics of Islam.

The Kharijites. The Kharijites originated in the time of the caliphs Uthman and Ali. They represent the earliest example of radical dissent in Islam and were the first, in a series of movements, to offer a different concept of the nature of the community and its leadership. Combining a rigorous puritanism and religious fundamentalism with an "exclusivist egalitarianism," the Kharijites emerged as revolutionaries who, despite their seeming lack of success in their own times, continue to inspire contemporary radical groups like Egypt's Takfir wal Hijra and Jamaat al-Jihad.

As previously noted, the occasion for the Kharijite secession from the main body of the community was Ali's submission to arbitration in his struggle with Muawiyah. For the Kharijites the situation was simple. Muawiyah had challenged the legitimate authority of the caliph; this grave sin rendered him an apostate or infidel, and thus Ali, and all true Muslims, had an obligation to wage jihad until Muawiyah desisted or was subdued. When the arbitration was announced, the Kharijites shouted, "Only God can decide." It was not the job of human beings to counter God's command and sit as judge. As a result, the Kharijites believed that Ali too was now guilty of a grave sin and no longer the legitimate head of the community. This early incident illustrates the basic Khariji beliefs. The Kharijites were extremist. They were very pious believers who interpreted the Quran and Sunna (example) of the Prophet literally and absolutely. Therefore, they believed that the Quranic mandate to "command the good and prohibit evil" must be applied rigorously and without compromise. Acts were either good or bad, permitted or forbidden. Similarly, their world was divided neatly into the realms of belief and un-belief, Muslim (followers of God) and non-Muslim (enemies of God), peace and warfare. Faith must be informed by action; public behavior must rigorously conform to Islamic principles if one was to be a Muslim. Therefore, any action contrary to the letter of the law constituted a grave sin that rendered a person a non-Muslim, subject to excommunication (exclusion), warfare, and death unless the person repented. Sinners were not simply backsliders but apostates who were guilty of treason against the community-state. All true believers were obliged to fight and subdue these nominal or self-styled Muslims.

Within their exclusivist view of the world and the nature of the Muslim community, the Kharijites incorporated an egalitarian spirit that maintained that any good Muslim, even a slave, could be the leader, or imam, of the community, provided he had community support. Their puritan absolutism demanded that a leader guilty of sin be deposed.

When the Kharijites broke with Ali, they went about establishing their vision of the true charismatic community based strictly and literally on the Quran and Sunna. Modeling themselves on the example of the Prophet, they first withdrew (hijra) to live together in a bonded community. From their encampments, they waged battle (jihad) against their enemies, seeing themselves as the instruments of God's justice. They were the people of God (paradise) fighting against the people of evil (hell). Since they were God's army struggling in a heavenly crusade against the forces of evil, violence, guerrilla warfare, and revolution were not only legitimate but obligatory in their battle against the sinful usurpers of God's rule. Defeated by Ali at Nahrawan in 658, they continued to lead uprisings and join in revolts against Muawiyah's Umayyad descendants and engaged in guerrilla warfare against subsequent Abbasid caliphs. A moderate branch of the Kharijites, known as the Ibadiyya, followers of Abd Allah ibn Ibad, founded Ibadi imamates in North (Tripolitania and Tahert) and East (Zanzibar) Africa, Yemen, and

Oman. Their descendants still exist in small numbers in North Africa and in Oman, where the Ibadi faith is the offical state religion.

Shii Islam. The first civil war between Ali and Muawiyah, which had resulted in the secession of the Kharijites and the alienation of Ali's supporters, came back to haunt the Umayyads. During the reign of Muawiyah's son, Yazid, a second round of civil wars broke out. One of these, the revolt of Ali's son Husayn, would lead to the division of the Islamic community into its two major branches, Sunni and Shii, and shape the worldview of Shii Islam.

When Yazid came to power in 680, Husayn, the son of Ali, was persuaded by a group of Alids in Kufa (Iraq) to lead a rebellion. However, when popular support failed to materialize, Husayn and his small band of followers were slaughtered by an Umayyad army at Karbala. The memory of this tragedy, the "martyrdom" of Alid forces, provided the paradigm of suffering and protest that has guided and inspired Shii Islam. For these partisans (*shia*) of Ali, the original injustice that had denied Ali his succession to Muhammad had been repeated, thwarting the rightful rule of the Prophet's family. Thus, the Shii developed their own distinctive vision of leadership and of history, centered on the martyred family of the Prophet and based on a belief that leadership of the Muslim community belonged to the descendants of Ali and Husayn.

The fundamental difference between Sunni and Shii Muslims is the Shii doctrine of the imamate as distinct from the Sunni caliphate. As we have seen, the caliph was the selected or elected successor of the Prophet. He succeeded to political and military leadership but not to Muhammad's religious authority. By contrast, for the Shii, leadership of the Muslim community is vested in the Imam (leader), who, though not a prophet, is the divinely inspired, sinless, infallible, religiopolitical leader of the community. He must be a direct descendant of the Prophet Muhammad and Ali, the first Imam. He is both political leader and religious guide, the final authoritative interpreter of God's will as formulated in Islamic law. Whereas after the death of Muhammad, Sunni Islam came to place final religious authority for interpreting Islam in the consensus (*ijma*) or collective judgment of the community (the consensus of the *ulama*, the traditional religious scholars), the Shii believe in continued divine guidance through their divinely inspired guide, the Imam.

Sunni and Shii Muslims also developed differing doctrines concerning the meaning of history. For Sunni historians, early Islamic success and power were signs of God's guidance and rewards to a faithful community as well as validation of Muslim belief and claims. For the Shii, history was the theater for the struggle of an oppressed and disinherited minority community to restore God's rule on earth over the entire community under the Imam. A righteous remnant was to persist in God's way against the forces of evil (Satan), as had Ali against Muawiyah and Husayn against the army of Yazid, to reestablish the righteous rule of the Imam. The lives of the suffering Imams, like that of Husayn, were seen as embodying the oppression and injustice experienced by a persecuted minority community. Realization of a just social order under the Imam was to remain a frustrated hope and expectation for centuries as the Islamic community remained under Sunni caliphal governments.

Rule of the Imam over the entire Muslim community was frustrated not only by "usurper" Sunni caliphs, but also by disagreements within the Shii community over succession. This led to three major divisions: Zaydi, Ismaili, and Ithna Ashari or Imami. The Zaydis claimed that Zayd ibn Ali, a grandson of Husayn, was the fifth Imam. The majority of the Shii recognized Muhammad al-Baqir and his son Jafar al-Sadiq as rightful heirs to the imamate. Unlike other Shii, who restricted the imamate to the descendants of Ali by his wife Fatima, the Prophet's daughter, Zaydis believed that any descendant of Ali could become Imam. They were political activists who, like the Kharijites, believed that the duty to enjoin the good and prohibit evil was encumbent on all Muslims at all times. They, too, rebelled against both Umayyad and Abbasid rule. The Zaydis were the first Shii to gain independence when Hasan ibn Zayd founded a Zaydi dynasty in Tabaristan, on the Caspian, in 864. Another Zaydi state was established in Yemen in 893, where it continued to exist until 1963.

In the eighth century, the majority of the Shii community split again into its two major branches in a dispute over whom the sixth Imam, Jafar al-Sadiq (d. 765), actually designated as his heir. While most accepted his younger son, Musa al-Kazim, some followed Ismail, the elder son. This resulted in the two major Shii communities, the Ithna Asharis, or Twelvers, and the Ismailis (sometimes called the Seveners). The numerical designation of each group stems from a crisis caused by the death or disappearance of their Imam and thus the disruption of hereditary succession. For the Twelvers, or Ithna Asharis, the end of imamate succession occurred in 874 with the disappearance of the twelfth Imam, the child Muhammad al-Muntazar (Muhammad, the awaited one). Shii theology resolved this dilemma with its doctrines of the absence or occultation of the Imam and his return in the future as the Mahdi (the expected one). For Shii, the Imam had not died but had disappeared and gone into hiding or seclusion. He would return as a messianic figure, the

Mahdi, at the end of the world to vindicate his loyal followers, restore the community to its rightful place, and usher in a perfect Islamic society in which truth and justice will prevail. During the absence of the hidden Imam, the community was to await his return and be guided by its religious experts, *mujtahids*, those *ulama* (religious scholars) who interpret God's will, Islamic law, for the community. The Ismaili split into a number of subdivisions. For a major group of Ismailis, the line of Imams ended in 760 when Ismail, the designated seventh Imam, died before his father. Another group believed that Ismail had not died but was in seclusion and would return as the Mahdi. Others accepted Ismail's son, Muhammad, as Imam.

The Ismailis. The image of the Ismaili today as a prosperous merchant community, led by the Aga Khan, belies their early revolutionary origins.[10] The early Ismaili were a revolutionary missionary movement. They attacked and assassinated Sunni political and religious leaders, seized power, and at their peak, ruled an area that extended from Egypt to the Sind province of India. For the Ismaili, as for Shii in general, the Quran had two meanings, an exoteric, literal meaning and an esoteric, inner teaching. This secret knowledge was given to the Imam and through a process of initiation to his representatives and missionaries. The followers of the Imam, as distinguished from the majority of Muslims, constituted a religious elite who possessed the true guidance necessary for salvation and a mission to spread or propagate, by force if necessary, the message and rule of the Imam. Often functioning as secret organizations to avoid the Abbasid police, Ismaili also used *taqiyya* (to shield or guard), a common Shii practice that permits concealment of one's belief for self-protection or survival as a persecuted minority. The Ismaili consisted of a variety of such missionary communities or movements. During the early tenth century, one branch, the Qarmatians, attacked Syria, Palestine, and southern Mesopotamia, and set up their own state in Bahrain. Other groups spread to North Africa and India. It was in North Africa and Egypt that the Ismaili Fatimid dynasty (named for Fatima, the Prophet's daughter, from whom the ruler claimed descent) was created. After an abortive attempt to conquer Syria, Ubayd Allah had fled to Qairawan (Tunisia), where he successfully seized power in 909, declaring himself the Mahdi and establishing a line of Fatimid Imams. In 969, Egypt was conquered and a new capital, Cairo (al-Qahiro, the victorious), was built outside the older city of Fustat to celebrate the conquest of Egypt. The Fatimids established an absolute hereditary monarchy. The infallible Imam ruled over a strong, centralized monarchy that relied on its military and religious missionaries.

From the tenth to the twelfth centuries, the Fatimids successfully competed with a weakened, fragmented Abbasid empire, spreading their influence and rule across North Africa, Egypt, Sicily, Syria, Persia, and Western Arabia to the Sind province of India. Although the state was Fatimid, the majority of the population remained Sunni. During this period, the Fatimid caliphate flourished culturally and commercially as well as militarily. Among its most enduring monuments was its religious center, the al-Azhar mosque in Cairo, which served as a training center for its missionary propagandists. Reputed to be one of the world's oldest universities, al-Azhar has remained an internationally recognized center of (Sunni) Islamic learning, training students from all over the Islamic world and issuing authoritative religious judgments on major issues and questions.

Although the Fatimids even managed to briefly capture Baghdad, their attempt to rule all of the *dar al-Islam* (abode of Islam) came to an abrupt end in 1171 when Salah al-Din (Saladin) conquered Egypt and restored the Sunni rule of the (Seljuq) Abbasid caliphate. However, the Ismaili persist through several offshoots. The Nizari Ismaili began as a Persian-based sect under Hasan al-Sabah that broke away from the Fatimids in 1094. Called the assassins and guided by a series of Grand Masters who ruled from a stronghold on Mt. Alamut in northern Persia (thus each becoming known as the Old Man of the Mountain), they were particularly effective in murdering Abbasid princes, generals, and leading *ulama* in the name of their hidden Imam.[11] They struck such terror in the hearts of their Muslim and Crusader enemies that their exploits in Persia and Syria earned them a name and memory in history long after they were overrun and driven underground by the Mongols in 1258. A descendant of Hasan al-Sabah, Hasan Ali Shah, received the honorary title Aga Khan through marriage to the daughter of the shah. He fled to India in 1840 after a failed revolt in Persia. Centered in Bombay, these Nizari (Khoja) Ismailis were led by a series of Imams, known as the Aga Khan, whose personal fortunes have been matched by the wealth of remarkably successful and thriving Ismaili communities in East Africa, South Asia, Britain, and Canada. Currently, the Aga Khan oversees the spiritual and cultural life of the community. As its living Imam, he has been able to reinterpret Islam to respond to modern life. At the same time, he oversees extensive commercial and industrial Ismaili investments and supervises the many educational, medical, and social welfare projects of its philanthropic foundation.

The Druze. Among the sectarian offshoots of Ismailism were the Druze of Lebanon. The Druze date back to two Fatimid missionaries named

Darazi (d. 1019) and Hamza ibn Ali, who had been encouraged by the Fatimid caliph al-Hakim (reigned 996–1021) to spread the Ismaili faith in southern Lebanon. Al-Hakim was an eccentric ruler who took the title Imam and progressively came to believe that he was not only the divinely appointed religiopolitical leader but also the cosmic intellect, linking God with creation. Darazi and Hamza became leaders of a movement centered on recognition of al-Hakim as a divine incarnation, the highest or first cosmic intellect. This supernatural status became the excuse for his erratic, authoritarian behavior, which at times included the persecution of Ismaili, Sunni, and Christian leaders alike. When al-Hakim disappeared or was killed, they maintained that he had gone into seclusion to test the faith of his followers and would return to restore justice in the world. After Darazi's death, Hamza, now claiming to be the leader (imam) in Hakim's absence, organized and developed Hakim's cult into what became a separate religion. Hamza then disappeared, and was expected to return as the Mahdi at a later date with al-Hakim. In the interim, Baha al-Din al-Muktana served as the earthly link between Hamza and the community.

The Druze call themselves the unitarians, followers of al-Hakim who embodied and revealed the one true God. Forming a distinct religion, the Druze possess their own Scripture, the *Risail al-Hikma* (the Book of Wisdom), and law. The Book of Wisdom is a collection of letters from al-Muktana, al-Hamza, and al-Hakim. The Sharia, mosque, and *ulama* were replaced by Druze law, places of prayer, and religious leadership. The community is hierarchically organized. The two major divisions are the majority of ordinary members, the so-called ignorant, and the wise, those men and women who are initiated and as such can read the Scriptures and are expected to lead an exemplary life of regular prayer and abstention from wine, tobacco, and other stimulants. They can be recognized by the quality of their lives and their special dress or white turbans. Among the wise are a group of religious leaders called shaykhs, noted for their learning and piety, who preside over meetings, weddings, and funerals. The head of the community is the *rais* (chief), who is selected from one of the leading families.

Historically, the Druze have been a secretive and closed community. They have steadfastly kept their texts, beliefs, and practices secret, carefully guarding them from outsiders. Regarded by both Sunni and Shii as heretics and living in a Sunni-dominated world, they too have followed the Shii doctrine of *taqiyya*, with its double meaning of caution and dissimulation for survival in a hostile world. Thus, although they do not observe the fast of Ramadan or pilgrimage to Mecca, when necessary they have outwardly followed the prevailing Sunni faith and a modified form of Hanafi (Islamic) law. Druze beliefs and practices emphasize solidarity; they neither accept converts nor marry outside the faith. They practice monogamy and endogamy and discourage divorce. The seven pillars or basic religious obligations reinforce a strong sense of community. They include speaking the truth to other members (though not necessarily to nonbelievers), mutual defense, and living separately from unbelievers. Unlike other monotheistic faiths, the Druze believe in the trasmigration of souls until perfected souls cease to be reborn and ascend to the stars. At the end of time, when Hakim and Hamza return to establish a reign of justice, the faithful will be rewarded by being placed close to God. The Druze have survived in Syria, Israel, and especially Lebanon, where they number several hundred thousand.

LAW AND MYSTICISM

Dissatisfaction with Umayyad rule also resulted in the development of nonrevolutionary reform movements within society. The rapid geographic expansion and conquests brought the rise of new centers of power and wealth, an influx of "foreign" ways, and greater social stratification. The very success of the Umayyad empire contained the seeds of its downfall. With wealth and power came corruption and abuse of power, symbolized by the new lifestyle of its flourishing, cosmopolitan capital and the growth of new cities. This was accompanied by the infiltration of new ideas and practices. The strengths that came with acculturation were offset, in the eyes of some, by innovations that were seen as undermining the older Arab way of life. In addition to the disaffected Kharijites and Alids, a host of other critics sprang up who contrasted an idealized Medinan Islamic community with the realities of Umayyad life. This gave rise, in particular, to the growth of two Islamic movements or institutions, the *ulama* (religious scholars) and the Sufis (mystics).

For a growing number of pious Muslims, who would become a religious and social class in the Muslim community known as the *ulama* (plural of *alim*, "learned" or scholar), Umayyad practice seemed more indebted to foreign innovations than to the practice of the Prophet and the early community. Arab power and wealth, not Islamic commitment and ideals, inspired and unified the empire. The behavior of many caliphs, the intrigues of court life, and the privileged status of new elites were regarded as having little to do with Islam. What the Umayyads had done was pragmatically necessary, because the Arabs had not had the institutions and trained personnel required for empire building, but their critics believed that the Umayyad system of incorporating the indigenous bureaucracy of the conquered lands inevitably produced an un-Islamic society based more on the command of the caliph than the command of God. The problem was epitomized by the application of Islamic law. God's law, they argued, should provide the blueprint for Muslim society. Yet, conquest and empire had introduced a diversity of cultures, lifestyles, and customs. The differing customary laws of Medina, Damascus, Kufa, and Basra, coupled with the caliph's decision and his judges' ability to settle disputes on the basis of their own discretion, resulted in a confused and often contradictory body of laws. Many asked, "Can God's will be discerned through so subjective a process; can His law for Muslims in Medina be so different from that in Kufa?" They responded that if all Muslims were bound to submit to and carry out God's law, then Islamic law ought to be defined clearly and with more uniformity. Maintaining that Islam offered a self-sufficient, comprehensive way of life based on the Quran and *sunna*, or custom, they argued that Islam must permeate every area of life. Umayyad practice and law should be brought into line with Islamic principles, and the institutions of the state should have as their source Islam and not the precedents of Byzantium.

The outcome of this movement was a burst of activity that would result in the development of Islamic religious sciences. Pious Muslims from all walks of life devoted themselves to the study of the Quran, Arabic language and linguistics, and the collection and examination of Prophetic traditions. In particular, in order to safeguard their beliefs and limit the power of the caliph, many devoted themselves to the formulation and explication of Islamic law. By the late Umayyad period, centers of law could be found in many cities of the empire.

Reaction to the excesses of empire contributed to the development of mysticism as well as law. Luxury, the pursuit of conquest and wealth, the transformation of the caliphate into a dynastic monarchy with the trappings of imperial court life, and the doubtful moral character of some of the Umayyad caliphs struck some pious Muslims as standing in sharp contrast to the early example of Muhammad and the Rightly Guided Caliphs and the relative simplicity of life in Medina. They believed that Umayyad goals of power and wealth conflicted with and distracted from the true center and goal of Muslim life, Allah. Therefore, the early mystics preached a message stressing renunciation and detachment from worldly concerns and attachments for the pursuit of the "real" God. As we shall see, mysticism or Sufism became a major popular force within Islam that swept across the Muslim world, spreading its spirit of love and devotion.

GROWTH OF "ISLAMIC" REVOLT

Despite the accomplishments of Umayyad rule, by the eighth century (720) anti-Umayyad sentiment had spread and intensified. It encompassed a variety of disaffected factions: non-Arab Muslims who denounced their second-class status vis-à-vis Arab Muslims as contrary to Islamic egalitarianism; Kharijites and Shii who continued to regard the Umayyads as usurpers; Arab Muslims in Mecca, Medina, and Iraq who resented the privileged status of Syrian families; and, finally, pious Muslims, Arab and non-Arab alike, who viewed the new cosmopolitan lifestyle of luxury and social privilege as foreign and an unwarranted innovation or departure from their established, Islamic way of life.

Opposition forces shared a discontent with Umayyad rule as well as a tendency to legitimate their own claims and agenda Islamically; they condemned Umayyad practice and policies as un-Islamic innovations and called for a return to the Quran and the practices of the Prophet and the early Medinan community:

> The ideology of a restoration of primitive Islam, with variants reflecting different trends, had conquered the masses, and, with the support of the majority of the learned men, became part of the programme of all, or nearly all, the leaders of parties. It triumphed when the Abbasids adopted it as their slogan.[12]

By 747, an opposition movement, with substantial Shii support, rallied behind Abu Muslim, a freed Abbasid slave. In 750, the Umayyads fell, and Abu al-Abbas, a descendant of the Prophet's uncle al-Abbas, was proclaimed caliph. Islam's capital was moved from Damascus to the newly created Baghdad, known in Arabic as the City of Peace. Under Abbasid rule, the Islamic community would become an empire remembered not only for its wealth and political power, but also for its extraordinary cultural activity and accomplishments.

The Abbasid Caliphate: The Flowering of Islamic Civilization

Abbasid rule of the Islamic community ushered in an era of strong centralized government, great economic prosperity, and a remarkable civilization. Abbasid caliphs could be as autocratic and ruthless as many of their Umayyad predecessors. Indeed, Abu al-Abbas did not hesitate to take the title "the blood shedder" (*al-saffah*); he came to be remembered as Abu Abbas al-Saffah. The Abbasid caliphs consolidated their power by crushing their Shii supporters as well as their opponents. This betrayal further alienated the Shii from the Sunni majority. The name Sunni comes from their self-designation as *ahl al-sunna wal jamaa*, those who follow the Prophet's example and thus belong to his society or community.

The Abbasids came to power under the banner of Islam. Their seizure of power and continued dynastic reign were Islamically legitimated. However, the Abbasids took great care publicly to align their government with Islam. They became the great patrons of an emerging religious class, the *ulama* (religious scholars). They supported the development of Islamic scholarship and disciplines, built mosques, and established schools.

The Abbasids refined Umayyad practice, borrowing heavily from Persian culture, with its divinely ordained system of government. The caliph's claim to rule by divine mandate was symbolized by the transformation of his title from Successor or Deputy of the Prophet to Deputy of God and by the appropriation of the Persian-inspired title, Shadow of God on Earth. The ruler's exalted status was further reinforced by his magnificent palace, his retinue of attendants, and the introduction of a court etiquette appropriate for an emperor. Thus, subjects were required to bow before the caliph, kissing the ground, a symbol of the caliph's absolute power. Persian influence was especially evident in the government and military. Preempting critics of the previous regime, the Arab Syrian-dominated military aristocracy was replaced by a salaried army and bureaucracy in which non-Arab Muslims, especially Persians, played a major role. The Abbasids explained this change in terms of Islamic egalitarianism. More often than not, however, it was royal favor and fear, symbolized by the royal executioner who stood by the side of the caliph, that brought him prestige and motivated obedience.

The early centuries of Abbasid rule were marked by an unparalleled splendor and economic prosperity whose magnificence came to be immortalized in the *Arabian Nights* (*The Thousand and One Nights*), with its legendary exploits of the exemplary caliph, Harun al-Rashid (reigned 786–809). In a departure from the past, Abbasid success was based not on conquest, but on trade, commerce, industry, and agriculture. The enormous wealth and resources of the caliphs enabled them to become great patrons of art and culture, and thus create the more significant and lasting legacy of the Abbasid period, Islamic civilization. The development of Islamic law, the Sharia, constitutes their greatest contribution to Islam. Since part of the indictment of the Umayyads had been their failure to implement an effective Islamic legal system, the Abbasids gave substantial support to legal development. The early law schools, which had begun only during the late Umayyad period (ca. 720), flourished under caliphal patronage of the *ulama*. Although Islam has no clergy or priesthood, by the eighth century the *ulama* had become a professional elite of religious leaders, a distinct social class within Muslim society. Their prestige and authority rested on a reputation for learning in Islamic studies: the Quran, traditions of the Prophet, law. Because of their expertise, they became the jurists, theologians, and educators in Muslim society, the interpreters and guardians of Islamic law and tradition. The judge (*qadi*) administered the law as it was developed by the early jurists, firmly establishing the Islamic court system.

In addition to law, the Abbasids were also committed patrons of culture and the arts. The process of Arabization, begun during the late Umayyad period, was completed by the end of the ninth century. Arabic language and tradition penetrated and modified the cultures of conquered territories. Arabic displaced local languages—Syriac, Aramaic, Coptic, and Greek—becoming the language of common discourse, government, and culture throughout much of the empire. Arabic was no longer solely the language of Muslims from Arabia but the language of literature and public discourse for the multiethnic group of new Arabic-speaking peoples, especially the large number of non-Arab converts, many of whom were Persian. Translation centers were created. From the seventh to the ninth centuries, manuscripts were obtained from the far reaches of the empire and beyond and translated from their original languages (Sanskrit, Greek, Latin, Syriac, Coptic, and Persian) into Arabic. Thus, the best works of literature, philosophy, and the sciences from other cultures were made accessible: Aristotle, Plato, Galen, Hippocrates, Euclid, and Ptolemy. The genesis of Islamic civilization was indeed a collaborative effort, incorporating the learning and wisdom of many cultures and languages. As in government administration, Christians and Jews, who had been the intellectual and bureaucratic backbone of the Persian and Byzantine empires, participated in the process as well as Muslims. This "ecumenical" effort was evident at the Caliph al-Mamun's (reigned 813–833) House of Wisdom and at the translation center headed by the renowned scholar Hunayn ibn Ishaq, a Nestorian Christian. This period of translation and assimilation was followed by one of Muslim intellectual and artistic creativity. Muslims ceased to be merely disciples and became masters, in the process producing Islamic civilization, dominated by the Arabic language and Islam's view of life: "It was these two things, their language and their faith, which were the great contribution of the Arab invaders to the new and original civilization which developed under their aegis."[13] Major contributions were made in many fields: literature and philosophy, algebra and geometry, science and medicine, art and architecture. Towering intellectual giants dominated this period: al-Razi (865–925), al-Farabi (d. 950), ibn Sina (known as Avicenna, 980–1037), ibn Rushd (known as Averroes, d. 1198), al-Biruni (973–1048), and al-Ghazali (d. 1111). Islam had challenged the world politically; it now did so culturally. Great urban cultural centers in Cordova, Baghdad, Cairo, Nishapur, and Palermo emerged and eclipsed Christian Europe, mired in the Dark Ages. The activities of these centers are reflected in the development of philosophy and science.

Islamic philosophy was the product of a successful transplant from Greek to Islamic soil, where it flourished from the ninth to the twelfth centuries. Muslim philosophers appropriated Hellenistic thought (Aristotle, Plato, Plotinus), wrote commentaries on and extended the teachings and insights of Greek philosophy within an Islamic context and worldview. The result was Islamic philosophy, indebted to Hellenism but with its own Islamic character. Its contribution was of equal importance to the West. Islamic philosophy became the primary vehicle for the transmission of Greek philosophy to medieval Europe. The West reappropriated its lost heritage as European scholars traveled to major centers of Islamic learning, retranslating the Greek philosophers and learning from the writings of their great Muslim disciples: men like al-Farabi, who had come to be known as "the second teacher or master" (the first being Aristotle), and ibn Sina (Avicenna), remembered as "the great commentator" on Aristotle. Thus we find many of the great medieval Christian philosophers and theologians (Albert the Great, Thomas Aquinas, Abelard, Roger Bacon, Duns Scotus) acknowledging their intellectual debt to their Muslim predecessors.

The enormous accomplishments of Islamic philosophy and science were the product of men of genius, multitalented intellectuals (who often mastered the major disciplines of medicine, mathematics, astronomy, and philosophy). They were the "renaissance" men of classical Islam. Avicenna's reflections on his own training typifies the backgrounds of many of the great intellectuals of this period:

> I busied myself with the study of the *Fusus al-Hikam* [a treatise by al-Farabi] and other commentaries on physics and mathematics, and the doors of knowledge opened before me. Then I took up medicine . . . Medicine is not one of the difficult sciences, and in a very short time I undoubtedly excelled in it, so that physicians of merit studied under me. I also attended the sick, and the doors of medical treatments based on experience opened before me to an extent that can not be described. At the same time I carried on debates and controversies in jurisprudence. At this point I was sixteen years old.

Then, for a year and a half, I devoted myself to study. I resumed the study of logic and all parts of philosophy. During this time I never slept the whole night through and did nothing but study all day long. Whenever I was puzzled by a problem . . . I would go to the mosque, pray, and beg the Creator of All to reveal to me that which was hidden from me and to make easy for me that which was difficult. Then at night I would return home, put a lamp in front of me, and set to work reading and writing. . . . I went on like this until I was firmly grounded in all sciences and mastered them as far as was humanly possible. . . . . Thus I mastered logic, physics, and mathematics.

The Sultan of Bukhara . . . was stricken by an illness which baffled the physicians. . . . . I appeared before him and joined them in treating him and distinguished myself in his service.

One day I asked his permission to go into their library, look at their books, and read the medical ones. . . . I went into a palace of many rooms, each with trunks full of books, back-to-back. In one room there were books on Arabic and poetry, in another books on jurisprudence, and similarly in each room books on a single subject. I . . . asked for those I needed . . . read these books, made use of them, and thus knew the rank of every author in his own subject. . . . When I reached the age of eighteen, I had completed the study of all these sciences. At that point my memory was better, whereas today my learning is riper.[14]

Islamic science was an integrated and synthetic area of knowledge. It was integrated in that Muslim scientists, who were often philosophers or mystics as well, viewed the physical universe from within their Islamic worldview and context as a manifestation of the presence of God, the Creator and source of unity and harmony in nature.[15] Islamic science was also a grand synthesis informed by indigenous and foreign sources (Arab, Persian, Hellenistic, Indian) and transformed by scholars and scientists in urban centers throughout the world of Islam. Thus, it constituted a major component of Islamic civilization, and in the eyes of many Muslims, a worthy complement to Islam's international political order. As one Muslim intellectual observed:

Islamic science came into being from a wedding between the spirit that issued from the Quranic revelation and the existing sciences of various civilizations which Islam inherited and which it transmuted through its spiritual power into a new substance, at once different from and continuous with what had existed before it. The international and cosmopolitan nature of Islamic civilization, derived from the universal character of the Islamic revelation and reflected in the geographical spread of the Islamic world, enabled it to create the first science of a truly international nature in human history.[16]

The legacy of Islamic civilization was that of a brilliant, rich culture. Its contributions proved to be as significant for the West, which in subsequent centuries appropriated and incorporated its knowledge and wisdom.

Thus during the Abbasid period, the comprehensiveness of Islam was clearly manifested and delineated:

> Islam—the offspring of Arabia and the Arabian Prophet—was not only a system of belief and cult. It was also a system of state, society, law, thought and art—a civilization with religion as its unifying, eventually dominating factor.[17]

For Muslim and non-Muslim alike, the political and cultural life of a vast empire, consisting of many tribal, ethnic, and religious groups, was brought within the framework of the Arabic language and Islamic faith.[18] Islamic civilization was the result of a dynamic, creative process as Muslims borrowed freely from other cultures. It proceeded from a sense of mission, power, and superiority. Muslims were the dominant force—masters not victims, colonizers not the colonized. The new ideas and practices were Arabized and Islamized. It was a process of change characterized by continuity with the faith and practice of Muhammad. Unlike the modern period, Muslims controlled the process of assimilation and acculturation. Their autonomy and identity were not seriously threatened by the specter of political and cultural domination. As with the early conquests and expansion of Islam, Muslims then (and now) regarded this brilliant period as a sign of God's favor and a validation of Islam's message and the Muslim community's universal mission.

The extraordinary spread and development of Islam was not without its religious conflicts. The same concern that had motivated the attempt by the *ulama* to preserve Islam in the face of caliphal whim and uncritical adoption of foreign, un-Islamic practices, led to conflicts between the *ulama* and those whom they sometimes regarded as their competitors, the Sufis and the philosophers. The *ulama* delineation of law as the embodiment of the straight path of Islam set the criteria for belief and behavior in intellectual, social, and moral life and the pattern for orthodoxy (correct belief) or, perhaps more accurately, orthopraxy (correct practice). This vision of Muslim life as the observance of God's law did not always coincide comfortably with the Sufi emphasis on the interior path of contemplation and personal religious experience or the tendency of philosophy to give primacy to reason over the unquestioned acceptance of revelation. The tension between religious scholars on the one hand and philosophers and Sufis on the other was reflected in the life and work of a towering giant in the history of Islam, indeed in the history of religions, Abu Hamid al-Ghazali.

Ironically, the golden age of Islamic civilization paralleled the progressive political fragmentation of the universal caliphate. The relative peace, prosperity, and unity of the Islamic community, epitomized during the rule of Harun al-Rashid, was challenged internally by competing groups and externally by the Fatimids and the Crusades.

Governing a vast empire extending from the Atlantic to central Asia proved impossible. Abbasid political unity deteriorated rapidly from 861 to 945 as religious (Khariji and Shii) and regional differences, and particularly competing political aspirations, precipitated a series of revolts and secessionist movements. In Morocco, Tunisia, Iran, Syria, and Iraq itself, local governors, who were often army commanders, asserted their independence as heads of semiautonomous states. These regional rulers (amirs, or commanders), while continuing to give formal, nominal allegiance to the caliph, exercised actual rule over their territories, establishing their own hereditary dynasties. By 945, the disintegration of the universal caliphate was evident when the Buyids (Buwayhids), a Shii dynasty from Western Persia, invaded Baghdad and seized power, and their leader assumed the title commander-in-chief or commander of the commanders. Although Shii, they did not change the Sunni orientation of the empire and left the caliph on his throne as a titular leader of a fictionally unified empire. The Abbasids continued to reign but not rule. With an Abbasid on the throne as a symbol of legitimate government and Muslim unity, real power passed to a series of Persian (Buyid) and Turkic (Seljuq) military dynasties or sultanates. The sultan ("power," ruler), as chief of the commanders, governed a politically fragmented empire as the caliph helplessly stood by.

Sunni Islam was also threatened by two other developments during the Abbasid caliphate—the rise of the Fatimid dynasty and the Crusades. The Ismaili rebellion in Tunisia and subsequent establishment of a Shii imamate in Egypt constituted a serious religiopolitical challenge. The Fatimids claimed to be Imams and were not content to simply govern Egypt, but, as we have seen, followed other Ismaili groups in sending their missionaries to spread their Shii doctrine. This Shii challenge elicited a religious as well as a military response as Sunni *ulama* moved to protect their version of orthodoxy in the face of Shii innovations. They were supported in their endeavors by the royal court, which wished to counter Shii anticaliphal sentiments. This contributed to a growing tendency among the Sunni *ulama* to preserve the unity of Islam through greater self-definition and standardization. In the face of the internal breakup of the central empire, this meant achieving a consensus on the corpus of Islamic law in order to protect and maintain the sociopolitical order.

Islam and the West: The Crusades and Muslim Response to Militant Christianity

Despite their common monotheistic roots, the history of Christianity and Islam has more often than not been marked by confrontation rather than peaceful coexistence and dialogue. For the Christian West, Islam is the religion of the sword; for Muslims, the Christian West is epitomized by the armies of the Crusades. From the earliest decades of Islamic history, Christianity and Islam have been locked in a political and theological struggle, because Islam, unlike other world religions, has threatened the political and religious ascendancy of Christianity. Muslim armies overran the Eastern Roman empire, Spain, and the Mediterranean from Sicily to Anatolia. At the same time, Islam challenged Christian religious claims and authority. Coming after Christianity, Islam claimed to supersede Christian revelation. While acknowledging God's revelation and revering God's messengers, from Adam through Jesus, as prophets, Islam rejected the doctrine of Christ's divinity, the finality of Christian revelation, and the authority of the church. Instead, it called on all, Jews and Christians as well, to accept finality of revelation and prophecy in Islam, to join the Islamic community, and to live under Islamic rule. Islam's universal mission had resulted in the spread of Muslim rule over Christian territories and Christian hearts. While conversions were initially slow, by the eleventh century large numbers of Christians living under Muslim rule were converting to Islam. Even those who had remained Christian were becoming Arabized, adopting Arabic language and manners. The European Christian response was, with few exceptions, hostile, intolerant, and belligerent. Muhammad was vilified as an imposter and identified as the anti-Christ. Islam was dismissed as a religion of the sword led by an infidel driven by a lust for power and women. This attitude was preserved and perpetuated in literature such as the *Divine Comedy,* where Dante consigned Muhammad to the lowest level of hell. Christian fears were fully realized as Islam became a world power and civilization while Christianity staggered and stagnated in its Dark Ages.

By the eleventh century, Christendom's response to Islam took two forms: the struggle to reconquer (the *Reconquista*) Spain (1000–1492) and Italy and Sicily (1061), and the undertaking of another series of Christian holy wars—the Crusades (1095–1453).

Two myths pervade Western perceptions of the Crusades: first, that the Crusades were simply motivated by a religious desire to liberate Jerusalem, and second, that Christendom ultimately triumphed.

Jerusalem was a sacred city for all three Abrahamic faiths. When the Arab armies took Jerusalem in 638, they occupied a center whose shrines had made it a major pilgrimage site in Christendom. Churches and the Christian population were left unmolested. Jews, long banned from living there by Christian rulers, were permitted to return, live, and worship in the city of Solomon and David. Muslims proceeded to build a shrine, the Dome of the Rock, and a mosque, the al-Aqsa, near the area formerly occupied by Herod's Temple and close by the Wailing Wall, the last remnant of Solomon's temple.

Five centuries of peaceful coexistence elapsed before political events and an imperial-papal power play led to centuries-long series of so-called holy wars that pitted Christendom against Islam and left an enduring legacy of misunderstanding and distrust.

In 1071, the Byzantine army was decisively defeated by a Seljuq (Abbasid) army. The Byzantine emperor, Alexius I, fearing that all Asia Minor would be overrun, called on fellow Christian rulers and the pope to come to the aid of Constantinople by undertaking a "pilgrimage" or crusade to free Jerusalem and its environs from Muslim rule. For Pope Urban II, the "defense" of Jerusalem provided an opportunity to gain recognition for papal authority and its role in legitimating the actions of temporal rulers. A divided Christendom rallied as warriors from France and other parts of Western Europe (called "Franks" by Muslims) united against the "infidel" in a holy war whose ostensible goal was the holy city. This was ironic because, as one scholar has observed, "God may indeed have wished it, but there is certainly no evidence that the Christians of Jerusalem did, or that anything extraordinary was occurring to pilgrims there to prompt such a response at that moment in history."[19] In fact, Christian rulers, knights, and merchants were driven primarily by political and military ambitions and the promise of the economic and commercial (trade and banking) rewards that would accompany the establishment of a Latin kingdom in the Middle East. However, the appeal to religion captured the popular mind and gained its support.

The contrast between the behavior of the Christian and Muslim armies in the First Crusade has been etched deeply in the collective memory of Muslims. In 1099, the Crusaders stormed Jerusalem and established Christian sovereignty over the Holy Land. They left no Muslim survivors; women and children were massacred. The Noble Sanctuary, the Haram al-Sharif, was desecrated as the Dome of the Rock was converted into a church and the al-Aqsa mosque, renamed the Temple of Solomon, became a residence for the king. Latin principalities were established in Antioch, Edessa, Tripoli, and Tyre. The Latin Kingdom of Jerusalem lasted less than a century. In 1187, Salah al-Din (Saladin), having reestablished Abbasid rule over Fatimid Egypt, led his army in a fierce battle and recaptured Jerusalem. The Muslim army was as magnanimous in victory as it had been tenacious in battle. Civilians were spared; churches and shrines were generally left untouched. The striking differences in military conduct were epitomized by the two dominant figures of the Crusades: Saladin and Richard the Lion-Hearted. The chivalrous Saladin was faithful to his word and compassionate toward noncombatants. Richard accepted the surrender of Acre and then proceeded to massacre all its inhabitants, including women and children, despite promises to the contrary.

By the thirteenth century the Crusades degenerated into intra-Christian wars, papal wars against its Christian enemies who were denounced as heretics and schismatics. The result was a weakening, rather than a strengthening, of Christendom. As Roger Savory has observed:

> An ironical but undeniable result of the Crusades was the deterioration of the position of Christian minorities in the Holy Land. Formerly these minorities had been accorded rights and privileges under Muslim rule, but, after the establishment of the Latin Kingdom, they found themselves treated as "loathsome schismatics." In an effort to obtain relief from persecution by their fellow Christians, many abandoned their Nestorian or Monophysite beliefs, and adopted either Roman Catholicism, or—the supreme irony—Islam.[20]

By the fifteenth century, the Crusades had spent their force. Although they were initially launched to unite Christendom and turn back the Muslim armies, the opposite had occurred. Amid a bitterly divided Christendom, Constantinople fell in 1453 before Turkish Muslim conquerors. This Byzantine capital was renamed Istanbul and became the seat of the Ottoman empire.

The Sultanate Period: Medieval Muslim Empires

By the thirteenth century, the Abbasid empire was a sprawling, fragmented, deteriorating commonwealth of semiautonomous states, sultanates, governed by military commanders. It was an empire in name only. The fictional unity of a united Islamic community symbolized by the caliph in Baghdad, stood in sharp contrast to the underlying reality of its political and religious divisions. Invaded and ruled successively by the Buyids and then the Seljuks, Baghdad was completely overrun in the thirteenth century by the Mongols. Pouring out of Central Asia, the armies of Genghis Khan had subjugated much of Central Asia, China, Russia, and the Near East. In 1258, the Mongol army under Hulagu Khan, the grandson of Genghis Khan, captured Baghdad, burned and pillaged the city, slaughtered its Muslim inhabitants, and executed the caliph and his family. Only Egypt and Syria escaped the Mongol conquest of the Muslim empire. In Egypt, the Mamluks ("the owned ones"), Turkish slave soldiers who served as a sort of praetorian guard, seized power from their Ayyubid masters. The Mamluk sultanate successfully resisted the Mongols and ruled until 1517.

Although the destruction of Baghdad and the abolition of the Abbasid caliphate brought an end to the caliphal period and seemed to many an irreversible blow to Muslim power, by the fifteenth century Muslim fortunes had been reversed. The central caliphate was replaced by a chain of dynamic Muslim sultanates, each ruled by a sultan, which eventually extended from Africa to Southeast Asia, from Timbuktu to Mindanao, as Islam penetrated Africa, Central and Southeast Asia, and Eastern Europe. Among the principal missionaries of Islam were traders and Sufi brotherhoods.

Muslim power peaked in the sixteenth century. Three major Muslim empires emerged in the midst of the many sultanates: the Ottoman Turkish empire, centered in Istanbul but encompassing major portions of North Africa, the Arab world, and Eastern Europe; the Persian Safavid empire, with its capital in Isfahan, which effectively established Shii Islam as the state's religion; and the Mughal empire, centered in Delhi and embracing most of the Indian subcontinent (modern-day Pakistan, India, and Bangladesh). Baghdad's successors were the imperial capitals of Istanbul, Isfahan, and Delhi. Political ascendancy was accompanied by a cultural florescence. As in Abbasid times, great sultans, such as the Ottoman Sulayman the Magnificent (reigned 1520–1566), Shah Abbas in Persia (reigned 1587–1629), and the Mughal emperor Akbar (reigned 1556–1605) in India, were patrons of learning and the arts.

The Ottoman empire was the heir to the Mongol-Turkish legacy of Ghengis Khan and his successors. The fall of Constantinople (Istanbul) in 1453 to the Ottoman sultan Mehmet II and the conquest of Byzantium realized the cherished dream of Muslim rulers and armies since the seventh century. The acknowledgment of Mehmet as "The Conqueror" throughout the Islamic world and his cosmopolitan capital at Istanbul, which sat astride both Europe and Asia, symbolized the power and mission of an emerging imperial giant.

The Ottomans drew on their Mongol-Turkish and Islamic roots and traditions, combining a warrior heritage with an Islamic tradition that believed in Islam's universal mission and sacred struggle (jihad), to establish themselves as worldwide propagators and defenders of Islam. They became the great warriors of Islamic expansion through military conquest. The titles taken by Ottoman sultans, such as "Warrior of the Faith" and "Defender of the Sharia," reflected this religiopolitical justification and rationale. Ottoman suzerainty was extended to the Arab Middle East and North Africa, incorporating such major Islamic cities as Mecca, Medina, Cairo, Damascus, and Tunis along with great centers of Islamic learning like Egypt's Al-Azhar and Tunisia's Zaytouna Mosque-University. Greece, Malta, Cyprus, Tripoli, the Balkans, and much of Eastern Europe were also absorbed. A besieged Europe struggled for its existence. After two centuries of confrontation, Ottoman forces were decisively turned back by the navies of Christian Europe at the Battle of Lepanto in 1571. The Ottoman defeat and the truce of 1580 in the Mediterranean "confirmed the frontier between Christian and Muslim civilizations that has lasted to the present day." In 1629 Ottoman expansion in Eastern Europe was checked by the failure of the siege of Vienna.

During the 1600s the Ottoman empire fully evolved. Istanbul, whose population of 500,000 was more than twice the size of any European capital, became once again an international but now Islamized center of power and culture. Scholars, artists, and architects from all over the Islamic world and Europe were commissioned, as Muslim conquerors also proved to be great builders of civilization as well. The skyline of Istanbul was transformed by the distinctive cupolas of palaces and mosques. The royal family lived in splendor in the Topkapi palace, preserved today as a great museum. An imperial monarchy governed subjects of many tribal, ethnic, linguistic, and religious backgrounds from the Mediterranean to Iran.

Both Byzantine and Turkish-Muslim influences informed the development of the political, legal, economic, and social institutions of the state. The ruling class was comprised of the Ottoman family and a special cadre of Balkan slaves who had been Turkified and Islamized through a sophisticated educational system so that they might serve as government administrators and members of the elite military, the Janissaries. Ottoman sultans relied on a strong military of slave-soldiers supported by gunpowder technology; the empire was governed by means of a centralized administration and a well-organized bureaucracy. Alongside the political establishment was a structured religious establishment. The *ulama*, schools, and the courts were brought within the state's bureaucracy. Through royal patronage, the empire developed a hierarchy of Islamic institutions: local Quran schools, mosque-universities (*madrasas*), and courts. At the apex of the state's religious bureaucracy was the *shaykh al-Islam,* who like the chief *qadi* (judge), was appointed by the sultan. Thus, Ottoman *ulama* families became a religious aristocracy.

A distinctive feature of the Ottoman sultanate was the millet system, a variation on the earlier Islamic institution of the *dhimmi,* or protected non-Muslim peoples, which recognized and regulated the rights and duties of religious communities. (Whatever the Ottoman desire was to forge a broader identity, the basic units of society were the empire's religious communities, which provided the primary source of identity and loyalty.) Leaders of religious communities (Christian patriarchs and chief rabbis) were appointed by the sultan to collect the taxes due the royal household and to rule over their communities. Religious communities enjoyed limited autonomy. They could operate their own churches and synagogues, schools, and domestic religious courts, train and govern their clergy, and oversee their charitable institutions.

As the Ottoman empire prospered in its imperial fortunes, new rival Muslim empires were emerging in the sixteenth century: the Safavid dynasty (1501–1722) in Iran and the Moghul empire (1520–1857) in the Indian subcontinent. The Safavids had begun as a revivalist Sufi brotherhood in the thirteenth century, calling for a restoration of a purified Islam. By the fifteenth century, the brotherhood was transformed into a religiopolitical movement, combining Shii messianism and a call for armed struggle (jihad) against other Muslim regimes, which it denounced as un-Islamic. In 1501, Ismail (1487–1524), head of the Safavid family, invaded and occupied Tabriz, proclaiming himself shah of Iran. Within a decade, he had conquered the rest of Iran, rapidly building an empire east of the Ottoman frontier. The creation of the Safavid dynasty made Shii Islam the official religion of an Islamic empire.

Shii Islam was effectively imposed in Iran through a process of persecution and doctrinal interpretation. Shah Ismail imposed Twelver Shii Islam upon Iran's Sunni majority to unify his rule. He sought religious legitimacy and leadership by asserting that he was a descendant of the twelfth (hidden) imam and a *mahdi,* or divinely guided reformer. Thus, the shah was both temporal and spiritual ruler, emperor and messianic messenger. The religious pretensions of Safavid rulers were symbolized by their title, "Shadow of God on Earth." Rival Islamic groups or interpretations of Islam (Sunni and Sufi) as well as non-Muslim communities were suppressed. The Safavids enforced their own brand of Shii religiopolitical ideology and identity in an attempt to legitimate their political authority and to forge a new Safavid Shii Iranian bond of solidarity. A full-blown Shii alternative to Sunni Islam was skillfully developed. Sufi ideas, philosophical doctrines, and popular religious practices such as saint veneration were selectively appropriated. Emphasis was placed on the veneration of sacred "Shii" persons: Husayn, the imams, and their families. Visits to their shrines replaced popular Sufi village shrines. Sunni persecution of Ali and his family were commemorated, while the first three caliphs were ritually cursed as usurpers. The martyrdom of Husayn at Karbala, the scene of the original massacre of Husayn and his followers by Sunni forces, became a central religious symbol, ritually reenacted during the sacred month of Muharram in passion plays which emphasized mourning, self-sacrifice and atonement. Karbala served as an alternative pilgrimage site to Mecca, which was under Ottoman control. Shii *ulama* from Iraq, southern Lebanon, and Bahrain were brought to Iran as missionaries and became part of the state-created and controlled Shii religious establishment, responsible for preaching Shii doctrine and manning the schools, universities, seminaries, and courts.

The Safavid empire reached its zenith guided by the genius of its most celebrated sultan, Shah Abbas (1588–1629). From his capital in Isfahan, he oversaw an ambitious program of state building, implementing administrative, military, economic and religious reforms. Generous religious endowments supported the building of major religious monuments, schools, mosques, and hospitals. As with the Ottomans, the *ulama* and their educational and judicial institutions were brought within the Safavid state bureaucracy.

The splendor and accomplishments of the Ottomans in the Arab Middle East and Eastern Europe and the Safavids in Iran were matched by those of India's Mughal dynasty, which was founded in the sixteenth century. North India had long been the scene of Muslim penetration and conquest, with the invasions of Arab soldiers in the seventh century and the establishment of the Turkish and Afghan dynasties of the Delhi sultanate (1211–1556). Muslims in the Indian subcontinent were a minority ruling a vast Hindu majority. In fact, Muslims never actually ruled all of India.

The Emperor Akbar (1565–1605) made the Mughal empire a reality. During his long reign, through conquest and diplomacy he significantly extended Muslim rule into major areas of the subcontinent. The emperor initiated policies to foster greater political centralization and the social integration of his Muslim and Hindu subjects. Religious learning, tolerance, harmony, and syncretism were hallmarks of Akbar's reign. Royal patronage sponsored the building of schools and libraries. A policy of universal tolerance and abolition of the poll tax as well as a tax on Hindu pilgrims fostered loyalty among Hindus, who constituted the majority of his subjects. Akbar encouraged the study of comparative religions and built a House of Worship, where religious scholars from various faiths engaged in theological discussion and debate. Sufi brotherhoods who followed a more flexible, eclectic approach in their encounter with other faiths enjoyed court favor. Their emphasis on religious synthesis, which stressed similarities rather than religious differences, was preferred to the rigid legalism of the more conservative *ulama*. The power of the *ulama* was circumscribed, and their ire incurred by a state-sponsored religious cult, the religion of God or divine religion (*din illahi*), which emphasized the truth to be found in all religions. They took special offense at the Infallibility Decree of 1579, which recognized the emperor, rather than the *ulama*, as the final authority in religious matters.

Ulama opposition to Akbar's eclectic religious approach and legacy was joined to that of religious reformers such as Shaykh Ahmad Sirhindi (1564–1624), a member of the Naqshbandi Sufi brotherhood, who rejected religious assimilation and advocated a more pronounced emphasis on the Islamic basis and character of state and society. However, it was the emperor Aurangzeb (1658–1707) who dismantled Akbar's pluralistic system of governance. Aurangzeb implemented the *ulama*'s more exclusive (rather than Akbar's inclusive) religiopolitical order, which emphasized implementation of Islamic law (including the prohibition of alcohol and gambling), a subordinate political and social status for non-Muslims, reimposition of the poll tax, and the destruction of Hindu temples.

The political and religious accomplishments of Akbar and his successors were accompanied by the fluorescence of Mughal art. Mughal painting and architecture reflected both Persian and Ottoman influences. As with its Safavid and Ottoman counterparts, Mughal art reached great heights in manuscript illustration and miniature paintings as well as the design and building of religious and public monuments— grand mosques, forts, and palaces. Perhaps the most famous product of this period is the Taj Mahal, built in Agra by Shah Jahan, a grandson of Akbar, as a memorial to his beloved wife.

Despite the divison of the Muslim world into separate sultanates, a Muslim traveler across this vast area could experience an international Islamic order that transcended state boundaries, particularly in the urban/intellectual culture of cities and towns. All Muslim citizens were members of a transnational community of believers, citizens of the *dar al-Islam* (abode of Islam) who, despite differences of interpretation, professed faith in one God, His Prophet, and revelation. All were bound by the Sharia, Islamic law, and obligated to observe the Five Pillars of Islam. The Islamic city reflected this common framework and culture in its organization and institutions (mosques, legal codes and courts, schools and universities, Sufi convents, religious endowments, a political establishment of sultans, military commanders, and soldiers as well as a religious establishment of *ulama* and Sufi shaykhs or *pirs*—scholars and mystics).

Despite variations and the individual policies of some rulers, the imperial Ottoman, Safavid, and Mughal sultanates demonstrated a somewhat common Islamic ideological outlook and approach to state organization, support, and use of Islam. Rulers bore the title sultan (the one who possesses power or authority). Their rule was based on a blend of military strength and religious legitimacy. The sultan appropriated the caliph's charge as defender and protector of the faith. Islamic law continued to enjoy pride of place as the official law of the state. Religion not only supported the state but was itself supported by state patronage. In particular, many of the *ulama* became part of a prosperous religious establishment that assisted the sultan's attempt to centralize and control the educational, legal, and social systems. They educated the military, bureaucratic, and religious elites in their schools, supervised and guided the interpretation and application of Islamic law in the Sharia courts, and oversaw the disbursement of funds from religious endowments (*waqf*) for educational and social services from the building of mosques and schools to hospitals and lodges for travelers. During this time, a number of the nonofficial *ulama* in particular developed strong international linkages. Many people came from far and wide to study at Mecca and Medina or at the renowned al-Azhar University in Cairo. After years of study and interchange, they returned to their home territories or took up residence in other parts of the Islamic world. Scholars, in particular, often traveled throughout the Muslim world to study with great masters and collect Prophetic traditions and reports about the Prophet's words and deeds. Islamic learning and interpretation possessed truly international character due to the sacrifice and commitment of these learned men. As the *ulama* developed and prospered, so too did the Sufis. Their eclectic, syncretistic tendencies enabled Islam to adapt to new environments and absorb local religious beliefs and customs. This complemented and enhanced the general process of adaptation pursued by the sultans and attracted droves of converts as Islam spread at an astonishing rate in Africa, India, and Southeast Asia. Established Sufi orders, like the Naqshbandi, spread from the Indian subcontinent to the Mediterranean, becoming vast international networks, and new orders sprang up and prospered.

Within the diversity of states and cultures, Islamic faith and civilization provided an underlying unity, epitomized by a common profession of faith and acceptance of the Sharia, Islamic law. Islam provided the basic ideological framework for political and social life, a source of identity, legitimacy, and guidance. A sense of continuity with past history and institutions was maintained. The world was divided into Islamic (*dar al-Islam*, the abode of Islam) and non-Islamic (*dar al-harb*, the abode of warfare). All Muslims were to strive to extend Islam wherever possible. Thus, merchants and traders as well as soldiers and mystics were the early missionaries of Islam. The sultan was the protector and defender of the faith charged with extending the Islamic domain. Citizenship, taxation, law, education, social welfare, defense, and warfare were based on Islam. The *ulama* for their part successfully asserted their role as protectors and interpreters of the tradition. Thus, both the political and the religious authorities, the "men of the sword" and the "men of the pen," appealed to Islam to legitimate their authority. For the majority of believers, there was a continuum of guidance, power, and success that transcended the contradictions and vicissitudes of Muslim life, and validated and reinforced the sense of a divinely mandated and guided community with a purpose and mission.

By the turn of the eighteenth century, the power and prosperity of the imperial sultanates were in serious decline. The decline of the great Muslim gunpowder empires coincided with the Industrial Revolution and modernization in the West. The emergence of modern Europe as a major military, economic, and political power ushered in the dawn of European colonialism. Internal political disintegration (the rise of semi-autonomous regional and provincial governments), military losses, a deteriorating economy affected by European competition in trade and manufacturing, and social disruption signaled the dénouement of Muslim imperial ascendancy. The Safavid empire fell in 1736; dynastic rule would not be reestablished until the end of the century under the relatively weak Qajar dynasty. The Mughal empire lingered on in name only, subservient to Britain, until 1857, when India was formally declared a British colony. Only the Ottoman empire survived into the twentieth century, when it collapsed and was dismembered by the British and the French during the post–World War I Mandate period. As we shall see, the social and moral decline of these great Muslim empires would contribute to a wave of Islamic revivalist movements throughout much of the Muslim world in the eighteenth and nineteenth centuries.

3

Religious Life: Belief and Practice

For Christianity, the appropriate question is "What do Christians believe?" In contrast, for Islam (as for Judaism), the correct question is "What do Muslims *do*?" Whereas in Christianity, theology was the "queen of the sciences," in Islam, as in Judaism, law enjoyed pride of place, for "to accept or conform to the laws of God is *islam*, which means to surrender to God's law."[22]

Because Islam means surrender or submission to the will of God, Muslims have tended to place primary emphasis on obeying or following God's will as set forth in Islamic law. For this reason, many commentators have distinguished between Christianity's emphasis on orthodoxy, or correct doctrine or belief, and Islam's insistence on orthopraxy, or correct action. However, the emphasis on practice has not precluded the importance of faith or belief. Faith (*iman*) and right action or practice are intertwined.

Theology

As the confession of faith or basic creed ("There is no god but God and Muhammad is the messenger of God") illustrates, faith in God and the Prophet is the basis of Muslim belief and practice. As discussed in Chapter 1, the Quran established a set of basic beliefs that are the foundation of its worldview and the criterion for belief versus unbelief: belief in God and His Prophet, previous prophets and revealed Scripture, angels, and the Day of Judgment (4:136). Acceptance of these beliefs renders one a believer (*mumin*); to reject them is to be an unbeliever (*kafir*). Faith places the Muslim on the straight path; acts demonstrate commitment and faithfulness. In Islam, the purpose of life is not simply to affirm but to actualize; not simply to profess belief in God but to realize God's will—to spread the message and law of Islam. Faith without works is empty, without merit; indeed, it is the Book of Deeds that will be the basis for divine judgment. Thus the primacy of law over theology in the Islamic tradition.

Kalam: Dialectical Theology

Islamic theology, unlike Christian theology, was not developed systematically, nor was it the product of theoretical reflection or speculation. Theology (kalam, "speech" or discourse) emerged as a reaction to specific debates or issues that grew out of early Islam's sociopolitical context, for example, the Kharijite split with Ali, early Christian–Muslim polemics, and the penetration of Greek thought during the Abbasid period. Although theological issues and discourse began during the early caliphal years, the science of theology, sometimes referred to as the science of (divine) unity, developed as an Islamic discipline during Abbasid times under royal patronage. Its scope reflected the mixing of faith and politics: questions of belief, sin, eschatology, legitimate governance. Among the key theological issues were the relationship of faith to works, the nature of God and the Quran, predestination, and free will.

The relationship of faith to works was the first major theological issue confronting the early community. It involved both the question of grave sin and its effect on membership in the community (does a Muslim guilty of a grave sin remain a Muslim?) and the legitimacy of its ruler or caliph. The occasion was the Kharijite rejection of the third caliph, Uthman, and of Ali's agreement to arbitration with Muawiyah. The Kharijites insisted on total commitment and observance of God's will. They equated faith with works. There could be no compromise, no middle ground. A Muslim was either rigorously observant, a true believer, or not a Muslim at all. Their worldview admitted of only two categories: believer and unbeliever, or infidel. For the Kharijites, Uthman had sinned seriously in his favoritism toward members of his family. Muawiyah, an Umayyad relative of Uthman, was an infidel due to his rebellion against the authority of Uthman's successor, the Caliph Ali. However, Ali's acceptance of arbitration, and thus failure to move decisively against the enemy of God, was also a grave sin. He, too, ceased to be a true Muslim and forfeited his right to rule. The Kharijites regarded these leaders as renegade Muslims (apostates), whose grave sin rendered them infidels and illegitimate rulers, against whom jihad was mandatory.

The majority of the community steered away from the extremism of the Kharijites and followed the more moderate position of the Murjiites, who refused to judge, maintaining that only God on the Last Day could judge sinners and determine whether they were excluded from the community and from paradise. This attitude came to prevail in mainstream Islam. Faith, not specific acts, determined membership in the Islamic community. Except for obvious acts of apostasy, sinners remained Muslims. Non-Muslims were the object of Islam's universal mission to call (*dawa*, "the call," propagation of the faith) all humanity to the worship and service of the one true God.

The Murjia position also provided a justification for Umayyad legitimacy and rule. The caliphs had asserted that, whatever sins and injustices they may have committed, they remained Muslims; they ruled by divine decree and their rule was predetermined by God. This belief gave rise to a second theological issue, determinism versus free will. The opposition to the Umayyads maintained that it was not God but human beings who committed injustices and thus were responsible for their acts. The theological question was, "Does an omnipotent and omniscient God predetermine all acts and events and thus constitute the source of evil and injustice; or are human beings free to act and therefore responsible for sin?" The determinists argued that to attribute free will to human beings limited an omnipotent God. The advocates of free will countered that to deny free will ran counter to the sense of human accountability implicit in the notion of the Last Day and Judgment. Both sides were able to utilize Quranic texts to justify their positions. On the one hand, human freedom is affirmed in such passages as, "Truth comes from your Lord. Let anyone who will, believe, and let anyone who wishes, disbelieve" (18:29). On the other hand, there are many verses that portray an all-powerful God who is responsible for all events: "God lets anyone He wishes go astray while He guides whomever He wishes" (35:8). The issue of free will versus predestination became a major theological issue, with the majority accepting a divinely determined universe. Among the chief advocates of free will were the Mutazila, who developed into a major theological movement.

The Mutazila

The origins of the Mutazila have often been traced back to the early discussion and debate over the status of a grave sinner during the Umayyad dynasty. The word *mutazila*, "those who stand aloof," may well refer to those who espoused a middle or intermediate position, regarding the grave sinner as neither a Muslim nor a non-Muslim. In any case, the Mutazila emerged as a formal school of theology during the Abbasid period. The Mutazila were especially strong during the reign of the Caliph Mamun (reigned 813–833), who attempted in vain to force their theological position on the majority, initiating an inquisition that persecuted and imprisoned its opposition. One of its most famous victims was Ahmad ibn Hanbal, the traditionist leader and legal scholar.

The Mutazila called themselves "the people of (divine) justice and unity," the defenders of divine unity (monotheism) and justice. Influenced by the influx of Greek philosophical and scientific thought during the Abbasid period, with its emphasis on reason, logical argumentation, and study of the laws of nature, they relied on reason and rational deduction as tools in Quranic interpretation and theological reflection. Reason and revelation were regarded as complementary sources of guidance from a just and reasonable God.

The Mutazila took issue with the majority of *ulama* over the doctrines of the divine attributes or names of God and the eternal, uncreated nature of the Quran. Both beliefs were seen as contradictory and as compromising God's unity (Islam's absolute monotheism). How could the one, transcendent God have many divine attributes (sight, hearing, power, knowledge, will)? The Mutazila maintained that the Quranic passages that affirmed God's attributes were meant to be understood metaphorically or allegorically, not literally. Not to do so was to fall into anthropomorphism, or worse, *shirk*, associationism or polytheism. Similarly, the Islamic doctrine that the Quran is the speech or word of God should not be taken literally, for how could both God and His word be eternal and uncreated? The result would be two divinities. The Mutazila interpreted metaphorically those Quranic texts that spoke of the Quran as preexisting in heaven. Contrary to majority opinion, they taught that the Quran is the *created* word of God, who is its uncreated source. The Mutazila critique of those like Ahmad ibn Hanbal, who believed in the eternity of the Quran, was ably summarized by Caliph Mamun in a letter to his governor in Baghdad:

> Everything apart from Him is a creature from His creation—a new thing which He has brought into existence. [This perverted opinion they hold] though the Koran speaks clearly of God's creating all things, and proves to the exclusion of all differences of opinion. They are, thus, like the Christians when they claim that Isa bin Maryam [Jesus, the son of Mary] was not created because he was the word of God. But God says, "Verily We have made it a Koran in the Arabic language," and the explanation of that is, "Verily, We have created it," just as the Koran says, "And He made from it His mate that he might dwell with her."[23]

For the Mutazila, belief in God's justice required human free will and responsibility. How could God be a just judge if people were not free, if human action was predetermined? How could there be divine justice if God was solely responsible for all acts, including evil and injustice? They rejected the image of an all-powerful divinity who arbitrarily and unpredictably determined good and evil, and instead declared that a just God could command only that which is just and good. His creatures bore the responsibility for acts of injustice. Thus, the Mutazila provided a counterweight to the Murjia; Mutazila teachings provided a rationale for critics of Umayyad policies and rule.

The Asharite Response

Muslim theology was pulled in two seemingly irreconcilable directions by those who asserted the unqualified, absolute power of God and by their adversaries, the Mutazila, who maintained that God's actions followed from His just and reasonable nature and that all people were free and morally responsible. Once again, someone arose to bring about a new synthesis. Ironically, it was Abu al-Hasan Ali al-Ashari (d. 935), one of the great Mutazila thinkers of his time, who was the father of the Asharite school of theology, which came to dominate Sunni Islam.

Al-Ashari used the rational dialectic of the Mutazila to expose the deficiencies of their system and to defend the nonrational aspects of belief, which, he maintained, transcended human categories and experience. A critique of the Mutazila tendency to rationalize God and theology is contained in the story of al-Ashari's break with his Mutazila teacher, al-Jubbai, which underscores the limits of human reason and human concepts of justice in explaining divine justice. Al-Ashari is reported to have said:

> Let us imagine a child and a grown-up person in Heaven who both died in the True Faith. The grown-up one, however, has a higher place in Heaven than the child. The child shall ask God: "Why did you give that man a higher place?" "He has done many good works," God shall reply. Then the child shall say, "Why did you let me die so soon that I was prevented from doing good?" God will answer, "I knew that you would grow up into a sinner; therefore, it was better that you should die a child." Thereupon a cry shall rise from those condemned to the depths of Hell, "Why, O Lord! did You not let us die before we became sinners?"[24]

Al-Ashari, like al-Shafii in law and al-Ghazali in theology, undertook a synthesis of contending positions. He staked a middle ground between the extremes of ibn Hanbal's literalism and the Mutazila's logical rationalism. He reasserted the doctrines of the omnipotence of God, His attributes, the uncreatedness of the Quran, and predestination. However, he did this with some reinterpretation, drawing on the language and categories of Greek thought that had now become an integral part of Muslim theological discourse. Al-Ashari used reason to provide a rational defense for that which transcended, and at times seemed contrary to, reason. Thus, while reason and logic might be used to explain and defend belief, revelation was not subordinate to the requirements of reason. The stark divinity of the Mutazila's attributeless God was countered by a reaffirmation of God's eternal attributes, which, al-Ashari maintained, were neither His essence nor accidents. Al-Ashari's universe was controlled by a transcendent, omnipotent God who could intervene in every place and at every moment. Yet he maintained a qualified law of causality by stating that God customarily allowed many events to follow from certain causes. Although al-Ashari's God decreed (willed and created) all actions and events, this determinism was accompanied by a theory of "acquisition," which maintained that people acquire responsibility and thus accountability by their actions.

Al-Ashari and his successors produced a school of theology that by the eleventh century had attracted many adherents, including followers of the Shafii law school, and had become a major stream of Muslim learning. Despite its success, for many of the traditionists, in particular Ahmad ibn Hanbal, al-Ashari and scholastic theology in general remained suspect. Whatever the accomplishments of theology, its use of reason, even if subordinated to revelation, was unacceptable. However, in time the followers of al-Ashari came to be regarded as the dominant school of Sunni theology, including among its members perhaps the most influential Muslim intellectual, al-Ghazali. Mutazila fortunes were more limited. Always a small minority, they failed to attract a substantial following. Their association with the excesses of Caliph Mamun's attempt to impose Mutazila theology as orthodoxy and their use of a rational dialectic struck the majority of *ulama* as a blasphemous attempt to limit God's power. However, much of their thought continued to influence Shii Islam, and many of the issues they raised remain influential today.

At the same time that Greek philosophy and science influenced the development of scholastic theology, philosophy developed as a separate Muslim discipline. Because of the movement to translate classical texts into Arabic, Muslim thinkers were able to appropriate Aristotle, Plato, Plotinus, and the Stoics, and rework these materials within their own context, producing an extraordinarily rich contribution to Islamic civilization. Men like the Arabs Abu Yusuf al-Kindi (d. 873) and al-Farabi

(d. 950), the Persian Ibn Sina (Avicenna, d. 1037), and the Spaniard Ibn Rushd (Averroes, d. 1198) were among the intellectual giants of their times. Their ideas challenged their Muslim contemporaries.

Ironically, despite the genius of Muslim philosophers, their impact on Islamic thought was marginal. If the use of reason in scholastic theology had been suspect, how much more was philosophy, which, in contrast to theology, took reason and not revelation as its starting point and method. The *ulama* (scholars of tradition, law, and theology alike) viewed philosophy as embodying the conflict between reason and revelation, a direct threat to faith. Talk of creation through a process of emanation, reason as the surest means to the truth, and philosophy as the superior path to the real drove a wedge between the philosophers and the bulk of orthodoxy. Al-Ghazali, the great theologian, legal scholar, and mystic, mastered philosophy simply to refute it in his *Incoherence of the Philosophers*, which became a standard work. Ibn Rushd countered with his ringing defense *The Incoherence of the Incoherence*, in which he argued that the differences between philosophy and religion were only apparent, since both pursued the real, the former relying on the language of reason and science and the latter on the metaphorical language of revelation. The measure of the gulf between the philosophers and the community could be seen in the response to Ibn Rushd and the philosophical tradition. Despite the accomplishments of many great philosophers, not only in philosophy but also in medicine and the sciences (for they were truly renaissance men), more often than not they were viewed as rationalists and nonbelievers. Philosophy never established itself as a major discipline. In contrast, Muslim philosophy had a major impact on the West. By transmitting Greek philosophy to medieval Europe, it influenced the curriculum of its universities and the work of such scholars as Albertus Magnus, Thomas Aquinas, Duns Scotus, and Roger Bacon.

Islamic Law

Law is the primary religious science in Islam. Once committed to Islam, the believer's overriding concern and question is "What do I do; what is God's will/law?" Law is essentially religious, the concrete expression of God's guidance (*sharia*, path or way) for humanity. Throughout history, Islamic law has remained central to Muslim identity and practice, for it constitutes the ideal social blueprint for the "good society." The Sharia has been a source of law and moral guidance, the basis for both law and ethics. Despite vast cultural differences, Islamic law has provided an underlying sense of identity, a common code of behavior, for Muslim societies. As a result, the role of Islamic law in Muslim society has been and continues to be a central issue for the community of believers.

Historical Development

For the early Muslim community, following the Sharia of God meant obedience to God's continuing revelation and to His Prophet. Issues of worship, family relations, criminal justice, and warfare could be referred to Muhammad for guidance and adjudication. Both Quranic teaching and Prophetic example guided and governed the early Islamic state. With the death of Muhammad, divine revelation ceased; however, the Muslim vocation to follow God's will did not. Knowledge and enforcement of God's law were continuing concerns. The first four caliphs, assisted by their advisers, carried on, rendering decisions as new problems and questions arose. With the advent of the Umayyad dynasty, an Islamic legal system began gradually to take shape, replacing this ad hoc approach. Part of the new administrative structure established by the Umayyads was the office of the *qadi,* or judge. The *qadi* was originally an official appointed by the caliph as his delegate to provincial governors. He was to see that government decrees were carried out and to settle disputes. In rendering a decision, judges relied on the prevailing Arab customary laws of the particular province and the Quran as well as their own personal judgment. A rudimentary legal code developed, consisting of administrative decrees and judicial decisions. The result was a body of laws that differed from one locale to another, given the cultural diversity of the empire's provinces and the independent judgment exercised by judges.

Growing dissatisfaction with Umayyad practice led to a new page in the history of Islamic law. Critics of the Umayyads charged that the differing customary laws, coupled with caliphal decrees and the personal opinions of judges, had resulted in a confused and often contradictory body of laws. Many asked, "Can God's will be discerned through so subjective a process; can His law for Muslims in Medina be so different from that in Kufa?" They argued that if all Muslims were bound to submit to and carry out God's law, then Islamic law ought to be defined clearly and more uniformly. By the eighth century, such critics, eager to limit the autonomy of Muslim rulers and to standardize the law, could be found in major cities: Medina, Damascus, Basra, Kufa, Baghdad. In time, these great early legal scholars, such as Abu Hanifa (d. 767), Malik ibn Anas (d. 796), Muhammad al-Shafii (d. 819), and Ahmad ibn Hanbal (d. 855), who came to be viewed respectively as the founders or leaders of the Hanafi, Maliki, Shafii, and Hanbali law schools, attracted followers. They began to systematically review Umayyad law and customs in light of Quranic teachings. Maintaining that Islam offered a comprehensive way of life, they sought to apply Islam to all aspects of life. These loosely organized endeavors were the beginnings of early law centers or schools.

The major development of Islamic law and jurisprudence took place during the Abbasid caliphate. Having justified their revolution in the name of Islam, the Abbasid caliphs became the great patrons of Islamic learning. Study of the Quran, traditions of the Prophet, and law excelled in the hands of a new class of scholars (*ulama*), who sought to discover, interpret, and apply God's will to life's situations. Islamic law was not the product of government decrees or judges' decisions but the work of jurists or scholars who struggled from 750 to 900 C.E. to set out a religious ideal, to develop a comprehensive law based on the Quran. Jurists interpreted and formulated Islamic law, while judges were restricted to the application of the law. The consensus of jurists during this period produced the binding legal formulations that were to govern Muslim life down through the centuries.

Despite their common purpose and goals, differences soon arose during Abbasid times, pitting one law school against another and causing divisions within the law schools themselves. This divergence resulted from a combination of factors. The Quran is not a law book. About six hundred of the six thousand verses in the Quran are concerned with law, many of them covering matters of prayer and ritual. Approximately eighty verses treat legal topics in the strict sense of the term: crime and punishment, contracts, family laws.[25] Therefore, in many instances the doctrines of the law schools remained dependent on the interpretation or opinion of jurists who were, in turn, influenced by the differing customs of their respective social milieux. Medina and Kufa provide instructive examples of this stage in the process of legal development. The legal interpretations in both cities shared a common starting point—the Quran was interpreted in light of the precedents of the Prophet and the early caliphs. However, where the Quran was silent, jurists in each city relied on local practice in elaborating the law. The older Arab patrilineal system of Medina contrasted with the more recently established, cosmopolitan Arab and non-Arab urban society of Kufa. Legal scholars who lived in Medina tended to identify their way of life with that of the Prophet and his early companions. Thus, customary tribal law (*sunna*, trodden path or practice) became associated or equated with the practice of the Prophet (what the Prophet said, did, or permitted) and his companions. For the Medinans, law in Islam was based on the Quran and the Prophetically informed practice or local consensus of the Medinan community. This perspective was epitomized by Malik ibn Anas, who wrote the first compendium of Islamic law. Malik was a scholar of both tradition (hadith, written reports about the practice or Sunna of Muhammad and his companions) and law. His treatise, the Muwatta, is a collection of traditions and laws. Legal argument and conclusions are justified or supported by citations from the Quran and traditions. Where differences existed, the local consensus of Medina remained authoritative. In contrast, legal scholars in the much younger community of Kufa, followers of Abu Hanifa and al-Shaybani (d. 804), relied on jurist opinion and local law. The law of equality in marriage is a clear example of the differences that followed from this approach. Because Kufa was a far more diverse and class-conscious society, influenced by Persian practice, a husband was required to be the equal of his wife's family in terms of lineage, financial status, and so forth. However, no such law developed in the more homogeneous society at Medina.

By the end of the eighth century, Muslims again found that despite their best efforts to bring uniformity to the law, significant differences in their legal doctrines continued to exist, given the number of law schools, differences of cultural milieux, and the diversity of legal techniques or criteria employed by jurists (personal opinion, tradition, equity, public welfare). Two contending camps emerged: those who wished to bring uniformity to the law by restricting the use of reason and relying primarily on the traditions of the Prophet versus those who vigorously asserted their right to reason for themselves in the light of such criteria as equity or public interest. Into the fray stepped Muhammad ibn Idris al-Shafii (d. 819), the father of Islamic jurisprudence.

Born in Mecca, al-Shafii studied with Malik ibn Anas at Medina. He spent the early part of his career traveling through Syria and Iraq, thoroughly familiarizing himself with the legal schools and the thinking of his time before settling in Egypt. It was here that his own thought crystallized, and he emerged as the champion of those who sought to curb the diversity of legal practice. Al-Shafii was primarily responsible for the formulation that, after great resistance and debate, became the classical doctrine of Islamic jurisprudence, establishing a fixed, common methodology for all law schools. According to al-Shafii, there are four sources of law (usul al-fiqh, roots or sources of law): the Quran, the example (Sunna) of the Prophet, consensus (ijma) of the community, and analogical reasoning or deduction (qiyas).

Al-Shafii taught that there were only two material sources of law: the Quran and the Sunna of the Prophet, as preserved in the hadith. He maintained that Muhammad was divinely inspired, and thus his example was normative for the community. He restricted the use of the term *sunna* to the Prophet. Henceforth, it came to be identified solely with the divinely inspired practice of Muhammad and no longer with tribal custom or the consensus of law schools. Al-Shafii also transferred the authority for legal interpretation from individual law schools to the consensus of the community. Basing his opinion on a tradition of the Prophet—"My community will not agree upon an error"—the agreed on practice of the community (*ijma*) became the third infallible source of law. Finally, the role of personal reasoning in the formulation of law was restricted. Where no explicit revealed text or community consensus existed, jurists were no longer free to rely on their own judgment to solve new problems. Instead, they were to use deductive reasoning (*qiyas*) to seek a similar or analogous situation in the revealed sources (Quran and Sunna), from which they were to derive a new regulation. Reasoning by analogy would eliminate what al-Shafii regarded as the arbitrary nature of legal reasoning prevalent in the more inductive approach of those who relied on their own judgment.

The Sources of Law

The literal meaning of Sharia is "the road to the watering hole," the clear, right, or straight path to be followed. In Islam, it came to mean the divinely mandated path, the straight path of Islam, that Muslims were to follow, God's will or law. However, because the Quran does not provide an exhaustive body of laws, the desire to discover and delineate Islamic law in a comprehensive and consistent fashion led to the development of the science of law, or jurisprudence (*fiqh*). *Fiqh*, "understanding," is that science or discipline that sought to ascertain, interpret, and apply God's will or guidance (Sharia) as found in the Quran to all aspects of life. As a result of al-Shafii's efforts, classical Islamic jurisprudence recognized four official sources, as well as other subsidiary sources.

QURAN

As the primary source of God's revelation and law, the Quran is the sourcebook of Islamic principles and values. Although the Quran declares, "Here is a plain statement to men, a guidance and instruction to those who fear God," it does not constitute a comprehensive code of laws. While it does contain legal prescriptions, the bulk of the Quran consists of broad, general moral directives—what Muslims ought to do. It replaced, modified, or supplemented earlier tribal laws. Practices such as female infanticide, exploitation of the poor, usury, murder, false contracts, fornication, adultery, and theft were condemned. In other cases, Arab customs were gradually replaced by Islamic standards. Quranic prescriptions governing alcohol and gambling illustrate this process. At first, the use of alcohol and gambling had not been expressly prohibited. However, over a period of years, a series of revelations progressively discouraged their use. The first prescription against the old custom is given in the form of advice: "They ask thee concerning wine and gambling. Say: in them is great sin and some use for man; but the sin is greater than the usefulness" (2:219). Then, Muslims were prohibited from praying under the influence of alcohol: "Approach not prayer with a mind befogged until you can understand all that you say" (4:43). Finally, liquor and gambling were prohibited: "Satan's plan is to incite enmity and hatred between you with intoxicants and gambling, and hinder you from the remembrance of God and from prayer: Will you not then abstain?" (5:93).

Much of the Quran's reforms consist of regulations or moral guidance that limit or redefine rather than prohibit or replace existing practices. Slavery and women's status are two striking examples. Although slavery was not abolished, slave owners were encouraged to emancipate their slaves, to permit them to earn their freedom, and to "give them some of God's wealth which He has given you" (24:33). Forcing female slaves into prostitution was condemned. Women and the family were the subjects of more wide-ranging reforms affecting marriage, divorce, and inheritance. Marriage was a contract, with women entitled to their dower (4:4). Polygamy was restricted (4:3), and men were commanded to treat their wives fairly and equally (4:129). Women were given inheritance rights in a patriarchal society that had previously restricted inheritance to male relatives.

SUNNA OF THE PROPHET

Quranic principles and values were concretized and interpreted by the second and complementary source of law, the Sunna of the Prophet, the normative model behavior of Muhammad. The importance of the Sunna is rooted in such Quranic injunctions as "obey God and obey the Messenger. . . . If you should quarrel over anything refer it to God and the Messenger" (4:59) and "In God's messenger you have a fine model for anyone whose hope is in God and the Last Day" (33:21). Belief that Muhammad was inspired by God to act wisely, in accordance with God's will, led to the acceptance of his example, or Sunna, as a supplement to the Quran, and thus, a material or textual source of the law. Sunna includes what the Prophet said, what he did, and those actions that he permitted or allowed.

The record of Prophetic deeds transmitted and preserved in tradition reports (*hadith*, pl. *ahadith*) proliferated. By the ninth century, the number of traditions had mushroomed into the hundreds of thousands. They included pious fabrications by those who believed that their practices were in conformity with Islam and forgeries by factions involved in political and theological disputes. Recognition that many of these traditions were fabricated led to the development of the science of tradition criticism and the compilation of authoritative compendia. The evaluation of traditions focused on the chain of narrators and the subject matter. Criteria were established for judging the trustworthiness of narrators—moral character, reputation for piety, intelligence, and good memory. Then a link by link examination of each of the narrators was conducted to trace the continuity of a tradition back to the Prophet. The process required detailed biographical information about narrators: where and when they were born, where they lived and traveled, and so forth. Such information might support or refute the authenticity of a narrator. For example, it might be shown that a reputed narrator could not have received a *hadith* from his predecessor because they did not live at the same time or because they neither lived nor traveled near each other.

The second criteria, evaluation of a tradition's subject matter, entailed an examination to determine whether, for example, a tradition contradicted the Quran, an already verified tradition, or reason. After traditions had been subjected to both external (narrators) and internal (subject matter) examination, they were categorized according to the degree of their authenticity (authority) or strength as sound, good or acceptable, and weak.

Throughout the ninth and tenth centuries, scholars traveled throughout the Muslim world collecting traditions and gathering information on their narrators or transmitters. Faced with the enormous corpus of traditions that had grown up, they sought to study and sift through them in order to authenticate and compile those traditions worthy of being conserved and followed by the Muslim community. Six collections came to be accepted as authoritative: those of Ismail al-Bukhari (d. 870), Muslim ibn al-Hajjaj (d. 875), Abu Dawud (d. 888), al-Nisai (d. 915), al-Tirmidhi (d. 892), and Ibn Maja (d. 896). Among these, the collections of al-Bukhari and Muslim have enjoyed an especially high status as authoritative sources.

Authenticity of Tradition Literature. Modern Western scholarship has seriously questioned the historicity and authenticity of the *hadith*, maintaining that the bulk of traditions attributed to the Prophet

Muhammad were actually written much later.[26] Joseph Schacht, the most influential modern Western authority on Islamic law, building on the work of his European predecessors, concluded that the term "Sunna of the Prophet" developed for the first time in the eighth century due to the influence of the Traditionist Movement and under the aegis of al-Shafii, and that this usage gave legal authority to later customary practices and traditions. On the basis of his research, Schacht found no evidence of legal traditions before 722, one hundred years after the death of Muhammad. Thus, he concluded that the Sunna of the Prophet is not the words and deeds of the Prophet, but apocryphal material originating from customary practice that was projected back to the eighth century to more authoritative sources—first the Successors, then the Companions, and finally the Prophet himself.

Most Muslim scholars, while critical of some Prophetic traditions, take exception to Schacht's conclusions.[27] To state that no tradition goes back prior to 722 creates an unwarranted vacuum in Islamic history. Schacht's "first century vacuum" with regard to the existence of Prophetic traditions is a theory or conclusion that completely overlooks or dismisses the Muslim science of tradition criticism and verification and does violence to the deeply ingrained sense of tradition in Arab culture, which all scholars, Muslim and non-Muslim, have acknowledged. As Fazlur Rahman notes:

> The Arabs, who memorized and handed down the poetry of their poets, sayings of their soothsayers and statements of their judges and tribal leaders, cannot be expected to fail to notice and narrate deeds and sayings of one whom they acknowledged as the Prophet of God.[28]

Accepting Schacht's conclusion regarding the many traditions he did examine does not warrant its automatic extension to all the traditions. To consider all Prophetic traditions apocryphal until proven otherwise is to reverse the burden of proof. Moreover, even where differences of opinion exist regarding the authenticity of the chain of narrators, they need not detract from the authenticity of a tradition's content and common acceptance of the importance of tradition literature as a record of the early history and development of Islamic belief and practice. As H.A.R. Gibb observed regarding the significance of tradition literature:

> It serves as a mirror in which the growth and development of Islam as a way of life and the larger Islamic community are truly reflected. . . . [I]t is possible to trace in *hadiths* the struggle between the supporters of the Umayyads and the Medinan opposition, the growth of Shiism and the divisions between its sects . . . the rise of theological controversies, and the beginnings of the mystical doctrines of the Sufis.[29]

ANALOGICAL REASONING

Throughout the development of Islamic law, reason had played an important role as caliphs, judges, and, finally, jurists or legal scholars interpreted law where no clear, explicit revealed text or general consensus existed. The general term for legal reasoning or interpretation was *ijtihad* (to strive or struggle intellectually). It comes from the same root as jihad (to strive or struggle in God's path), which included the notion of holy war. The use of reason (legal reasoning or interpretation) had taken a number of forms and been described by various terms: personal opinion, jurist preference, and analogical reasoning (*qiyas*). Reasoning by analogy was a more restricted, systematic form of *ijtihad*. When faced with new situations or problems, scholars sought a similar situation in the Quran and Sunna. The key is the discovery of the effective cause or reason behind a Sharia rule. If a similar reason could be identified in a new situation or case, then the Sharia judgment was extended to resolve the case. The determination of the minimum rate of dower offers a good example of analogical deduction. Jurists saw a similarity between the bride's loss of virginity in marriage and the Quranic penalty for theft, which was amputation. Thus, the minimum dower was set at the same rate that stolen goods had to be worth before amputation was applicable.

CONSENSUS OF THE COMMUNITY

The authority for consensus (*ijma*) as a fourth source of law is usually derived from a saying of the Prophet, "My community will never agree on an error." Consensus did not develop as a source of law until after the death of Muhammad, with the consequent loss of his direct guidance in legislative matters. It began as a natural process for solving problems and making decisions; one followed the majority opinion or consensus of the early community as a check on individual opinions. However, two kinds of consensus came to be recognized. The consensus of the entire community was applied to those religious duties, such as the pilgrimage to Mecca, practiced by all Muslims. But despite al-Shafii's attempt to define the fourth source of law as this general consensus, classical Islamic jurisprudence defined the community in a more restricted sense as the community of legal scholars or religious authorities who act in behalf of and guide the entire Muslim community.

Consensus played a pivotal role in the development of Islamic law and contributed significantly to the corpus of law or legal interpretation. If questions arose about the meaning of a Quranic text or tradition or if revelation and early Muslim practice were silent, jurists applied their own reasoning (*ijtihad*) to interpret the law. Often this process resulted in a number of differing legal opinions. Over time, perhaps several generations, certain interpretations were accepted by more and more scholars, endured the test of time, while others disappeared. Looking back upon the evolving consensus of scholars, it was concluded that an authoritative consensus had been reached on the issue. Thus, consensus served as a brake on the vast array of individual interpretations of legal scholars and contributed to the creation of a relatively fixed body of laws.

While all came to accept the four sources of law, Islamic jurisprudence recognized other influences, designating them subsidiary principles of law. Among these were custom, public interest, and jurist preference or equity. In this way, some remnant of the inductive, human input that had characterized the actual methods of the law schools in their attempt to realize the Sharia's primary concern with human welfare, justice, and equity was acknowledged. However, the ultimate effect of the acceptance of al-Shafii's formulation of the four sources of law, with its tendency to deny independent interpretation and derive all laws directly from revelation, the inspired practice of Muhammad, or the infallible consensus of the community, was the gradual replacement of the real by the ideal. The actual, historical development of the law was forgotten.

By the tenth century, the basic development of Islamic law was completed. The general consensus (ijma) of Muslim jurists was that Islamic law (Islam's way of life) had been satisfactorily and comprehensively delineated in its essential principles, and preserved in the regulations of the law books or legal manuals produced by the law schools. This attitude led many to conclude that individual, independent interpretation (ijtihad) of the law was no longer necessary or desirable. Instead, Muslims were simply to follow or imitate (taqlid) the past, God's law as elaborated by the early jurists. Jurists were no longer to seek new solutions or produce new regulations and law books but instead study the established legal manuals and write their commentaries. Islamic law, the product of an essentially dynamic and creative process, now tended to become fixed and institutionalized. While individual scholars like Ibn Taymiyya (d. 1328) and al-Suyuti (d. 1505) demurred, the majority position resulted in traditional belief prohibiting substantive legal development. This is commonly referred to as the closing of the gate or door of ijtihad. Belief that the work of the law schools had definitively resulted in the transformation of the Sharia into a legal blueprint for society reinforced the sacrosanct nature of tradition; change or innovation came to be viewed as an unwarranted deviation (bida) from established sacred norms. To be accused of innovation—

deviation from the law and practice of the community—was equivalent to the charge of heresy in Christianity.

There is a danger in overemphasizing the unity and fixed nature of Islamic law. First, while an overall unity or common consensus existed among the law schools with regard to essential practices such as the confession of faith, fasting, and pilgrimage to Mecca, the divergent character of the law schools was preserved by differences in such areas as the grounds for divorce, the levying of taxes, and inheritance rights. Acknowledgment of this diversity within the unity of law was sanctioned by the reported saying of the Prophet, "Difference of opinion within my community is a sign of the bounty of Allah." This diversity continued in practice as judges applied the laws of the various law schools in their courts. Second, some limited legal development and change did occur where scholars interpreted and clarified details of legal doctrine. This was especially true as regards the activity of the *mufti*, a legal expert or consultant. These experts advised both judges and litigants on matters of law. Their formal, written legal opinions (*fatwa*), based on their interpretation of the law, were often relied on in judicial matters. Many of the more important opinions became part of collections of *fatwas*, which became authoritative in their own right.

Schools of Law

Although there had been many law schools, by the thirteenth century the number became stabilized. For Sunni Islam, four major schools predominated: the Hanafi, Hanbali, Maliki, and Shafii. Today, they are dominant in different parts of the Islamic world—the Hanafi in the Arab Middle East and South Asia; the Maliki in North, central, and West Africa; the Shafii in East Africa, southern Arabia, and Southeast Asia; and the Hanbali in Saudi Arabia.

Shii Islam also generated its own schools, the most important of which is the Jafari, named for Jafar al-Sadiq. The doctrine of the imamate resulted in fundamental differences in Islamic jurisprudence. While both Sunni and Shii accept the Quran and Sunna of the Prophet as inspired authoritative textual sources, the Shii have maintained their own collections of traditions that include not only the Sunna of the Prophet but also that of Ali and the Imams. In addition, the Shii reject analogy and consensus as legal sources, since they regard the Imam as the supreme legal interpreter and authority. In his absence, qualified religious scholars serve as his agents or representatives, interpreters (*mujtahids*) of the law. Their consensus guides the community and is binding during the interim between the seclusion of the Imam and his return as the Mahdi. In contrast to Sunni Islam, Shii Islam did not curb the use of *ijtihad*. In practice, Shii religious leaders, although not formally accepting the Sunni doctrine of imitation, tended to follow their medieval legal manuals as well. In the eighteenth century, the right to *ijtihad* was challenged in the conflict between the Akbari and Usuli schools over the question of religious authority. Were the sacred texts sufficient or was there still need for jurist interpretation of the law? The Akbari (a synonym for tradition, or *hadith*) took a more rigid approach and maintained that the sacred texts were sufficient. Therefore, they sought to curb the authority of jurists by maintaining that independent interpretation was not necessary. The Usuli, defending the right and authority of jurists to interpret the law, asserted the need for *mujtahids*. In the end, the Usuli school won out. Moreover, Shii Islam also developed its own distinctive doctrine of emulation or imitation. This was the belief that in the absence of the Imam, leading *mujtahids*, those publicly acknowledged for their learning, piety, and justice, should serve as a religious guide whose example and teachings believers should follow.

Courts of Law

The application of Islamic law was the task of the Sharia courts and their judges (*qadis*). The judiciary was not independent, for judges were appointed by the government, and were paid and served at the pleasure of the caliph. Although originally judges had been interpreters and makers of law, their role came to be restricted to the application of law—that body of laws developed by the jurists and enshrined in the law books. Sharia judges were not to interpret or add to the law. Thus, Islamic law does not recognize a case law system of legally binding precedents. This reflected the belief that jurists, not judges, were to interpret the law. Judges served under a chief judge appointed by the caliph. They were assisted in their work by experts or legal consultants, *muftis*. Among the notable judicial procedures were rules of evidence that required an oath sworn before God in the absence of two adult male Muslim witnesses to a crime, the exclusion of circumstantial evidence, and the absence of cross examination of witnesses. Legal decisions were final. There was no system of judicial appeal. In reality, however, all decisions could be reviewed by the political authority, the caliph or his provincial governor. The *ulama* were the backbone of the legal system. While these scholars were experts in a number of fields, many specialized in law. A specialist in law, or jurist, was called a *faqih* (pl. *fuqaha*). They dominated the Sharia system, serving as lawyers, teachers, judges, and *muftis*.

In addition to the Sharia courts, a class of officials or religious police were charged with the supervision and enforcement of public morals. The office of *muhtasib* originally referred to a market inspector who was to regulate business transactions and practices in the marketplaces or bazaars. However, the office was extended to ensuring public morality in general: the observance of prayer times, fasting, modesty between the sexes. Islamic justification for his activities was rooted in the Quranic command to the Muslim community to encourage good and prohibit evil (3:104, 9:71). The *muhtasib* was empowered to impose penalties for violation of Islamic laws, flogging for public drunkenness, and amputation for theft. The institution continues to exist in a number of Muslim countries like Saudi Arabia and Kuwait. It has been reintroduced more recently in other countries, such as Pakistan and Iran.

While the Sharia system remained integral to state and society, it was not the sole system of law. Though in theory the Sharia was the only officially recognized system of law, in practice a parallel system of caliphal laws and courts existed from earliest times. Both legal idealism and imperial absolutism contributed to the development of an alternative, or rather, supplementary system. An idealism that accepted in good faith an oath sworn before God and excluded circumstantial evidence and cross examination of witnesses proved cumbersome. More importantly, the Sharia system limited the powers of strong and often autocratic rulers. The caliph's desire to exercise absolute power clashed with the belief that God was the only lawmaker. An Islamic rationale was created to circumvent the problem. Citing the caliph's obligation to uphold and ensure governance according to the Sharia, the Umayyads asserted broad discretionary legislative and judicial powers. They issued administrative ordinances and created Grievance courts, ostensibly to enhance the proper administration and implementation of the Sharia in society. Carefully avoiding the term "law," government regulations were called ordinances; the only requirement was that they not be contrary to the Sharia. The Grievance courts were initially established to permit the caliph or his representative to hear complaints against senior officials whose status or power might have inhibited the judges. They soon became a system of courts whose scope and function were determined by the ruler. As a result, Islamic society possessed a dual system of laws and courts (Sharia and Grievance), religious and secular, with complementary jurisdictions. Sharia courts were increasingly restricted to the enforcement of family laws (marriage, divorce, inheritance) and the handling of religious endowments. The Grievance courts dealt with public law, especially criminal law, taxation, and commercial regulations. This approach continued throughout Islamic history. In modern times, it has been employed in countries like Saudi Arabia to provide the rationale for the introduction of a series of modern ordinances, such as the Civil Service Law (1971) and the Mining Code (1963), that supplement the Sharia. Similarly, the creation of Grievance courts made possible the broadening of the judicial system and the introduction of a hierarchy of courts.

Despite the differences between the ideal and the reality, Islamic law endured as the officially recognized cornerstone of the state. When Sunni Muslim jurists and theologians faced the issue of what to do about tyrants and despots, they concluded that it was not the moral character of the caliph but the ruler's acknowledgment of the Sharia as official state law that preserved the unity of the community and determined the Islamic nature and acceptability of a state.

The Content of Law

Law in Islam is both universal and egalitarian. The Sharia is believed to be God's law for the entire Islamic community, indeed for all humankind. In the final analysis, God is the sovereign ruler of the world, head of the human community, and its sole legislator. As a result, Islamic law is as much a system of ethics as it is law, for it is concerned with what a Muslim ought to do or ought not to do. All acts are ethically categorized as: (1) obligatory; (2) recommended; (3) indifferent or permissible; (4) reprehensible but not forbidden; or (5) forbidden. To break the law is a transgression against both society and God, a crime and a sin; the guilty are subject to punishment in this life and the next. The idealism of the law can be seen in the fact that ethical categories such as recommended and reprehensible were not subject to civil penalties. Islamic law is also egalitarian; it transcends regional, family, tribal, and ethnic boundaries. It does not recognize social class or caste differences. All Muslims, Arab and non-Arab, rich and poor, black and white, caliph and craftsman, male and female, are bound by Islamic law as members of a single, transnational community or brotherhood of believers.

The belief that Islamic law was a comprehensive social blueprint was reflected in the organization and content of law. Legal rights and duties are divided into two major categories: (1) duties to God (ritual observances), such as prayer, almsgiving, and fasting, and (2) duties to others (social transactions), which include penal, commercial, and family laws. The heart of the former is the so-called Five Pillars of Islam; that of the latter is family law.

THE FIVE PILLARS

Despite the rich diversity in Islamic practice, the Five Pillars of Islam remain the core and common denominator, the five essential and obligatory practices all Muslims accept and follow.

1. *The Profession of Faith.* A Muslim is one who proclaims (*shahada,* witness or testimony): "There is no god but the God [Allah] and Muhammad is the messenger of God." This acknowledgment of and commitment to Allah and His Prophet is the rather simple means by which a person professes his or her faith and becomes a Muslim, and a testimony that is given throughout the day when the muezzin calls the faithful to prayer. It affirms Islam's absolute monotheism, an unshakable and uncompromising faith in the oneness or unity (*tawhid*) of God. As such, it also serves as a reminder to the faithful that polytheism, the association of anything else with God, is forbidden and is the one unforgivable sin:

> God does not forgive anyone for associating something with Him, while He does forgive whomever He wishes to for anything else. Anyone who gives God associates [partners] has invented an awful sin. (4:48)

The second part of the confession of faith is the affirmation of Muhammad as the messenger of God, the last and final prophet, who serves as a model for the Muslim community. Molding individuals into an Islamic society requires activities that recall, reinforce, and realize the word of God and the example of the Prophet. The praxis orientation of Islam is witnessed by the remaining four pillars or duties.

2. *Prayer.* Five times each day, Muslims are called to worship God by the muezzin (caller to prayer) from atop a mosque's minaret:

> God is most great (Allahu Akbar), God is most great, God is most great, I witness that there is no god but Allah (the God); I witness that there is no god but Allah. I witness that Muhammad is His messenger. I witness that Muhammad is His messenger. Come to prayer, come to prayer. Come to prosperity, come to prosperity. God is most great. God is most great. There is no god but Allah.

Facing Mecca, the holy city and center of Islam, Muslims, individually or in a group, can perform their prayers (*salat,* or in Persian, *namaz*) wherever they may be—in a mosque (*masjid,* place of prostration), at home, at work, or on the road. Recited when standing in the direction of Mecca, they both recall the revelation of the Quran and reinforce a sense of belonging to a single worldwide community of believers. Although the times for prayer and the ritual actions were not specified in the Quran, they were established by Muhammad. The times are daybreak, noon, mid-afternoon, sunset, and evening. Ritually, prayer is preceded by ablutions that cleanse the body (hands, mouth, face, and feet) and spirit and bestow the ritual purity necessary for divine worship. The prayers themselves consist of two to four prostrations, depending on the time of day. Each act of worship begins with the declaration, "God is most great," and consists of bows, prostrations, and the recitation of fixed prayers that include the opening verse of the Quran (the *Fatihah*) and other passages from the Quran:

> In the name of God, the Merciful and Compassionate. Praise be to God, Lord of the Universe, the Merciful and Compassionate. Ruler on the Day of Judgment. You do we worship and call upon for help. Guide us along the Straight Path, the road of those whom You have favored, those with whom You are not angry, who are not lost. (1:1–7)

At the end of the prayer, the *shahada* is again recited, and the "peace greeting"—"Peace be upon all of you and the mercy and blessings of God"—is repeated twice.

On Friday, the noon prayer is a congregational prayer and should be recited preferably at the official central mosque, designated for the Friday prayer. The congregation lines up in straight rows, side by side, and is led in prayer by its leader (*imam*), who stands in front, facing the niche (*mihrab*) that indicates the direction (*qibla*) of Mecca. A special feature of the Friday prayer is a sermon (*khutba*) preached from a pulpit (*minbar*). The preacher begins with a verse from the Quran and then gives a brief exhortation based on its message. Only men are required to attend the Friday congregational prayer. If women attend, for reasons of modesty due to the prostrations, they stand at the back, often separated by a curtain, or in a side room. Unlike the Sabbath in Judaism and Christianity, Friday was not traditionally a day of rest. However, in many Muslim countries today, it has replaced the Sunday holiday, usually instituted by colonial powers and therefore often regarded as a Western, Christian legacy.

3. *Almsgiving (zakat).* Just as the performance of the *salat* (prayer) is both an individual and a communal obligation, so payment of the *zakat* instills a sense of communal identity and responsibility. As all Muslims share equally in their obligation to worship God, so they all are duty-bound to attend to the social welfare of their community by redressing economic inequalities through payment of an alms tax or poor tithe. It

is an act both of worship or thanksgiving to God and of service to the community. All adult Muslims who are able to do so are obliged to pay a wealth tax annually. It is a tithe or percentage (usually 2½ percent) of their accumulated wealth and assets, not just their income. This is not regarded as charity since it is not really voluntary but instead is owed, by those who have received their wealth as a trust from God's bounty, to the poor. The Quran (9:60) and Islamic law stipulate that alms are to be used to support the poor, orphans, and widows, to free slaves and debtors, and to assist in the spread of Islam. Although initially collected and then redistributed by the government, payment of the *zakat* later was left to the individual. In recent years, a number of governments (Pakistan, the Sudan, Libya) have asserted the government's right to a *zakat* tax.

4. *The Fast of Ramadan.* Once each year, Islam prescribes a rigorous, month-long fast during the month of Ramadan, the ninth month of the Islamic calendar. From dawn to sunset, all adult Muslims whose health permits are to abstain completely from food, drink, and sexual activity from sunrise to sunset. Ramadan is a time for reflection and spiritual discipline, for expressing gratitude for God's guidance and atoning for past sins, for awareness of human frailty and dependence on God, as well as for remembering and responding to the needs of the poor and hungry. The rigors of the fast of Ramadan are experienced during the long daylight hours of summer when the severe heat in many parts of the Muslim world proves even more taxing for those who must fast while they work. Some relief comes at dusk, when the fast is broken for the day by a light meal (popularly referred to as breakfast). Evening activities contrast with those of the daylight hours as families exchange visits and share a special late evening meal together. In some parts of the Muslim world, there are special foods and sweets that are served only at this time of the year. Many will go to the mosque for the evening prayer, followed by a special prayer recited only during Ramadan. Other special acts of piety, such as the recitation of the entire Quran (one-thirtieth each night of the month) and public recitation of the Quran or Sufi chantings, may be heard throughout the evening. After a short evening's sleep, families rise before sunrise to take their first meal of the day, which must sustain them until sunset. As the end of Ramadan nears (on the twenty-seventh day), Muslims commemorate the "Night of Power" when Muhammad first received God's revelation. The month of Ramadan comes to an end with a great celebration, the Feast of the Breaking of the Fast, *Id al-Fitr.* The spirit and joyousness remind one of the celebration of Christmas. Family members come from near and far to

feast and exchange gifts in a celebration that lasts for three days. In many Muslim countries, it is a national holiday. The meaning of Ramadan is not lost for those who attend mosque and pay the special alms for the poor (alms for the breaking of the fast) required by Islamic law.

5. *Pilgrimage: the Hajj.* Ramadan is followed by the beginning of the pilgrimage season. Every adult Muslim physically and financially able is expected to perform the annual pilgrimage (*hajj*) to Mecca at least once in his or her lifetime. The focus of the pilgrimage is the Kaba, the cube-shaped House of God, in which the sacred black stone is embedded. Muslim tradition teaches that the Kaba was originally built by the prophet Ibrahim (Abraham) and his son Ismail. The black stone was given to Abraham by the angel Gabriel and thus is a symbol of God's convenant with Ismail and, by extension, the Muslim community. The Kaba was the object of pilgrimage during pre-Islamic times. Tradition tells us that one of the first things Muhammad did when he marched triumphantly into Mecca was to cleanse the Kaba of the tribal idols that it housed, thus restoring it to the worship of the one true God.

The pilgrimage proper takes place during the twelfth month, Dhu al-Hijja, of the Muslim lunar calendar. As with prayer, the pilgrimage requires ritual purification, symbolized by the wearing of white garments. Men shave their heads, or have a symbolic tuft of hair cut, and don two seamless white sheets. Women may wear simple, national dress; however, many don a long white dress and head covering. Neither jewelry nor perfume is permitted; sexual activity and hunting are prohibited as well. These and other measures underscore the unity and equality of all believers as well as the total attention and devotion required. As the pilgrims near Mecca they shout, "I am here, O Lord, I am here!" As they enter Mecca, they proceed to the Grand Mosque, where the Kaba is located. Moving in a counterclockwise direction, they circle the Kaba seven times. During the following days, a variety of ritual actions or ceremonies take place—praying at the spot where Abraham, the patriarch and father of monotheism, stood; running between Safa and Marwa in commemoration of Hagar's frantic search for water for her son, Ismail; stoning the devil, three stone pillars that symbolize evil. An essential part of the pilgrimage is a visit to the Plain of Arafat, where, from noon to sunset, the pilgrims stand before God in repentance, seeking His forgiveness for themselves and all Muslims throughout the world. It was here, from a hill called the Mount of Mercy, that the Prophet during his Farewell Pilgrimage preached his last sermon or message. Once again, the preacher repeats Muhammad's call for peace and harmony among the believers. Standing together on the Plain of Arafat,

Muslims experience the underlying unity and equality of a worldwide Muslim community that transcends national, racial, economic, and sexual differences.

The pilgrimage ends with the Feast of Sacrifice (*Id al-Adha*), known in Muslim piety as the Great Feast. It commemorates God's command to Abraham to sacrifice his son Ismail (Isaac in Jewish and Christian traditions). The pilgrims ritually reenact Abraham's rejection of Satan's temptations to ignore God's command by again casting stones at the devil, here represented by a pillar. Afterward, they sacrifice animals (sheep, goats, cattle, or camels), as Abraham was finally permitted to substitute a ram for his son. The animal sacrifice also symbolizes that, like Abraham, the pilgrims are willing to sacrifice that which is most important to them. (One needs to recall the importance of these animals as a sign of a family's wealth and as essential for survival.) While some of the meat is consumed, most is supposed to be distributed to the poor and needy. In modern times, with almost 2 million participants in the pilgrimage, Saudi Arabia has had to explore new methods for freezing, preserving, and distributing the vast amount of meat. The Feast of Sacrifice is a worldwide Muslim celebration that lasts for three days, a time for rejoicing, prayer, and visiting with family and friends. At the end of the pilgrimage, many of the faithful visit the mosque and tomb of Muhammad at Medina before returning home. The enormous pride of those who have made the pilgrimage is reflected in a number of popular practices. Many will take the name Hajji, placing it at the beginning of their name. Those who can will return to make the pilgrimage.

In addition to the *hajj*, there is a devotional ritual, the *umra* (the "visitation") or lesser pilgrimage, which Muslims may perform when visiting the holy sites at other times of the year. Those who are on the pilgrimage often perform the *umra* rituals before, during, or after the *hajj*. However, performance of the *umra* does not replace the *hajj* obligation.

The Struggle (Jihad). Jihad, "to strive or struggle" in the way of God, is sometimes referred to as the sixth pillar of Islam, although it has no such official status. In its most general meaning, it refers to the obligation encumbent on all Muslims, as individuals and as a community, to exert themselves to realize God's will, to lead virtuous lives, and to extend the Islamic community through preaching, education, and so on. As discussed earlier, a related meaning is the struggle for or defense of Islam, holy war. Despite the fact that jihad is not supposed to include aggressive warfare, this has occurred, as exemplified by early extremists like the Kharijites and contemporary groups like Egypt's Jihad Organization (which assassinated Anwar Sadat) as well as Jihad organizations in Lebanon, the Gulf states, and Indonesia.

MUSLIM FAMILY LAW

As the Five Pillars are the core of a Muslim's duty to worship God, family law is central to Islam's social laws. Because of the centrality of the community in Islam and the role of the family as the basic unit of Muslim society, family law enjoyed pride of place in the development of Islamic law as well as in its implementation throughout history. While caliphs and modern Muslim rulers might limit, circumvent, and replace penal or commercial laws, Muslim family law has generally remained in force. Today, as in the past, the subject of women and the family remains an important and extremely sensitive topic in Muslim societies.[30]

The special status of family law reflects the Quranic concern for the rights of women and the family (the greater part of its legislation concerns these issues) as well as that of the patriarchal society in which the law was elaborated. The traditional family social structure, the roles and responsibilities of its members, and family values may be identified in the law. The Quran introduced substantial reforms affecting the position of women by creating new regulations and modifying customary practice. These reforms and customary practice constitute the substance of classical family law. To understand the significance of Quranic reforms as well as the forces that influenced the development of family law, some appreciation of the social context in pre-Islamic Arabia is necessary.

The extended family had one head or leader, the father or senior male, who controlled and guided the family unit. The family consisted of the father, his wife or wives, unmarried sons and daughters, and married sons with their wives and children, all of whom had specific roles within the family structure. It served as the basic social and economic unit of the tribe within a male-dominated (patriarchal) society. The paramount position of males was reflected in family matters: their unlimited right to marry or divorce at will and an inheritance system that excluded women. A woman was regarded as little more than a possession, first of her father and her family, and subsequently, of her husband and his family.

The status of women and the family in Muslim family law was the product of Arab culture, Quranic reforms, and foreign ideas and values assimilated from conquered peoples. These regulations and practices—organized in Islamic law under the categories of marriage, divorce, and inheritance—have guided Muslim societies and determined attitudes and values throughout the history of Islam.

The centrality of marriage in Islam is captured by the tradition of the Prophet, which says, "There shall be no monkery in Islam." Marriage is encumbent on every Muslim man and woman unless they are financially or physically unable. It is regarded as the norm for all, a safeguard on chastity, and essential to the growth and stability of the family, the basic unit of society. Marriage is regarded as a sacred contract or covenant, but not a sacrament, legalizing intercourse and the procreation of children. It is not simply a legal contract between two individuals, but between two families. Thus, in the traditional practice of arranged marriages, the families or guardians, not the prospective bride and groom, are the primary actors. They identify suitable partners and finalize the marriage contract. The official marriage ceremony is quite simple. It consists of an offer and acceptance by the parties (the representatives of the bride and groom) at a meeting before two witnesses. This is followed later by a family celebration. The preferred marriage is between two Muslims and within the extended family. While a Muslim man can marry a non-Muslim woman (i.e., a Christian or a Jew, "People of the Book") (5:6), Muslim women are prohibited from marrying non-Muslims (5:6).

Islamic law embodies a number of Quranic reforms that significantly enhanced the status of women. Contrary to pre-Islamic Arab customs, the Quran recognized a woman's right to contract her own marriage. In addition, she, not her father or other male relatives as had been the custom, was to receive the dower from her husband (4:4). She became a party to the contract rather than simply an object for sale. The right to keep and maintain her own dowry was a source of self-esteem and wealth in an otherwise male-dominated society. Women's right to own and manage their own property was further enhanced and acknowledged by the Quranic verses of inheritance (4:7, 11–12, 176), which granted inheritance rights to wives, daughters, sisters, and grandmothers of the deceased in a patriarchal society where all rights were traditionally vested solely in male heirs. Similar legal rights would not occur in the West until the nineteenth century.

Although it is found in many religious and cultural traditions, polygamy (or more precisely, polygyny) is most often identified with Islam in the minds of Westerners. In fact, the Quran and Islamic law sought to control and regulate the number of wives rather than give free license. In a society where no limitations existed, Muslims were not told to marry four wives but instead to marry no more than four. The Quran permits a man to marry up to four wives, provided he can support and treat them all equally. Muslims regard this Quranic command (4:3) as strengthening the status of women and the family, for it sought to ensure the welfare of single women and widows in a society whose male population was diminished by warfare, and to curb unrestricted polygamy: "If you are afraid you shall not be able to deal justly with the orphans, marry women of your choice, two or three or four; but if you shall not be able to deal justly [with them] only one."

Islamic law prescribes that co-wives are to be treated equally in terms of support and affection. This includes separate housing (depending on finances, a room, an apartment, or a house) and maintenance. As we shall see, a subsequent verse of the Quran ("You are never able to be fair and just between women even if that is your ardent desire" [4:129]) has been used in modern times by some Muslims to reject the possibility of equal justice among wives and to therefore argue that the Quran preached a monogamous ideal.

The relationship of a husband and wife is viewed as complementary, reflecting their differing characteristics, capacities, and dispositions, and the roles of men and women in the traditional patriarchal family. The primary arena for men is the public sphere; they are to support and protect the family and to deal with the "outside" world, the world beyond the family. Women's primary role is that of wife and mother, managing the household, raising children, supervising their religious and moral training. While both are equally responsible before God to lead virtuous lives, in family matters and in society women are subordinate to men by virtue of their more sheltered lives, protected status, and the broader responsibilities of men in family affairs. Because men were responsible for the economic well-being of all of the women in the extended family, their portion of inheritance was twice that of women. Similarly, because men had more extensive experience in society, in legal affairs the testimony of two women was regarded as equal to that of one man.

Divorce. Alongside the popular images of polygamy, veiling, and seclusion, is that of a man's unilateral right to dismiss his wife simply by declaring, "I divorce you." However, ideally divorce is a last resort, discouraged rather than encouraged in Islam. This attitude is preserved in an often-cited tradition of the Prophet that states that "of all the permitted things, divorce is the most abominable with God."[31] The Quran counsels arbitration between spouses: "If you fear a split between a man and his wife, send for an arbiter from his family and an arbiter from her family. If both want to be reconciled, God will arrange things between them" (4:35). One of the clearest indications of the negative attitude toward divorce, yet reluctant acceptance of it by jurists as a last resort, occurs in the *Hedaya,* a legal manual, which describes divorce as a dangerous and disapproved procedure as it dissolves marriage, an institution which involves many circumstances as well of a temporal as a spiritual nature; nor is its propriety at all admitted, but on the ground of urgency of relief from an unsuitable wife.[32]

However, the Islamic ideal was often compromised by social realities.

Faced with a situation in which Arab custom enabled a man to divorce at will and on whim while women had no grounds for divorce, the Quran and Islamic law established guidelines for men and rights for women based on considerations of equity and responsibility, values that exemplified the Quranic admonition to husbands who were separated and contemplating divorce to "either retain them [their wives] honorably or release them honorably" (65:2).

Several methods of divorce were introduced to constrain a man's unbridled right to repudiate his wife and to establish a woman's right to a judicial (court) divorce. The most common form of divorce is a man's repudiation (*talaq*) of his wife. The approved forms were: (1) a husband's single pronouncement of divorce ("I divorce you"), to take effect after a three-month mandatory waiting period had elapsed in order to make sure the wife was not pregnant (to determine paternity and maintenance) and to allow time for reconsideration and reconciliation; (2) the pronouncement of the words of divorce three times, once each in three successive months. At any time during the three months, the couple can nullify the divorce by word or action, such as resuming to live together. However, at the end of the three months, the second form of divorce becomes final and irrevocable. The couple may not remarry unless there is an intervening marriage—that is, the wife must have remarried, consummated the marriage, and then divorced. The third form of divorce, more common and problematic, is the husband's pronouncement of the words of divorce three times at once. In this case, the divorce takes effect immediately rather than at the end of a three-month waiting period, bypassing the Quranically mandated waiting period for determining paternity and maintenance obligations and the opportunity for reconciliation. Although this form of divorce is regarded as an unapproved innovation or deviation (*talaq al-bida,* a deviant repudiation) and therefore sinful, it is legally valid. The allowance of this disapproved, though legal, form of divorce is a good example of the extent to which custom was able at times to contradict and circumvent revelation in the development of law:

> When you divorce women, divorce them when they have reached their period. Count their periods . . . and fear God your Lord. Do not expel them from their houses. . . . Those are limits set by God. (65:1)

The strong influence of custom is also evident in the more limited divorce rights of women. In pre-Islamic times, Arab women had no divorce rights. In contrast the Quran states, "Women have rights similar to those [men] over them; while men stand a step above them" (2:228). In the elaboration of Islamic law, the *ulama* extended rights to women while retaining the dominant status of men. In contrast to men, women who wished a divorce had to go before a court and had to have grounds for their action. A wife can sue for divorce if her husband has previously delegated a right to divorce in their marriage contract. She may also request a judicial divorce on such grounds as impotence, insanity, desertion, or nonmaintenance. These grounds varied within the law schools; some were more liberal than others in their interpretation.

Historically, divorce rather than polygamy has been the more serious social problem. This situation has been compounded by the fact that many women have been unable to exercise their legal rights because they were unaware of them or because of pressures in a male-dominated society.

Inheritance. Prior to Islam, the rules of inheritance were concerned solely with the strength and solidarity of the male-dominated tribe. Therefore, inheritance was kept within the male line (patrilineal). Women in Arabia, as in many cultures, were excluded from inheritance, which passed in its entirety to the nearest male relative of the deceased, on whom they were totally dependent. However, Quranic reforms in inheritance strengthened the rights of individual family members, especially women. New rules of inheritance were superimposed on existing practices. The Quran gave rights of inheritance to wives, daughters, sisters, and grandmothers of the deceased, all of whom had previously had no rights. These new "Quranic heirs" received a fixed share from the estate before the inheritance passed to the nearest male relative of the deceased. Only after these Quranic claims were satisfied was the residue of the estate awarded to the senior male.

Custom and Law

VEILING AND SECLUSION

Nothing illustrates more the interaction of Quranic prescription and customary practice than the development of the veiling (*hijab, burqa,* or *chador*) and seclusion (*purdah,* harem) of women in early Islam. Both are customs assimilated from the conquered Persian and Byzantine societies and viewed as appropriate expressions of Quranic norms and

Completed in 691, the Dome of the Rock in Jerusalem is the earliest remaining Islamic monument.

Ali, the cousin and son-in-law of the Prophet Muhammad, was the fourth caliph (successor) of Sunni Islam and the first Imam (leader) of Shii Islam. The Shrine of Imam Ali, Kufa, Iraq, remains one of the most important religious centers in the Islamic world. (*Courtesy of Mehmet Biber*)

The "Golden Mosque," in Baghdad, Iraq, reflects the grandeur of mosque architecture as found throughout the Islamic world. (*Courtesy of ARAMCO World*)

Although according to Islamic belief the grave for Muslims is to be simple, the burial sites for the wealthy and powerful often were marked by elaborate architectural masterpieces, such as Sultan Barquq's Mausoleum and Mosque in Cairo, Egypt. (*Courtesy of ARAMCO World*)

The mosque of Süleyman the Magnificent dominates the Istanbul skyline. Completed in 1557, the vast mosque and its surrounding complex of buildings epitomize the artistic creativity of the Ottoman period. (*Courtesy of Walter B. Denny*)

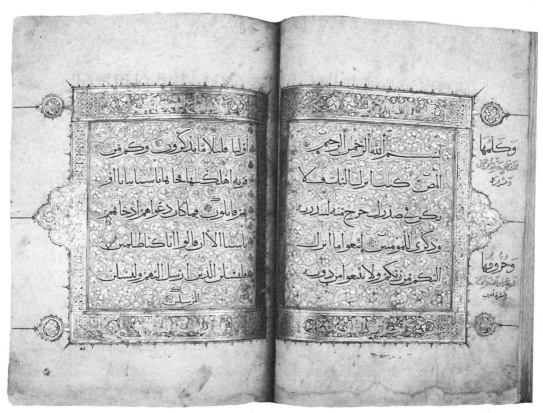

Calligraphy and text illumination are major Islamic art forms. Opening of Sura VII of the Quran. Arabic Ms. OR., 1401, ff.116v–117r, Egyptian, fourteenth century. (*Courtesy of The British Library*)

Dome of the Mosque of Shaykh Lutfallah, Isfahan, Iran, built during the Safavid period when Shii Islam was established as the state religion and a major source of Iranian identity and culture. (*Courtesy of Islamic Art Archive, University of Michigan, Ann Arbor*)

The Great Mosque at Cordoba. One of the few remaining religious monuments commemorating Muslim rule in Spain and the presence of Islam in the Iberian Peninsula from the eighth to the fifteenth centuries. A major center of culture and civilization, Spain served as an intermediary in the transmission of Arabic science and philosophy to the West.

Built during the Mughal period by Shah Jahan in memory of his wife Mumtaz Mahal, the Taj Mahal in Agra, India, is one of the masterpieces of Islamic art as well as one of the seven wonders of the world. (*Courtesy of Walter B. Denny*)

Islam spread throughout much of the Muslim world due to the efforts of Muslim mystics. Shrines, such as the Mian Mir Sufi Shrine in Lahore, Pakistan, serve as centers of pilgrimage for the disciples of great Sufi masters.

The mystics of Islam used music and dance to "remember" (*dhikr*) or experience the presence of God. Perhaps the most famous example is that of the whirling dervishes, disciples of the great Sufi master Jalal al-Din Rumi, whose dance imitated the order of the universe. (*Courtesy of Mehmet Biber*)

The martyrdom of Husayn (grandson of the Prophet Muhammad) at Karbala is a central religious paradigm, ritually reenacted annually in Shii Islam. His shrine at Karbala, Iraq, is a major center for pilgrimage. (*Courtesy of Mehmet Biber*)

Once each week Muslims come together for the Friday congregational prayer as seen here at the Blue Mosque, Istanbul, Turkey. (*Courtesy of Mehmet Biber*)

Women praying in mosque. Men and women are equally responsible to worship and obey God. However, women have tended to pray at home. Today, in many parts of the Muslim world, women are seen in greater numbers worshipping at the mosque. (*Courtesy of Mehmet Biber*)

Wherever Muslims are, as individuals or in a group, they face Mecca and prostrate before God to perform their daily prayer or worship (*salat*).

Five times each day the muezzin calls Muslims throughout the world to worship God. (*Courtesy of ARAMCO World*)

The Kaba, believed by Muslims to have been built originally by the Prophet Ibrahim (Abraham) and his son Ismail, has been a focal point of the annual pilgrimage to Mecca since the days of the Prophet Muhammad. (*Courtesy of the Middle East Institute*)

values. The Quran does not stipulate veiling or seclusion. On the contrary, it tends to emphasize the participation and religious responsibility of both men and women in society. However, the Quran does say that the wives of the Prophet should speak to men from behind a partition and admonishes women to dress modestly:

> And say to the believing women that they should lower their gaze and guard their modesty; that they should not display their beauty and charms except what [normally] appears of them; that they should draw their veils over their bosoms and display their beauty only to their husbands, their fathers. (24:31)

It should be noted that in the previous verse, modesty is enjoined for men as well: "Tell the believing men to lower their gaze and be modest (24:30).

The extent to which foreign practices were adopted and legitimated by Quranic interpretation may be seen in the exegesis of al-Baydawi, a thirteenth-century Persian Muslim and one of the most renowned Quranic scholars, who wrote regarding this verse of the Quran:

> Indeed the whole of the body is to be regarded as pudental and no part of her may lawfully be seen by anyone but her husband or close kin, except in case of need, as when she is undergoing medical treatment or giving evidence.[33]

Veiling and seclusion had as their original intent the protection, honor, and distinction of women. They were adopted by upper-class urban women who lived in great palaces and courts and enjoyed considerable mobility and opportunity to participate in the activities within their environment. Village and rural women were slower to adopt these practices, as they interfered with their ability to work in the fields. Over the centuries, as the segregation of women in the home spread to every stratum of society, it had unforeseen and deleterious effects. Poorer women were confined to small houses with limited social contacts. They were effectively barred from community life. Since the mosque served as the center of community life, to the extent that women ceased to worship publicly in the mosque, they were cut off from social and educational activities. The negative effects of this process are attested to in modern times by the Egyptian religious scholar Muhammad al-Ghazzali: "Ninety percent of our women do not pray at all; nor do they know of the other duties of Islam any more than their names."[34]

To the extent that tribal customs prevailed in the development of Islamic law and in Muslim practice, both the letter and the spirit of

Quranic reforms were weakened or subverted by practices such as the *talaq al-bida*. Similarly, despite Quranic passages that talk about the rights of women and counsel that they be treated justly and equitably, regulations were enacted such as the "house of obedience," which requires that a woman obtain her husband's permission to leave the house. If she fails to do so, he may ask the police to forcibly return her and may confine her until she becomes more obedient.

The force of custom can also be seen in the ways in which social customs often contradicted the precepts of Islamic law. Despite a woman's Quranic and legal right to contract her marriage and receive the dower, marriage was often simply arranged by the bride's father and the dower functioned as a bride price given to her family. Thus, she remained the object of sale rather than the subject of a contractual agreement. Women's inheritance rights were also often ignored. Given the social structure of the family, awarding married daughters their rightful share in their father's estate was often regarded as giving wealth to another, her husband's family. Finally, the pressures of a strong patriarchal society often militated against women exercising their legal right to divorce. As a result, in practice, men could still legally divorce at will and for any reason (a wife's sickness, failure to produce a son), free from legal, though not moral, sanction.

Historically, although the Sharia technically was the sole law and a ruler's source of legitimacy, in fact Islamic empires and states had two complementary legal systems—Sharia courts, which were increasingly restricted to family law and the handling of religious endowments, and Grievance courts, which dealt with public law (criminal, land, and commercial regulations). While the Sharia remained an essential and integral part of Islamic government, it was only part of a legal system in which the ruler was able to exercise his authority and influence through his power to restrict the scope and jurisdiction of Sharia courts, appoint and fire its judges, issue his own ordinances, and guide his courts. The Sharia set out the law to be followed, but it did not provide constitutional or (independent) judicial restraints. Its ideal nature was reflected in a law that presumed a good Muslim ruler. When faced with the question of what to do about a tyrant, the majority (Sunni) position accepted obedience to the ruler rather than the disorder of civil strife, provided the ruler recognized the supremacy of the Sharia. Acknowledgment by the ruler that the Sharia was the state's official law preserved both the unity and the Islamic character or framework of the community. The supremacy of Islamic law as the eternally valid expression of the straight path of Islam for state and society prevailed both as an ideal and in the practice of official government recognition.

Popular Religion

Sufism: The Mystic Path of Love

Alongside the exterior path of law (*sharia*) is the interior path or way (*tariqa*) of Sufi mysticism, a major popular religious movement within Sunni and Shii Islam. While the Sharia provided the exoteric way of duties and rights to order the life of the individual and community, Sufism offered an esoteric path or spiritual discipline, a method by which the Sufi sought not only to follow but to know God. Like other mystical movements in Christianity, Judaism, Hinduism, and Buddhism, the Sufi path is a way of purification (*tasawwuf*), a discipline of mind and body whose goal is to directly experience the ultimate reality. In later generations, Sufism swept across the Islamic world as Sufis became the great missionaries and popular preachers of Islam in Asia and Africa.

While the traditional Islamic way of life was expressed officially and formally in Islamic law, there developed within the Islamic community individuals for whom mere following or obedience to the will of God was not totally satisfying. Reacting with disdain and dismay to the worldly seductions of imperial Islam, they were motivated by a desire to return to what they regarded as the purity and simplicity of the Prophet's time and driven by a deep devotional love of God that culminated in a quest for a direct, personal experience of the presence of God in this life. These men and women pursued an ascetic lifestyle that emphasized detachment from the material world, which, they believed, distracted Muslims from God, repentance for sins, fear of God, and the Last Judgment. Many took to wearing simple, coarse woolen garments; their detachment from material concerns earned them the name *faqir* or, in Persian, *darwish* (poor or mendicant). Dedicated to a life of prayer and fasting, they meditated on the words of the Quran, seeking deeper or hidden guidance, and scrupulously gathered and imitated the example of the Prophet, strongly motivated by fear of God and His judgment on the Last Day.

Many of the early Sufis were critics and opponents of the Umayyads, among those early *ulama* (*hadith* scholars, jurists, and theologians) who sought to check Umayyad extravagances and refocus the vision and goals of the community. Hasan al-Basri (643–728), an eminent scholar, typifies the ascetic reaction to what they regarded as the decadence of imperial Islam:

> The lower (material) world is a house whose inmates labor for loss, and
> only abstention from it makes one happy in it. He who befriends it in
> desire and love for it will be rendered wretched by it, and his portion
> with God will be laid waste. . . . For this world has neither worth nor
> weight with God, so slight it is.[35]

The early emphasis on ascetic detachment (worldly renunciation)
and meditation was complemented by the contribution of Rabia al-
Adawiyya (d. 801), who fused asceticism with an undying devotional
love of God. Her joining of the ascetic with the ecstatic permanently
influenced the nature and future development of Sufism. An attractive
and desirable woman, Rabia declined offers of marriage, not willing to
permit anyone or anything to distract her from dedication and total
commitment to God. She attracted a circle of followers for whom she
served as an example and a guide. Perhaps nothing captures better the
selfless devotion she espoused than the following words attributed to
her:

> O my Lord, if I worship Thee from fear of Hell, burn me in hell, and if
> I worship Thee in hope of Paradise, exclude me thence, but if I worship
> Thee for Thine own sake, then withhold not from me Thine Eternal
> Beauty.[36]

The joining of devotionalism with asceticism transformed Sufism
from its relatively limited elite base into a movement that attracted and
embraced all strata of society. Throughout the ninth and tenth centuries, Sufism grew in Arabia, Egypt, Syria, and Iraq. Though its origins
and sources (Sufi interpretation of the Quran and life of the Prophet)
were clearly Islamic, outside influences were absorbed from the Christian hermits of Egypt and Lebanon, Buddhist monasticism in Afghanistan, Hindu devotionalism, and Neoplatonism. Mystics like al-Muha-
sibi of Baghdad (d. 857) Dhu al-Nun of Egypt (d. 859), Junayd of
Baghdad (d. 910), and the Persians Abu Yazid al-Bistami (d. 874) and
Mansur al-Hallaj (d. 922) made major contributions to the formation of
the Sufi way. Their lives and teachings provided the core of beliefs and
practices on which later generations would build. They represented a
range of mystical doctrines from the "sober" to the "intoxicated," from
the doctrinally safe followers of the law and a path of selfless love and
service of God to ecstatic rebels like Abu Yazid and al-Hallaj, whose
experience of God as indwelling in their souls moved them to actions
and statements that scandalized many and drew the ire of the *ulama*.
Abu Yazid's consciousness of the transience of the material world and
the inner presence of God led him to declare, "Glory to me. How great
is my majesty!" Equally blasphemous to orthodox ears was al-Hallaj's
claim, "I am the Truth," for which he was crucified.

As Sufism spread in Muslim societies, becoming a mass movement, the gap widened between the Sufi movement and many of the *ulama,* who were often seen by Sufis as co-opted by power, tolerating and supporting the sociopolitical abuses and excesses of the government. As a religious establishment, the *ulama* felt Sufism challenged their authority and prerogatives. Sufis claimed their own authority and guides. They often rejected as religious formalism the official, legal-moral Islam of the *ulama,* seeking to go beyond the letter of the law to its spirit. Sufism claimed to go back beyond religious forms, institutions, and laws to the divine source itself. While some members of the *ulama* were Sufis, the majority dismissed Sufi doctrine and practice as heretical, as an unwarranted deviation or innovation from the orthodox consensus of the community. Deep-seated suspicions and hostility led to persecution and even executions, as in the martyrdom of al-Hallaj.

Abu Hamid al-Ghazali: Reconciler and Revivalist

The eleventh and twelfth centuries were a particularly turbulent time in Muslim history. The universal caliphate had disintegrated into a system of decentralized and competing states whose only unity was the symbolic, though powerless, Abbasid caliph in Baghdad. The Ismaili missionary propagandists were actively undermining the Sunni consensus. Muslim philosophers, deeply indebted to Hellenism and Neoplatonism, were offering alternative, and sometimes competing, answers to philosophical and theological questions that often strained or tested the relationship between reason and faith. Sufism had become a mass movement with a strong emotional component and an eclectic propensity to accept superstitious practices. Much of what was taking place seemed out of the reach and control of the *ulama,* many of whom felt that these movements threatened their status and authority in the community. It was the genius and accomplishment of Abu Hamid al-Ghazali (1058–1111) to address all these issues. Amid the turmoil, al-Ghazali emerged, as had al-Shafii centuries earlier, to save the day by providing the needed religious synthesis. His reputed success may be measured by his popular designation as a great reviver (*mujaddid*) of Islam.

Born and raised in Iran, al-Ghazali received the best Islamic education available in his time. After studying at the mosque school in his village Tus, near modern-day Mashhad, he was trained at Nishapur by the most prominent theologian of the time, al-Juwayni. He mastered law, theology, and philosophy. At a relatively young age, he was appointed in 1091 to the faculty of the Nizamiyya, a theological institute in Baghdad. There, in a series of books, he responded to the challenges posed by the Ismailis and the philosophers. He wrote *The Incoherence of* the Philosophers, in which he refuted those aspects of the philosophy of Avicenna (d. 1037) that he found unacceptable. In particular, he maintained that while reason was most effective in mathematics and logic, its application to theological and metaphysical truths merely led to confusion and threatened the fabric of faith. Al-Ghazali's teaching and writings brought him fame and recognition. Yet, at the peak of his success, he had a spiritual crisis that was to change his life. The brilliant lecturer suddenly found himself unable to speak. Inexplicably, he deteriorated physically and psychologically. Despite his theological knowledge and extraordinary achievements, he felt lost:

> When I considered the circumstances, I saw I was deeply involved in affairs, and that the best of my activities, my teaching, was concerned with branches of knowledge which were unimportant and worthless. I also examined my motive in teaching and saw that it was not sincere desire to serve God but that I wanted an influential position and widespread recognition. I was in no doubt that I stood on an eroding sandbank, and in imminent danger of hell-fire if I did not busy myself with mending my ways. . . . Worldly desires were trying to keep me chained where I was, while the herald of faith was summoning, "To the road! To the road! Little of life is left, and before you is a long journey. Your intellectual and practical involvements are hypocrisy and delusion. If you do not prepare for the future life now, when will you prepare; if you do not sever your attachments now, when will you sever them?"[37]

Desperate, al-Ghazali resigned his position, left his home and family, and withdrew to Syria, where he studied and practiced Sufism:

> I turned to the way of the mystics. . . . [I] obtained a thorough intellectual understanding of their principles. Then I realized that what is most distinctive of them can be obtained only by personal experience ["taste"-dhawq], ecstasy and a change of character. . . . I saw clearly that the mystics were men of personal experience not of words, and that I had gone as far as possible by way of study and intellectual application, so that only personal experience and walking in the mystic way were left.[38]

For many years, al-Ghazali studied and practiced Sufism, traveling, after his initial stay in Syria, to Sufi centers in Palestine and Arabia. During this period, he wrote what many regard as his greatest work, *The Revivification of the Religious Sciences*, his great synthesis of law, theology, and mysticism. Law and theology were presented in terms which the *ulama* could accept, but these disciplines were grounded in direct religious experience and interior devotion. Rationalism was tempered by Sufism's emphasis on religious experience and love of God. It proved to be a brilliant tour de force, reassuring the *ulama* about the orthodoxy of Sufism and countering the rationalism of the philosophers.

In both his life and his work, al-Ghazali represented the intellectual and spiritual currents of his times. At the end, he had achieved an integration and religious synthesis that earned him a place as one of Islam's great scholars and the title, "Renewer of Islam," a designation based on the popular belief that in each century an individual (*mujaddid*) will come to restore and revitalize the Muslim community, to renew (*tajdid*) Islam by returning Muslims to the straight path.[39] Despite continued differences of opinion between the Sufis and many of the *ulama*, al-Ghazali had secured a place for Sufism within the life of the community.

SUFI ORDERS

The twelfth century proved to be an important turning point both for al-Ghazali's legitimation of Sufism and because of the formation of the first great Sufi orders. In the last years of his life, al-Ghazali had established one of the first Sufi centers or compounds (*zawiyya*), where followers gathered to live and be trained by their spiritual guide. As Sufism became a mass movement, attracting people of all social classes and educational backgrounds, similar centers sprang up and multiplied. Sufism began to be transformed from loose, voluntary associations into organized brotherhoods or religious orders (*tariqa*) of mendicants with their own distinctive institutions. Prior to this time, Sufism had tended to be concentrated in urban areas among religious elites who met at mosques or in private homes. Now the spiritual family was organized more formally as a community. By the thirteenth century, Sufi orders had created international networks of centers that transformed Sufism into a popular mass movement whose preachers were the great missionaries of Islam.

Organizationally, Sufi orders built on the already established relationship of master (*shaykh*, or Persian, *pir*) and student or disciple. Sufi masters drew their authority from their illustrious predecessors. As the authority of traditions was based on a system of links dating back to the Prophet, so too a similar system of linkages of pious predecessors was established going all the way back to Muhammad. Spiritual pedigree or lineage was the source of a master's religious authority, teachings, and practices. Because of his piety, reputation for sanctity, and often miraculous powers, the master was viewed as especially near to God, a friend of God. He served as a spiritual guide and a model to be emulated. His followers wished to be near him both to benefit from his teaching, advice, and example as well as to receive his blessing, the product of his spiritual power. Over time the teachings of masters were passed on through their disciples to future generations.

Sufi centers served as the spiritual, social, and cultural center of the community. They consisted of a collection or compound of buildings, which might include the residence of the shaykh and his family, a separate room for recollection, living quarters for his disciples, a mosque, kitchen, hospice for visitors, and school. The focal point was the master's residence. The shaykh would lead prayers, instruct and train, guide and advise individuals, and oversee communal life. Membership was of two kinds: full-time professed members and associate or affiliated members. Professed disciples were those who, after a period of training, were initiated into the order. This ceremony included investiture with the distinctive garb and cap of the order, which symbolized obedience to the rule of the order. The initiate swore an oath of allegiance to his shaykh and clasped his hand, receiving his blessing. Disciples lived nearby in the center, devoting themselves to study, spiritual exercises, and the upkeep and activities of the center. These included a soup kitchen to feed the poor and hungry, care for the sick, a hospice for visitors (travelers, pilgrims, other Sufis), and religious education. Centers were often established and subsidized by pious endowments that permitted the master and his disciples to pursue their spiritual path, free from secular employment and concerns. A large number, often the majority, of members had an associate status, somewhat like "third-order" members of Christian religious orders. These lay associates "lived in the world," engaged in the everyday activities of working and raising families. However, they were also subject to the authority of the shaykh, sought his guidance and advice, participated in community services, and performed the important task of financially supporting the center and its activities. Often associate members formed neighborhoods or even villages around Sufi centers.

Sufi orders developed their own forms of monastic rule that detailed the regulations by which the dervishes or *faqirs* were to live. These varied from order to order and from one geographic area to another. In one of the earliest set of rules, we find regulations common to many orders, such as:

> 1) The disciple should keep his garments clean and be always in a state of ritual purity. . . . 2) One should not sit in a holy place gossiping. . . . 5) At dawn a disciple should pray for forgiveness. . . . 6) Then, in the early morning, he should read the Koran, abstaining from talk until sunrise. . . . 7) Between the two evening prayers, he should be occupied with his recollection [*dhikr*] and the special litany [*wird*] which is given to him by his master. . . . 8) The Sufi should welcome the poor and needy, and look after them.[40]

Under the tutelage of a shaykh, disciples progressed along the Sufi path of virtue and spiritual knowledge. The master assigned them prayers to recite and meditate on, monitored and evaluated their progress, and, finally, authenticated their spiritual experiences and insights. He designated the more advanced as *khalifa*, successors. A *khalifa* might be designated to succeed the shaykh after his death or he might be sent to head one of the centers of the order. The spiritual power of the shaykh was passed on or inherited by his successor. While some orders retained the practice of selection or election of the shaykh's successor, many opted for hereditary succession. Leadership of the order often passed to a son or relative of the shaykh, keeping control of the order in family hands.

The focal point of a Sufi order was the domed tomb of its founder, who was venerated as a saint (*wali*, friend) of God. The tomb became a center for pilgrimage as visitors came to appeal to the saint for assistance. His spiritual power and intercession before God could be invoked for a safe pregnancy, success in exams, or a prosperous business, and offerings were made in thanksgiving for answered prayers. Once each year, a great celebration was held to commemorate the anniversary of his birth or death. Pilgrims would come from near and far for several days of rituals, songs or spiritual concerts, and celebration.

THE WAY: DOCTRINE AND PRACTICE

At the heart of Sufism is the belief that one's self must die, that is, one must undergo annihilation (*fana*) of the lower, ego-centered self in order to abide or rest (*baqa*) in God. Renunciation of that which is impermanent and transient, the phenomenal world, is a prerequisite to realization of the divine that indwells in all human beings. The goal of the Sufi is direct knowledge or personal religious experience of God's presence. This mystical knowledge or understanding is reached by means of a series of stages and states. The shaykh leads the disciple through successive stages—renunciation, purification, and insight. Along the way, God rewards and encourages the disciple by granting certain religious experiences or psychological states.

In order to obtain their goal, the Sufis adapted many practices, some of which were foreign, in the eyes of the *ulama*, to early Islamic values. One of the fundamental tensions between the *ulama* and the Sufis was the extent to which the religious brotherhood offered an alternative sense of community, and the shaykh constituted a threat to the religious authority of the *ulama*. Among the predominant Sufi practices employed to break attachment to the material world and rediscover or become aware of God's presence were: (1) Poverty, fasting, silence, celibacy, and other disciplines of mind and body whose object was the letting go of all attachment to and awareness of the self and the phenomenal world. Only then could the Sufi become aware of the divine,

which was always present but ordinarily hidden from view by a preoc-
cupation with the material world. While some orders practiced celibacy,
many did not. The interpretation and practice of poverty varied as well.
Each order and master had a distinctive approach. (2) Remembrance or
recollection of God through a rhythmic, repetitive invocation of God's
name(s), accompanied by breathing exercises, to focus consciousness on
God and place the devotee in His presence. By themselves or sitting
with their shaykh in community worship, Sufis repeated or recalled
God's name hundreds and thousands of times for hours during the day
or throughout the night. Another form of recollection is the recitation of
a litany of God's names or attributes, often counted on a string of prayer
beads, similar to a rosary. To become absorbed in recitation is to forget
about worldly attachments and rest in God. (3) The use of music and
song, spiritual concerts of devotional poems, as well as dance or bodily
movements to induce or trigger ecstatic states in which the devotee
could experience the presence of God or union with God. Though orthodoxy remained critical and Sufis like al-Ghazali warned of their dangers, music and dance proved especially popular among the people as a
quick way to become intoxicated on God, to experience deep feelings of
love for God and to feel His nearness. Groups of Sufis would gather to
sing God's praises and loving hymns to Muhammad, or other great leaders like Ali, begging their intercession and assistance. The most famous
example of the use of dance is that of the whirling dervishes, followers
of the order founded by Jalal al-Din Rumi. Their whirling dance imitated
the order of the universe. As dervishes spun in a circle around their
shaykh, so did the planets revolve around the sun, the axis or center of
the universe. (4) Veneration of Muhammad and Sufi saints as intermediaries between God and people. Muhammad had emphasized that he
was only a human being and not a miracle worker. Despite this emphasis in official Islamic belief, the role of the Prophet as a model for Muslim life had early led to extravagant stories about Muhammad's life and
extraordinary powers. This tendency became pronounced in Sufi piety.
Muhammad was viewed as the link between God and man. The most
extraordinary powers were attributed to him, given his closeness to
God. These wonders were extended to Sufi saints, the friends or protégés
of God. Miraculous powers (curing the sick, bilocation, reading minds,
multiplication of food) and stories of saintly perfection abounded. Sufi
theory organized the saints into a hierarchy, at the apex of which stood
Muhammad, the pole of the universe, supervising the world. Shaykhs
were venerated during their lifetime; they were honored, loved, and
feared because of their miraculous powers. After their death, their burial
sites or mausoleums became religious sanctuaries, objects of pilgrimage

and of petitions for success in this life as well as the next, for worldly gains as well as eternal life.

The very characteristics that accounted for the strength of Sufism and its effectiveness and success as a popular religious force, contributed to its degeneration. That same flexibility, tolerance, and eclecticism that had enabled Islam to spread and incorporate local customs and practices from Africa to Southeast Asia and attract many converts permitted the most bizarre and antinomian practices to enter and run wild. Sufism's healthy concern about legalism and ritual formalism gave way to the rejection by many of official religious observances and laws. Sacred song and dance resulted not in spiritual intoxication but in drunkenness and sensuality. Awareness of the divine presence in all of creation became a justification for the assimilation of saint worship, fetishism, and all manner of magical and superstitious practices. A movement that had emphasized poverty and asceticism became weighed down by shaykhs, whose playing on the credulity of poor and ignorant followers rather than their sanctity won them followers and financial fortune. The *faqir* (mystic/mendicant) became the faker; the spiritual heads of mendicant orders were transformed into dispensers of amulets, becoming wealthy feudal landlords. Emphasis on the limitations of reason and the need for direct knowledge to experience the divine became an excuse for the rejection of all Islamic learning and religious authority and the growth of superstition and fatalism. The high ground of sound and sober mysticism sank under the weight of ignorance and superstition, contributing significantly to the decline and decay of the Islamic community. The corrosive role of Sufi excesses came to be so much regarded as a primary cause of Muslim decline that from the seventeenth century onward, Sufism was subject to suppression and reform by premodern and modern Islamic revivalist and reformist movements.

Shii Religious Practices

In contrast to official Sunni Islamic ambivalence and/or rejection of popular religious practices, such as visiting the shrines or tombs of saints and belief in their intercession, Shii Islam's worldview incorporated a number of such beliefs and ritual practices. This difference was rooted in their different orientations. For Sunnis, God and human beings have a direct relationship; the *ulama* are not intermediaries but scholar-interpreters of religion. Thus, belief in saintly intermediaries was often viewed as heretical or, more precisely, dangerous deviation (*bida*). For Shii, intercession is an integral part of the divine plan for salvation. Ali and the other Imams were divinely inspired models, guides, and inter-mediaries between God and the believers. In their absence, the *ulama* or *mujtahids* and local religious leaders (*mullas*) served as community guides, though they had no intermediary or intercessory powers. This belief developed later into the notion that, in the absence of the Imam, a distinguished cleric (or clerics) might serve as the supreme guide and authority on law, the source of emulation.

The special place and veneration of the Imams generated a rich set of religious symbols and rituals that were accepted as integral to Shiism, rather than, as would have been the case in Sunni Islam, peripheral. The central figures are the Fourteen Pure or Perfect Ones. They consist of: (1) the Prophet, Ali and Fatima, and their sons Hasan and Husayn and; (2) the remaining nine Imams. Ali and the Imams are the means to an intellectual, esoteric, and legal understanding and interpretation of rev-elation. They serve as charismatic, infallible, divinely inspired leaders of the community as well as models of suffering and sacrifice in the face of tyranny and oppression. Veneration for the Holy Family is reflected in the special place and honorific title that their descendants have claimed throughout Islamic history, an attitude found in Sunni Islam as well.

Like Sufism, Shiism places great value on the intercession of saints, the "friends" of God who mediate God's grace and blessings to the believers. As in Christianity, suffering and compassion, martyrdom and sacrifice, atonement and redemption are central motifs in salvation his-tory. In contrast to the Sunni, Shii believe that the intercession of the Imams is a necessary part of history, from the redemptive death of Husayn to the return of the Hidden Imam at the end of time:

> The Imams are also the intermediaries between man and God. To ask
> for their succour is to appeal to the channel God placed before man so
> as to enable man to return to him.[41]

Along with those holy days that they share with their Sunni coreli-gionists, Shii also mourn and celebrate the birthdays and death anni-versaries of the Imams. Moreover, a major form of devotion is the vis-itation of the tomb-shrines of the Holy Family and Imams at Karbala, Kazimiyya, Najaf, Kufa, Qum, and Mashhad. These holy sites draw hun-dreds of thousands of pilgrims throughout the year. Historically, for financial reasons and ease of access, these pilgrimages have been more popular and common than the *hajj*.

Husayn and Fatima serve as major male and female religious symbols, on whom believers are to meditate and pattern their lives. Husayn's martyrdom at Karbala on the tenth day (*ashura*) of the Islamic month of Muharram in 680 is the paradigmatic event of Shii history. Remembrance and ritual reenactment of the tragedy of Karbala is a cornerstone of faith, personal and communal identity, and piety. It accounts for the special vision and character of Shii Islam as a disinherited, oppressed community, loyal to God and His Prophet, struggling throughout history to restore God's rule and a just society. The martyrdom motif was extended to all the Imams, who, with the exception of the twelfth, were believed to have been martyred. As a result, the "passion" of Husayn symbolized the historic struggle between the forces of good and evil, God and Satan, and the eschatological hope and belief in the ultimate triumph of justice over tyranny when the Imam will return at the end of time.

The pathos and meaning of Husayn's martyrdom—with its themes of oppression, tyranny, martyrdom, social justice, and atonement—are revealed in liturgical manuals which recount the fateful battle. Husayn was drawn into battle by a request from the citizens of Kufa to liberate them from a land

> where an oppressor now rules, who takes wedded wives and virgin daughters for his own pleasure, and extracts money with threats and violence. It is better to execute a tyrant than to allow the government of sinners. If you, Prince Husayn, do not rescue us from corruption and injustice, we shall accuse you on the Day of Judgment of neglecting your duty, we swear this by the Almighty.

Husayn then set out from Mecca to Kufa with but seventy-seven followers. Along the way he was tested by God but overcame all temptation. Husayn and his army encountered the Syrian forces of the Sunni Umayyad caliph Yazid:

> The Syrians avoided man-to-man battle because Husayn and his men had a reputation as warriors and the Syrians were cowards who limited themselves to shooting arrows at the Alids from behind safe positions. For the sake of the women and children who were with them, Husayn's men tried to fight their way through to the river in the hope of fetching water for those parched creatures . . .

However, after hours of battle, the small band of followers were overcome by the vast Syrian army. The casualties included Husayn's eldest and youngest sons as well as the son of Husayn's brother Hasan who, Shii tradition reports, had gallantly killed more than three thousand of the enemy before he too fell in battle. Finally, Husayn set out for his final confrontation. The meaning of this event and the intensity of religious belief and feeling it inspires is captured in a scene movingly recalled in Shii religious literature:

> In spite of his admonition, all the women wept bitter tears, and so did the children. Even the angels in heaven cried sadly, and the animals in

the wilderness and the birds in the sky lamented in mournful songs; even the fish in the ocean wept. . . . He mowed down his enemies like a fire raging through the tall grass of the savannah. The earth grew bloodied and the sky grew dark as if the Day of Judgment had begun. Dark clouds veiled the sun even in Mecca so that its people wondered what caused this gloom which covered Arabia, Syria, and Egypt, reaching as far as Iran and Khurasan. . . . A voice was heard: Husayn! The enemy has overrun your tent! / The women have been taken and the children killed! / . . . He turned his horse and hurried back to the camp. There in the shrubs the enemy were waiting. They shot at him without their faces showing / Hundreds of arrows flew into his face / Seventy arrows hit his tender body / and pierced the skin and spilled his precious blood. / He knew that he did not have long to live / Just enough time to say: There is no god / but God and Muhammed is His prophet. / His soul flew up into the cloudless sky where it was met by those who loved him most: / His parents and his brother and his sons. . . . Here ends the sad account of Prince Husayn / Who lived and died a witness for the faith / A ransom for his people, for Mankind.

Fatima, "the Mother of the Imams," has a special claim and role in Shii piety due to her special place in the family of the Prophet. She was the Prophet's only surviving child, the wife of Imam Ali, and the mother of the Imams Husayn and Hasan. Her unique status is captured by a widely cited tradition of the Prophet: "Fatima is a part of my body. Whoever hurts her, has hurt me, and whoever hurts me has hurt God."[45] Fatima is the primal mother figure, immaculate and sinless, the pattern for virtuous women, the object of prayer and petition. Like her son Husayn, she embodies a life of dedication, suffering, and compassion. Tradition portrays her as, despite often leading a life of poverty and destitution, sharing whatever she had with others. Like the Virgin Mary in Christian tradition, Fatima is portrayed as a woman of sorrow, symbolizing the rejection, disinheritance, and martyrdom of her husband and sons.

In addition to the *salat* (daily prayer), Shiism developed a number of ritual practices that became major forms of piety and were regarded as earning spiritual merit. All are centered on the tragedy of Karbala, commemorated each year during the month of Muharram through dramatic recitations, passion plays, (*taziya*), and street processions. The purpose of these ceremonies is remembrance and mourning. Participants experience profound grief, pain, and sorrow in emotional ceremonies marked by lamentation, breast beating, weeping, and flagellation as the tragedy and heroism of Husayn are relived. Some of its aspects are reminiscent of practices found at times in a number of Christian contexts—"The Muharram processions are, perhaps, more similar to the Passion Week celebrations which can still be seen in such Christian countries as Guatemala."[46]

Through ritual reenactment and identification with the suffering and patient endurance of Husayn and his family, Shii seek to atone for their sins, merit salvation, and hasten the final triumph:

> Thus lamentations for Husayn enable the mourners not only to gain assurance of divine forgiveness, but also to contribute to the triumph of the Shii cause. Accordingly, Husayn's martyrdom makes sense on two levels: first, in terms of a soteriology not dissimilar from the one invoked in the case of Christ's crucifixion: just as Christ sacrificed himself on the altar of the cross to redeem humanity, so did Husayn allow himself to be killed on the plains of Karbala to purify the Muslim community of sins; and second, as an active factor, vindicating the Shii cause, contributing to its ultimate triumph.[47]

Remembrance of the passion and death of Husayn, like that of Christ in Christianity, occurs not only annually, during the month of Muharram, but also daily. The recitation of sacred stories in homes and specially constructed halls and the performance of passion plays in special theaters, which focus on Husayn and other great Shii martyrs, take place throughout the year in villages, towns, and cities. They constitute popular forms of piety and entertainment and a distinctive way of preserving and reappropriating a sacred history and heritage.

While the Five Pillars and the Sharia remain the common basis of faith and practice for all Muslims, at the same time Islam incorporated a variety of beliefs and activities that grew out of religious and historical experience and the needs of specific Muslim communities. The inherent unity of faith, implicit in statements like "one God, one Book, one [final] Prophet," should not deter one from appreciating the rich diversity that has characterized the religious (legal, theological, and devotional) life of the Islamic community.

4

Modern Interpretations
of Islam

Though the sultanate period had marked a new and somewhat different beginning after the fall of Baghdad, it began to fall apart by the seventeenth and eighteenth centuries. Political disintegration and social and moral decline once more gripped much of the Muslim world. The internal breakdown of Muslim society was exacerbated by the growing threat from European presence and imperialist designs. Many concerned Muslims and Western observers at that time would have agreed that Islam was a spent force, helpless before the military and political cadres of Europe and rendered religiously impotent by the superstitious and fatalistic tendencies that had infected much of popular Islamic belief and practice. Yet, these internal and external threats to the life of the community proved once again to be stimuli for religious revival and reform. Premodern revivalist movements rose up in the eighteenth century to address the social and moral decline, while the nineteenth and twentieth centuries produced the Islamic modernist movement and Islamic societies like the Muslim Brotherhood, which offered Islamic responses to the challenges of European colonialism and modernization. These movements not only contributed to the revitalization of Islam in their own times, but also left a legacy that has informed much of the temper and mood of contemporary Islam. Understanding the background and context of revival and reform, its leadership, and their interpretations of Islam is essential for an appreciation of Islam's dynamism and diversity.

From Imperial Islam to Islamic Revivalism

The power, prosperity, and dynamic expansionism of imperial Islam had seriously declined by the eighteenth century. Military revolts and reversals, the decline of a strong central authority, and economic setbacks affected by European competition in trade and manufacturing proved costly. For many of the religiously minded, the causes for this political, military, and economic breakdown were to be found in the spiritual and moral decay that afflicted the community of believers. They believed that the fundamental failure of the community resulted from its departure from true Islam; its revitalization could only come from a return to the straight path of Islam. This call for a moral reconstruction of society did not occur in a vacuum. During the sultanate period, many of the nonofficial *ulama* had concluded that a religious renewal was desirable. This sentiment had an international dimension due to the contacts and exchanges that took place among those scholars who had traveled extensively in their search for knowledge and studied at major Islamic centers of piety and learning in Mecca, Medina, and Cairo (al-Azhar University). At the same time, a new wave of Neo-Sufism arose that sought to restrain and purify the excesses of pantheism and eclecticism that had infected Sufism. Influenced by the thought of men like al-Ghazali, Ibn Taymiyya, and Shaykh Ahmad Sirhindi, it reemphasized the importance of divine transcendence and the primacy of the Sharia.[48] These reformist tendencies grew and multiplied with astounding vitality during the eighteenth century, both because the sociohistorical conditions were ripe for reform and because the calls for religious renewal occurred within a religious tradition that had strong revivalist precedents and tendencies.

Revivalism in Islam

From its earliest days, Islam possessed a tradition of revival and reform. Muslims had been quick to respond to what they regarded as the compromising of faith and practice: Kharijite secession, Shii revolts, the development of Islamic law, and Sufism. In succeeding centuries, a rich revivalist tradition expressed itself in a variety of concepts and beliefs, in the lives and teachings of individual reformers, and in the activities of a host of movements.

The concepts of renewal (*tajdid*) and reform (*islah*) are fundamental components of Islam's worldview, rooted in the Quran and the Sunna of the Prophet.[49] Both concepts involve a call for a return to the fundamentals of Islam (the Quran and Sunna). *Islah* is a Quranic term (7:170; 11:117; 28:19) used to describe the reform preached and undertaken by the prophets when they warned their sinful communities and called on them to return to God's path by realigning their lives, as individuals and as a community, within the norms of the Sharia. This Quranic mandate, epitomized in the lives and preaching of the prophets, especially that of Muhammad, coupled with God's command to enjoin good and prohibit evil (3:104, 110), provides the time-honored rationale for Islamic reformism, however diverse its manifestations in history.

> In so far as it is on the one hand an individual or collective effort to define Islam solely in relation to its authentic sources (i.e. the Kuran and the Sunna of the Prophet) and on the other an attempt to work towards a situation in which the lives of Muslims, in personal and social terms, really would conform to the norms and values of that religion, *islah* is a permanent feature in the religious and cultural history of Islam.[50]

Tajdid is based on a tradition of the Prophet: "God will send to this *umma* [the Muslim community] at the head of each century those who will renew its faith for it."[51] The renewer (*mujaddid*) of Islam is believed to be sent at the beginning of each century to restore true Islamic practice and thus regenerate a community that tends, over time, to wander from the straight path. The two major aspects of this process are first, a return to the ideal pattern revealed in the Quran and Sunna; and second, the right to practice *ijtihad*, to interpret the sources of Islam. Implicit in renewal is: (1) the belief that the righteous community established and guided by the Prophet at Medina already possesses the norm; (2) the removal of foreign (un-Islamic) historical accretions or unwarranted innovations (*bida*) that have infiltrated and corrupted community life; and (3) a critique of established institutions, in particular the religious establishment's interpretation of Islam. Despite the general tendency in Sunni Islam after the tenth century to follow (*taqlid*) the consensus of the community, great renewers or revivalists like al-Ghazali, Ibn Taymiyya, Muhammad ibn Abd al-Wahhab, and Shah Wali Allah claimed the right to function as *mujtahids*, practitioners of *ijtihad*, and thus to reinterpret Islam in order to purify and revitalize their societies. Both Sufi excesses and prevailing *ulama* interpretations of Islamic law and belief were to be corrected by subordination to pristine Islam. In contrast to the Islamic modernist movement of the nineteenth and twentieth centuries, the purpose of reinterpretation (*ijtihad*) was not to accommodate new ideas but to get back to or reappropriate the unique and essentially complete vision of Islam as preserved in its revealed sources. However, Islamic revivalism is not so much an attempt to reestablish the early Islamic community in a literal sense as to reapply the Quran and Sunna rigorously to existing conditions. Thus, we see its militant, even revolutionary, potential as both a moral and a political force, as witnessed by the wave of eighteenth- and nineteenth-century religiopolitical revivalist movements that swept across the Islamic world from the Sudan to Sumatra. The orientation and diversity of revivalism are demonstrated by the cases of several movements in Arabia, Africa, and India.

Arabia: The Wahhabi Movement

The Wahhabi movement is perhaps the best known of the eighteenth-century revivalist movements. Its significance is due not only to its formative influence on Saudi Arabia but also, and more importantly, to its role as an example for modern revivalism. Its founder, Muhammad ibn Abd al-Wahhab (1703–1792), was trained in law, theology, and Sufism at Mecca and Medina, where he was drawn to the Hanbali school, the strictest of the Sunni law schools, and to the writings of the rigorous revivalist Ibn Taymiyya (d. 1328). Ibn Abd al-Wahhab regarded the condition of his society as little better than that of pre-Islamic Arabia, the *jahiliyya* or period of ignorance, with which he compared it. He was appalled by many of its popular religious practices, such as the veneration of saints and their tombs, which he condemned as pagan superstitions and idolatry, the worst of sins in Islam. Ibn Abd al-Wahhab denounced these beliefs and practices as unwarranted innovations. They compromised the unity of God (Islam's radical or absolute monotheism) and the Islamic community, as evidenced by the tribalism and tribal warfare that had returned to Arabia. Living in the Islamic heartland, the homeland of the Prophet and the site of the holy cities of Mecca and Medina, made these conditions all the more reprehensible. The diagnosis of ibn Abd al-Wahhab was similar to that of other revivalists. The political weakness of the community and its moral decline were due to a deviation from the straight path of Islam. Its cure was equally obvious; the task was clear. Muslims must return to true Islamic practice. This could be achieved only by a repetition of Islam's first great reformation, the social and moral revolution led by Muhammad, a return to a community life based strictly on the Quran and the example of Muhammad and the Medinan community.

Muhammad ibn Abd al-Wahhab joined with a local tribal chief, Muhammad ibn Saud (d. 1765), and a militant reformist movement was set in motion that would subdue large areas of Arabia. Although commonly referred to as Wahhabi, its self-designation was the Muwahiddun ("unitarians," those who uphold and practice monotheism). Religious zeal and military power were united in a religiopolitical movement that waged holy war with an uncompromising, Kharijite-like commitment that viewed all Muslims who resisted as unbelievers, enemies of God who must be fought. The tribes of Arabia were subdued and united in the name of Islamic egalitarianism; the Wahhabi missionary-warriors referred to themselves as the Ikhwan, or Brotherhood. In contrast to other revivalists, like the Mahdi of the Sudan and the Grand Sanusi of Libya, who reformed Sufism, ibn Abd al-Wahhab totally rejected it. As Muhammad had cleansed the Kaba of its idols, Wahhabi forces destroyed Sufi shrines and tombs. Their iconoclastic zeal against idolatrous shrines led to the destruction of sacred tombs in Mecca and Medina, including those of the Prophet and his companions. In addition, they destroyed the tomb of Husayn at Karbala, a major Shii holy place and pilgrimage center, an act that has never been forgotten by Shii Muslims and has affected their attitude toward the Wahhabi of modern-day Saudi Arabia.

For ibn Abd al-Wahhab, Islam's normative period was the time of Muhammad and the early community. All subsequent, post-Prophetic developments and the time-honored interpretations of the *ulama* and the law schools were subject to review and reevaluation in the light of Islam's fundamental sources. The purpose of *ijtihad* was a return to a purified Islam by weeding out those un-Islamic beliefs and practices that had infiltrated the law and life of Muslims. Because he was in Arabia, ibn Abd al-Wahhab's mode of revivalism was a more literalist re-creation of the life and customs of the early Medinan community, that of the pious forefathers. He equated "Arab" and "Islam." This differed somewhat from revivalist movements outside Arabia, where a return to the Quran and Sunna meant reform through the subordination of Muslim life to God's revelation, not simply the appropriation of Arab Islam in toto. It also differed from the process of reinterpretation espoused by the Islamic modernist movement in the next century, which sought to formulate Islamically acceptable solutions for new situations. For ibn Abd al-Wahhab, the Islamic way of life was to be found in its pure, unadulterated form in the seventh-century community.

The Wahhabi movement influenced other revivalists in Africa and India. In addition, its legacy may be found in the state and society of Saudi Arabia and the ideological worldviews of many contemporary Muslims.

African Jihad Movements

A series of jihad revivalist movements led to the establishment of Islamic states such as those of Uthman Dan Fodio in Nigeria (1754–1817), the Grand Sanusi in Libya (1787–1859), and the Mahdi of the Sudan (1848–1885). A distinctive characteristic was its Sufi leadership—reformist, militant, and politically oriented charismatic heads of Sufi orders. Their posture was in striking contrast to the syncretistic, passive, nonworldly image of mystic orders whose missionaries had brought Islam to much of Africa. Although much of the success of African Sufism had been attributed to its openness to cultural synthesis, blending Islam with indigenous African beliefs and practices, reformers now attempted to bring Sufism into conformity with the demands of Islamic law in order to stamp out what they regarded as idolatrous customs that had led to social and moral decline. Sufism was not suppressed but redefined, emphasizing a spirituality that incorporated militant activism with its willingness to fight and die to establish Islamically oriented states and societies. Prayer and political action were joined together in the earthly as well as the heavenly pursuit of the divine.

THE SANUSI AND MAHDI MOVEMENTS

Born in Algeria, Muhammad Ali ibn al-Sanusi (1787–1859) or, as he came to be known, the Grand Sanusi, studied in Cairo and Mecca, where he earned a reputation as a scholar of law and *hadith*. He rejected the political fragmentation of Muslims resulting from tribalism and regionalism and reasserted the need for Islamic unity and solidarity. A student in Mecca of Ahmad ibn Idris, the renowned scholar of Prophetic traditions and revivalist Sufi, al-Sanusi followed in the footsteps of this great Moroccan reformer in calling for the purification of Sufism and much of Islamic law, which, he believed, had been distorted by *ulama* interpretation. This and his claim to be a *mujtahid* (an independent interpreter of Islam) alienated him from many of the *ulama* and Sufi leaders. Al-Sanusi moved from Arabia to what is modern-day Libya after the death of his teacher and established the Sanusiyyah brotherhood, a reformist and missionary movement that created a network of settlements across central and western Africa.

The Sanusi program pursued a path of militant activism, consciously emulating the example of Muhammad. It involved the unification of tribal factions in the name of their common Islamic brotherhood and the establishment of Sufi centers, or lodges, which served as places of prayer and instruction as well as of military training and social welfare. They were committed to both the creation of an Islamic state and the spread of Islam. Although not hostile to the outside world, descendants of the Grand Sanusi resisted European colonialism. His grandson led the Sanusi resistance to Italian colonial rule and at independence became King Idris I of Libya.

In contrast to the Grand Sanusi, Muhammad Ahmad (1848–1885), the founder of the Mahdiyyah in the Sudan, proclaimed himself Mahdi in 1881. Although Sunni Islam, unlike the Shii, does not have a formal doctrine of the Mahdi, popular lore did accept the notion of a *mahdi* ("divinely guided one"), a messianic figure who will be sent by God to rescue the community from oppression and to restore true Islam and a just society. This eschatological belief should be distinguished from the more specific Shii expectation that the twelfth Imam will return at the end of time as the Mahdi. Unlike the renewer of Islam who claimed the status of *mujtahid* (one who is qualified to interpret Islam), the Sudanese Mahdi claimed to be the divinely appointed and inspired representative of God. He shared with other revivalist leaders the belief that he was reenacting the paradigmatic drama of early Islam—establishing, as the Prophet had done in the seventh century, God's rule on earth. As with Muhammad's victories, the gains of the Mahdi's forces were attributed to divine guidance and interpreted as divine validation of his mission. He established an Islamic community-state, and in common with other reformers, called for the purification of Islam and the unity of Muslims. Accomplishing this mission meant not only reforming Sufism, but also uniting his followers, who, like the Prophet's companions, were called the Ansar, in a struggle against fellow Muslims. Like the early Kharijites, the Mahdi justified waging holy war against other Muslims, in this case the Sudan's Ottoman Egyptian rulers, by declaring them infidels who

> disobeyed the command of His messenger and His Prophet . . . ruled in a manner not in accord with what God had sent . . . altered the Sharia of our master, Muhammad, the messenger of God, and blasphemed against the faith of God.[52]

Alcohol, gambling, music, and prostitution were all denounced as foreign (Ottoman Egyptian) and indigenous, un-Islamic practices that had corrupted Sudanese Islamic society.

When the Mahdist forces finally triumphed over Egyptian forces in 1885, an Islamic state was established in Khartoum, governed by Mahdist religious ideology. The Mahdi had supreme power as God's delegate, and the Sharia was its only law. The Mahdist state, which many regard as the forerunner of the modern Sudan, lasted until 1899.

The Indian Subcontinent

Two men in particular stand out in the premodern era of Muslim India: Shaykh Ahmad Sirhindi (1564–1624) and Shah Wali Allah of Delhi (1702–1762). Both provided the foundation for Indian revivalism and were formative influences on modern Indian Muslim thought.

Shah Wali Allah lived during a critical period for Indian Muslims. The power of the Mughal empire was in decline. A Muslim minority community faced not only the disintegration of its political rule, challenged by Hindu and Sikh uprisings, but also the internal disunity of conflicting factions: Sunni and Shii, *hadith* and legal scholars, *ulama* and Sufis. Educated in Mecca and a contemporary of Muhammad ibn Abd al-Wahhab, Wali Allah was also a member of the revivalist-oriented Naqshbandi order. He followed in the footsteps of the great revivalist of seventeenth-century India, Shaykh Ahmad Sirhindi. Like Shaykh Ahmad, he asserted the need for Muslims to purge their lives of un-Islamic practices and to reform popular Sufi practices, which he believed were responsible for much of the religious syncretism that threatened the identity, moral fiber, and survival of Indian Islam in its multiconfessional setting. As with other revivalists, the purification and renewal of Islam were contingent on a return to the pristine Sharia, grounded in its two infallible sources, the Quran and Sunna, which encompassed all areas of life. For Wali Allah, the revivification of Muslim society was a prerequisite for the restoration of Mughal power.

The genius of Wali Allah was his method of reconciliation. He eschewed the rigid, confrontative style of Muhammad ibn Abd al-Wahhab and Sirhindi. His surgery was less radical than that of the Wahhabi. Instead of rejecting the current to restore the past, he sought to modify and refashion present belief and practice in light of early Islamic practice. Like Sirhindi, he sought to reform rather than, as the Wahhabi had done, suppress or eradicate Sufism. Sirhindi's condemnation of error as unbelief was offset by Wali Allah's penchant for a synthesis of contending ideas. In reforming Sufism, Sirhindi had enthusiastically declared Ibn al-Arabi an infidel; Wali Allah softened the condemnation. He resolved the contradictions between the ontological monism of Ibn al-Arabi's unity of being, which denied all existence except God's and declared the ultimate unity of God and the universe, and Sirhindi's "unity of experience," which maintained that Ibn al-Arabi's pantheistic union with God was experiential (based on a subjective experience of illumination or ecstasy) rather than an ontological reality (a union with the divine reality). Wali Allah taught that the seemingly contradictory teachings of Ibn al-Arabi and Sirhindi were two different ways of speaking about the same underlying reality. He denied that there was any substantial difference between the two; instead, the problem was one of semantics. As a result, Shah Wali Allah was able to reconcile contending camps within Indian Sufism and to couple this reconciliation with an appeal to Sufi leaders to cleanse their practices of un-Islamic, idolatrous, and antinomian tendencies.

The great legacy of Wali Allah and his major contribution to Islamic modernist thought was his condemnation of blind imitation and his emphasis on reopening the gates of *ijtihad*, the right to reinterpret Islam. As he had used his principle of reconciliation to resolve differences among Sufis and between Sunni and Shii, his teaching regarding *ijtihad* was pivotal to the resolution of a long-standing conflict between jurists and traditionists.

From the tenth century, two opposing trends had developed among the scholars of India. One emphasized strict and exclusive adherence to a particular school of law, and the other opposed this method and instead stressed rigorous following of the clear meaning of the Sunna of the Prophet as found in the accepted compendia of Prophetic traditions (*hadith*). Competition and bitter clashes had become the norm rather than the exception. Wali Allah criticized the partisanship of jurists, which had hardened into a belief that their leaders' interpretations or rulings were infallible and resulted in a rigid doctrine of blind imitation (*taqlid*). He distinguished between blind imitation, which was prohibited, and a more flexible imitation, for those incapable of *ijtihad*, which was subject to change in light of a new understanding of the Quran and Sunna. Wali Allah followed Ibn Taymiyya in calling for the opening of the gates of *ijtihad*, since the rulings of the old jurists were open to correction in light of the Quran and the Sunna. He maintained that the nature of interpretation itself was susceptible to error because of human limitations or because new evidence might arise. In practice, wherever possible, he resolved questions of law by seeking a synthesis of points of agreement among the law schools. However, ultimately he sided with the traditionists, for in doubtful cases he subordinated the fallible opinion of the jurist to Prophetic tradition, since the Sunna of the Prophet, unlike legal opinion, was an infallible source of law.

Shah Wali Allah has often been regarded as the father of modern Indian Islamic thought because of his condemnation of blind imitation of the past and his advocacy of personal interpretation. In this, he opened the door for many reformers who followed, from modernists like Sayyid Ahmad Khan and Muhammad Iqbal to neorevivalists like Mawlana Abul Ala Mawdudi. While he established the acceptance in principle of the need for reinterpretation and reform, it is important to distinguish his meaning from that of others who later broadened and extended its use. For Wali Allah, as for other premodern revivalists, the purpose of reinterpretation was not to formulate new answers but to rediscover forgotten guidelines from the past. Thus, when Wali Allah spoke of the use of *ijtihad* to avoid the rigid particularistic following of one school of law, he did so with the objective of obtaining an answer solely from the "purified past," from a Sharia that was complete and final in its Arabian form, although in need of periodic purification from historical accretions by Islamic reformers or revivalists (*mujaddids*).

Wali Allah believed that the restoration of Mughal power, and thus assurance of Muslim rule, was dependent on the social and moral reform of Muslim society. It was Sayyid Ahmad Barelewi (1786–1831), a disciple of Wali Allah's son, who transformed a reformist school of thought into a jihad movement. For Sayyid Ahmad, effective response to the breakup of the Mughal empire required a jihad against the military threat of Sikh armies, and later, the colonial ambitions of the British. Loss of Muslim power meant that India was no longer an Islamic land but an abode of war. Thus, jihad was obligatory.

Sayyid Ahmad combined a program of religious purification with military power to establish an Islamic state based on social justice and equality for its Muslim citizens. He emphasized pristine monotheism and denounced all those practices (Sufi, Shii, and social customs borrowed from Hinduism) that compromised it. Patterning his revivalist movement on the example of Muhammad, he led a group of his followers on pilgrimage to Mecca. At Hudabiyya, the place where Muhammad's followers had sealed a pact to fight the Meccans, Sayyid Ahmad administered an oath of jihad to these new holy warriors for Islam. Revered as a renewer of Islam, he returned to India where, in 1826, he led his holy warriors 3,000 miles to the Northwest Frontier Province (Pakistan) to wage war against Sikh armies that had taken control of the area. Sayyid Ahmad regarded both a holy war against a non-Muslim regime that ruled a predominantly Muslim population and the restoration of Muslim rule as Islamically required and legitimate. After the Muslim warriors defeated the Sikhs at Balakot, they established a religiopolitical state based on Sharia law. Like the early caliphs, Sayyid Ahmad was proclaimed commander of the believers. Although he was killed in battle in 1831, Sayyid Ahmad's movement continued for some years, his followers waging jihad against the British.

Islamic revivalist movements sought to revitalize their societies through a process of moral reconstruction that transformed not only the religious but also the sociopolitical life of their communities. Despite some considerable differences, their strength and legacy included an ideological framework and example that strongly influenced subsequent developments in the history of Islam. This ideological worldview included belief that: (1) the process of renewal requires a reenactment of the first and paradigmatic Islamic revolution or reformation of the Prophet Muhammad; (2) religion is integral to state and society; (3)

departure from this norm leads to the fragmentation of the community and a decline in its fortunes; (4) only a purging of un-Islamic behavior and a return to the straight path of Islam, a life governed by Islamic law, can restore the community to its rightful place of ascendancy and power; (5) major causes of Muslim decline are the unchecked cultural syncretism of popular Sufism and the uncritical acceptance of tradition; (6) the reform of Sufism must be accompanied by the practice of *ijtihad*; (7) renewal is the task of both individuals and the community; (8) true believers, like the early Muslims, may need to separate themselves to preserve their faith and form a righteous society or brotherhood; (9) the struggle (jihad) to reassert the rightful place of Islam in society requires moral self-discipline and, where necessary, armed struggle; and (10) those Muslims who resist are no longer to be regarded as Muslim but numbered among the enemies of God.

Modern Islamic Movements

While premodern revivalist movements were primarily internally motivated, Islamic modernism was a response both to continued internal weaknesses and to the external political and religiocultural threat of colonialism. Much of the Muslim world faced a powerful new threat—European colonialism. The responses of modern Islamic reformers in the late nineteenth and early twentieth centuries to the impact of the West on Muslim societies resulted in substantial attempts to reinterpret Islam to meet the changing circumstances of Muslim life. Legal, educational, and social reforms were aimed at rescuing Muslim societies from their downward spiral and demonstrating the compatibility of Islam with modern Western thought and values. Because of the centrality of law in Islam and the importance of the Muslim family, Islamic modernists often focused their energies on these areas. In many modern Muslim states, governments used Islamic modernist thought to justify reform measures and legislation. For some Muslims, neither the conservative, the secular, nor Islamic modernist positions were acceptable. Their reaction to the the "Westernizing" of Islam and Muslim society led to the formation of modern Islamic societies or organizations, such as the Muslim Brotherhood and the Jamaat-i-Islami (the Islamic Society), that combined religious ideology and activism. These organizations served as catalysts for Islamic revivalism in the middle decades of the twentieth century and have had a major impact on the interpretation and implementation of Islam in recent years.

Islamic Modernism

European trade missions of the sixteenth and seventeenth centuries progressively expanded so that by the eighteenth century many areas of the Muslim world had felt the impact of the economic and military challenge of Western technology and modernization. A major shift in power occurred as declining Muslim fortunes reversed the relationship of the Muslim world to the West, from that of ascendant expansionism to one of defensiveness and subordination. By the nineteenth and early twentieth centuries, Europe (in particular, Great Britain, France, and Holland) had penetrated and increasingly dominated much of the Muslim world from North Africa to Southeast Asia (the French in North Africa, the British and French in the Middle East and South Asia, and the Dutch and British in Southeast Asia).

Western imperialism precipitated a religious as well as a political crisis. For the first time, much of the Muslim world had lost its political and cultural sovereignty to Christian Europe. Although the Muslim world had endured the Mongol conquests, in time the conquerors had embraced Islam. Colonial rule eclipsed the institutions of an Islamic state and society—the sultan, Islamic law, and *ulama* administration of education, law, and social welfare. Muslim subjugation by Christian Europe confirmed not only the decline of Muslim power but also the apparent loss of divine favor and guidance. For the believer, it raised a number of religious questions. What had gone wrong in Islam? Was the success of the West due to the superiority of Christendom, the backwardness of Islam, or the faithlessness of the community? How could Muslims realize God's will in a state governed by non-Muslims and non-Muslim law? In what ways should Muslims respond to this challenge to Muslim identity and faith?

A variety of responses emerged from Muslim self-criticism and reflection on the causes of decline. Their actions spanned the spectrum, from adaptation and cultural synthesis to withdrawal and rejection. Secularists blamed an outmoded tradition. They advocated the separation of religion and politics, and the establishment of modern nation-states modeled on the West. Islam should be restricted to personal life, and public life should be modeled on modern, that is, European, ideas and technology in government, the military, education, and law. Conservative religious leaders, including most of the *ulama*, attributed Muslim impotence to divergence from Islam and deviation from tradition. Many advocated withdrawal, noncooperation, or rejection of the West. Western (Christian) ideas and values were as dangerous as their governments and armies, for they threatened faith and culture. Some concluded that where Muslims no longer lived under Islamic rule in an Islamic territory, they were now in a land of warfare which, following the example of the Prophet, necessitated either armed struggle (jihad) or emigration (*hijra*) to an Islamically governed land. In India, the son of Shah Wali Allah, Shah Abdul Aziz, issued a *fatwa* declaring India a non-Islamic territory, a land of warfare in which to fight or to flee were Islamically appropriate responses. While some attempted to emigrate, more joined jihad movements. However, the majority of religious leaders advocated a policy of cultural isolation and noncooperation. They equated any form of political accommodation of Western culture with betrayal and surrender.

A third major Muslim response, Islamic modernism, emerged during the late nineteenth century. It sought to delineate an alternative to Western, secular adaptationism on the one hand and religiously motivated rejectionism on the other. A group of reform-minded Muslims sought to respond to, rather than react against, the challenge of Western imperialism. They proclaimed the need for Islamic reform. They blamed the internal decline of Muslim societies, their loss of power and backwardness, and their inability to respond effectively to European colonialism on a blind and unquestioned clinging to the past (*taqlid*). Islamic reformers stressed the dynamism, flexibility, and adaptability that had characterized the early development of Islam, notable for its achievements in law, education, and the sciences. They pressed for internal reform through a process of reinterpretation (*ijtihad*) and selective adaptation (Islamization) of Western ideas and technology. Islamic modernism was a process of internal self-criticism, a struggle to redefine Islam to demonstrate its relevance to the new situations that Muslims found themselves in as their societies modernized. The Middle East and South Asia produced major modernist movements. Their themes and activities are illustrated in several key figures—in the Middle East, Jamal al-Din al-Afghani and his disciples, Muhammad Abduh and Rashid Rida; and in South Asia, Sayyid Ahmad Khan and Muhammad Iqbal.

THE MIDDLE EAST

Jamal al-Din al-Afghani (1838–1897) was an outstanding figure of nineteenth-century Islam and a major catalyst for Islamic reform. A tireless activist, he roamed the Muslim world, calling for internal reform in order to defend Islam, strengthen the Muslim community and, eventually, drive out the West. An orator, teacher, journalist, and political activist, he lived and preached his reformist message in Afghanistan, Egypt, Turkey, Persia, India, Russia, France, and England. Afghani attempted to bridge the gap between secular modernists and religious traditionalists. He believed that Muslims could repel the West not by ignoring or rejecting the sources of Western strength (science and technology), but instead by reclaiming and reappropriating reason, science, and technology, which, he maintained, had been integral to Islam and the grand accomplishments of Islamic civilization. He was an ardent advocate of constitutionalism and parliamentary government to limit the power of rulers. Such statements appealed to many of the young who had had a traditional upbringing but were now also attracted by modern reforms. Afghani also appealed to the *ulama* with his assertion that Muslims needed to remember that Islam was the source of strength and that Muslims must return to a more faithful observance of its guidance.

Afghani rejected the passivity, fatalism, and otherworldliness of popular Sufism as well as the Western secular tendency to restrict religion to personal life or worship. He countered by preaching an activist, this-worldly Islam: (1) Islam is a comprehensive way of life, encompassing worship, law, government, and society; (2) the true Muslim struggles to carry out God's will in history, and thus seeks success in this life as well as the next.

> [T]he principles of Islamic religion are not restricted to calling man to the truth or to considering the soul only in a spiritual context which is concerned with the relationship between this world and the world to come. . . . There is more besides: Islamic principles are concerned with relationships among the believers, they explain the law in general and in detail, they define the executive power which administers the law. . . . Thus, in truth, the ruler of the Muslims will be their religious, holy, and divine law. . . . Let me repeat . . . that unlike other religions, Islam is concerned not only with the life to come. Islam is more: it is concerned with the believers' interests in the world here below and with allowing them to realize success in this life as well as peace in the next life. It seeks "good fortune in two worlds."[53]

Like the revivalists of the previous century, Afghani maintained that the strength and survival of the *umma* was dependent on the reassertion of Islamic identity and solidarity. He exhorted Muslims to realize that Islam was the religion of reason and science—a dynamic, progressive, creative force capable of responding to the demands of modernity:

> The Europeans have now everywhere put their hands on every part of the world. The English have reached Afghanistan; the French have seized Tunisia. In reality this usurpation, aggression, and conquest have not come from the French or the English. Rather it is science that everywhere manifests its greatness and power. . . . [S]cience, is continually changing capitals. Sometimes it has moved from the East to the West, and other times from West to East . . . all wealth and riches are

the result of science. In sum, the whole world of humanity is an industrial world, meaning that the world is a world of science. . . . The first Muslims had no science, but, thanks to the Islamic religion, a philosophic spirit arose among them. . . . This was why they acquired in a short time all the sciences . . . those who forbid science and knowledge in the belief that they are safeguarding the Islamic religion are really the enemies of that religion. The Islamic religion is the closest of religions to science and knowledge, and there is no incompatibility between science and knowledge and the foundation of the Islamic faith.[54]

Therefore, science and learning from the West did not pose a threat to Islam; they could, and should, be studied and utilized.

Central to Afghani's program for Islamic reform was his call for a reopening of the door of *ijtihad*. He denounced the stagnation in Islam, which he attributed both to the influence of Sufism and to the backwardness of the *ulama*, who lacked the expertise required to respond to modern concerns and discouraged others from obtaining scientific knowledge, erroneously labeling it "European science." The process of reinterpretation and reform that he advocated went beyond that of eighteenth-century revivalism. While he talked about a need to return to Islam, the thrust and purpose of reform were not simply to reappropriate answers from the past, but in light of Islamic principles, to formulate new Islamic responses to the changing conditions of Muslim societies. Reinterpretation of Islam would once again make it a relevant force in intellectual and political life. In this way, Islam would serve as the source of a renewal or renaissance that would restore Muslim political independence and the past glory of Islam.

In Afghani's holistic interpretation of Islam, the reform of Islam was inseparably connected with liberation from colonial rule. The reassertion of Muslim identity and solidarity was a prerequisite for the restoration of political and cultural independence. Although he preached a pan-Islamic message, he also accepted the reality of Muslim nationalism. National independence was the goal of reformism and a necessary step in revitalizing the Islamic community both regionally and transnationally.

Jamal al-Din al-Afghani articulated a cluster of ideas and attitudes that influenced Islamic reformist thought and Muslim anticolonial sentiment for much of the first half of the twentieth century. His disciples included many of the great political and intellectual leaders of the Muslim world. He is remembered both as the Father of Muslim Nationalism and as a formative influence on Egypt's Salafiyya ("pious ancestors," the early founding fathers of the Muslim community) reformist movement and later, the Muslim Brotherhood.

Muhammad Abduh and the Salafiyya. If Afghani was the catalyst, his disciples Muhammad Abduh (1849–1905) and Rashid Rida (1865–1935) were the great synthesizers of modern Islam. Their Salafiyya movement was to influence reform movements from North Africa to Southeast Asia. Muhammad Abduh was one of the earliest and most remarkable disciples of al-Afghani, destined to become one of Egypt's leading *ulama*, a reformer of al-Azhar University, and the Mufti (chief judge of the Sharia court system) of Egypt, and to be remembered as the Father of Islamic Modernism in the Arab world. During the 1870s and early 1880s, Abduh enthusiastically collaborated with Afghani in writing reformist articles, publishing a journal, and participating in the nationalist movement. He was exiled with Afghani to Paris after they participated in an unsuccessful nationalist revolt against British influence in Egypt. When Abduh returned, he turned his attention away from politics and focused instead on religious, educational, and social reform.

Abduh's theology and approach began with the unity of God, the cornerstone of Islamic belief and the source of the Muslim community's strength and vitality. One of his major reformist works was *The Theology of Unity*.[55] The basis for Abduh's reformist thought was his belief that religion and reason were complementary, and that there was no inherent contradiction between religion and science, which he regarded as the twin sources of Islam. The bases of Muslim decline were the prevalence of un-Islamic popular religious beliefs and practices, such as saint worship, intercession, and miracles, and the stifling of creativity and dynamism due to Sufi passivity and fatalism as well as to the rigid scholasticism of the traditionalist *ulama* who had forbidden fresh religious interpretation. He attributed the stagnation of Muslim society to blind imitation (*taqlid*), the dead weight of scholasticism:

> We must, however, believe that the Islamic religion is a religion of unity throughout. It is not a religion of conflicting principles but is built squarely on reason, while divine revelation is its surest pillar . . . the Quran directs us, enjoining rational procedure and intellectual inquiry into the manifestations of the universe. . . . It forbids us to be slavishly credulous. . . . Well is it said that traditionalism can have evil consequences as well as good. . . . It is a deceptive thing, and though it may be pardoned in an animal [it] is scarcely seemly in man.[56]

Abduh was convinced that the transformation of Muslim society depended on a reinterpretation of Islam and its implementation through national educational and social reforms. His writings and *fatwas* reflected his underlying message that Islam and science, revelation and reason, were compatible, and thus Muslims could selectively appropriate aspects of Western civilization that were not contrary to Islam.

Abduh sought to provide an Islamic rationale for the selective integration of Islam with modern ideas and institutions. He distinguished between Islam's inner core or fundamentals, those truths and principles which were unchanging, and its outer layers, society's application of immutable principles and values to the needs of a particular age. Therefore, he maintained that while those regulations of Islamic law that governed worship (*ibadat* such as prayer, fasting, pilgrimage) were immutable, the vast majority of regulations concerned with social affairs (*muamalat*, such as penal, commercial, and family laws) were open to change. As historical and social conditions warranted, the core of Islamic principles and values should be reapplied to new realities and, where necessary, the old layers of tradition discarded. Abduh believed that the crisis of modern Islam was precipitated by Muslim failure to uphold the distinction between the immutable and the mutable, the necessary and the contingent. Abduh followed this approach by championing reforms in law, theology, and education. His reformist ideas were incorporated in his legal rulings and set forth in a journal, *al-Manar* ("The Beacon" or "Lighthouse"), which he published with his protégé, the Syrian Rashid Rida. In education, he worked for national reforms and modernized the curriculum at al-Azhar University during his tenure as its rector. Employing the Maliki law school's principle of public welfare, he gave *fatwas* that touched on everything from bank interest to women's status.

Abduh was particularly critical of the lack of educational opportunities for women and the deleterious effects of polygamy on Muslim society. His handling of the issue reflects his methodology, which combined a modernist interpretation of Scripture and its employment in the name of the public interest. Abduh argued that polygamy had been permitted, not commanded, in the Prophet's time as a concession to prevailing social conditions:

> If you are afraid that you will not treat orphans justly, then marry such women as may seem good to you, two, three or four. If you feel that you will not act justly, then one. (Quran 4:3)

He maintained that the true intent of the Quran was monogamy because marriage to more than one wife was contingent on equal justice and impartial treatment of each wife, which the Quran notes, subsequent to verse 4:3, is not possible: "You will never manage to deal equitably with women no matter how hard you try" (4:129). Abduh maintained that since this was a practical impossibility, the Quranic ideal was monogamy. Abduh's Quranic interpretation and his use of public interest as an Islamic justification for legal reform were adopted by reformers in Egypt and in other Muslim countries to introduce changes in family law.

Rashid Rida has been called the "mouthpiece of Abduh."[57] He traveled from his home in Syria to Cairo in 1897 to become Abduh's close protégé. In 1898, they published the first edition of *al-Manar*, a periodical that became the principal vehicle for Abduh and Rida's Salafi reformism. Rida continued to publish *al-Manar* after Abduh's death (1905) until his own death in 1935. Although regarded as a journal devoted to Abduh's reformist thought, in fact it was greatly affected by Rida's interpretation of his master and Rida's own growing conservatism in later years. It covered the range of reformist concerns—Quranic exegesis, articles on theological, legal, and educational reform, *fatwas* on contemporary issues.

In general, Rida adopted and carried on the Afghani–Abduh legacy of calling for a reinterpretation of Islam. The development of a modern Islamic legal system was a fundamental priority, given the challenges and requirements of the modern world. Rida, too, rejected the unquestioned authority of medieval formulations of law and regarded much of the social sphere as subject to change. Reform in Islam required more than the eclectic selection of appropriate regulations from one of the established schools of law. New regulations were necessary. He utilized a number of sources to justify this claim. Following Abduh, Rida relied on the Maliki principle of the public interest or general welfare. In classical jurisprudence public interest was a subsidiary legal principle used in deducing new laws by analogy from the Quran and Sunna. Reformers now employed it as an independent source of law to formulate regulations where no clear scriptural text prevailed. Rida also relied on Hanbali law and Ibn Taymiyya. Although Hanbalism is normally regarded as the most rigid of the law schools, its strict formalism pertains to acts of worship, the unchanging essence of Islam based on the Quran and Sunna, as distinct from social laws that are subject to change. Thus, Ibn Taymiyya had been able to maintain the right to exercise *ijtihad* in social affairs. Rida adopted this distinction:

> Creed and ritual were completed in detail so as to permit neither additions nor subtractions, and whoever adds to them or subtracts from them is changing Islam and brings forth a new religion. As for the *muamalat* (social laws), beyond decreeing the elements of virtue and establishing penalties for certain crimes, and beyond imposing the principle of consultation, the Law Giver delegated the affair in its detailed applications to the leading ulama and rulers.[58]

Rashid Rida believed that the implementation of Islamic law required an Islamic government, since law was the product of consultation between the ruler (caliph) and the *ulama,* the guardian-interpreters of law. Like Afghani, Rashid Rida concerned himself with the restoration of the caliphate and pan-Islamic unity. He also shared the modernist belief that the *ulama* were backward and ill-equipped to understand the modern world and to reinterpret Islam. Therefore, he advocated the development of a group of progressive Islamic thinkers to bridge the gap between the conservative *ulama* and Westernized elites.

Rida shifted the Salafi movement's orientation toward a more conservative position during the thirty years after the death of Abduh in 1905. Although strongly drawn to Afghani and Abduh, Rida had a much more limited exposure to the West. He neither traveled much in the West nor spoke a Western language. He remained convinced that the British continued to be a political and religious threat: "The British government is committed to the destruction of Islam in the East after destroying its temporal power."[59] He became more critical of the West with the growing influence of Western liberal secular nationalism and culture in Egypt, ironically at the hands of former students of Afghani and Abduh, who wished to restrict religion to private life. An admirer of the Wahhabi movement in Arabia, he was more inclined to emphasize the self-sufficiency and comprehensiveness of Islam. Muslim reformers must not look to the West, but single-mindedly return to the sources of Islam—the Quran, the Sunna of the Prophet, and the consensus of the Companions of the Prophet. Rida's conservatism was reflected in his more restricted understanding of the term *salaf,* ancestors or pious forefathers. For Abduh, it was a general reference to the early Islamic centuries; Rida followed eighteenth-century revivalism's restriction of the term to the first generation of Muslims, the Companions of the Prophet, whose example was to be emulated.

During the post–World War I period, Rida became more wary of modernism and more drawn to the *ulama.* The example of Egyptian nationalism reinforced his fear that modernist rationalism in the hands of intellectuals and political elites would degenerate into the secularization and Westernization of Muslim societies. As a result, he cast his reformism more and more in the idiom of a defense of Islam against the dangers of the West. His rejection of Western secular liberalism and emphasis on the comprehensiveness and self-sufficiency of Islam aligned him more closely with eighteenth-century revivalism and influenced the thinking and ideological worldviews of Hasan al-Banna (1906–1949), founder of Egypt's Muslim Brotherhood, and other contemporary Islamic activists.

The Indian Subcontinent

Two men dominate the Islamic modernist movement in India—Sir Sayyid Ahmad Khan (1817–1898), a contemporary of al-Afghani and Abduh, and Muhammad Iqbal (1875–1938). As the eighteenth century had produced Islamic revivalists like Shah Wali Allah and Sayyid Ahmad Barelewi, the aftermath of the "Mutiny" of 1857, what some Indian historians have called the first war of independence, proved a turning point in Indian Muslim history. The threat to Muslim power, the decline of its society, the question of whether India was any longer a Muslim empire, were all moot points now. The war resulted in British rule and the end of Muslim dominance of India. The Muslim community stood defeated, powerless, and demoralized. Although both Hindus and Muslims had participated in the uprising, the British held the Muslims primarily responsible. In the aftermath, they questioned the loyalty of Muslims in a non-Muslim state. At the same time, the majority of the *ulama* would have nothing to do with these "enemies of Islam." Both British doubts about the loyalty of Muslims and Muslim withdrawal undermined the future of Indian Muslims vis-à-vis their British masters and the Hindu majority. Into the void stepped Sayyid Ahmad Khan. Like al-Afghani and Abduh, he was convinced that the survival of the Muslim community necessitated a bold reinterpretation of Islam and the acceptance, not rejection, of the best in Western thought. However, unlike al-Afghani and Rida, Ahmad Khan preached acceptance of the political reality of British rule and restricted his Islamic concerns to the Muslims of India. He was convinced that both political resistance and appeals to pan-Islam were impractical, given the political reality.

Like his Salafi coreligionists in the Middle East, Sayyid Ahmad Khan believed that the survival of Islam depended on the rejection of unquestioned acceptance (*taqlid*) of medieval interpretations of Islam and the exercise of *ijtihad* in order to produce fresh interpretations of Islam to demonstrate its relevance and validity for modern life. On the one hand, he placed himself within the revivalist tradition of Shah Wali Allah by maintaining that a return to pristine Islam necessitated purifying Islam of many of the teachings and interpretations of the *ulama*. His goal was to

> justify without any wavering, what I acknowledge to be the original religion of Islam which God and the messenger have disclosed, not that religion which the ulama and the preachers have fashioned.[60]

On the other hand, he differed with Shah Wali Allah and other eighteenth-century revivalists in his method. His exercise of *ijtihad* was not simply to use reason to get back to original interpretations of Islam covered over by *ulama* scholasticism, but to boldly reinterpret Islam in light of its revealed sources.

The extent of his use of reason, the degree to which he reinterpreted Islam, and his borrowing from the West marked him off from revivalists of the previous century. However, Ahmad Khan did see a continuity between his own work and that of previous scholars. Just as in the past Muslim theology had developed out of the need to respond to a social context, so the Muslims of modern India required a new interpretation of Islam to demonstrate the compatibility of Islam and modern science: "Today we need, as in former days, a modern theology by which we either render futile the tenets of modern sciences or [show them to be] doubtful, or bring them into harmony with the doctrines of Islam."[61] Ahmad Khan's use of reason was far more rationalist than that of Muhammad Abduh. Muhammad Abduh believed that there was no necessary contradiction between true religion and science, but he believed that religion and reason functioned on two different levels or in two different spheres. Ahmad Khan, influenced by nineteenth-century European rationalism and natural philosophy, much of which he regarded as consonant with the rationalist principles of the Mutazila and Ibn Rushd (Averroes), believed that Islam was the religion of reason and nature. There could be no contradiction between the word of God and the work of God (nature): "If that religion is in conformity with human nature . . . then it is true."[62] Islam was in total harmony with the laws of nature and therefore compatible with modern scientific thought. These premises, reason and the laws of nature, governed Ahmad Khan's interpretation of the Quran and Sunna and his treatment of such questions as evolution, miracles, and the existence of angels. Though he maintained that the Quran was the final authority, in practice his rationalist approach meant that where a seeming conflict existed between text and reason, reason prevailed. Quranic texts that contained miraculous or supernatural language were interpreted metaphorically or allegorically, since miracles were contrary to the laws of nature. Yet, even here, he used his interpretation of the Quran to support his rationalist position: "I do not deny the possibility of miracles because they are against reason, but because the Quran does not support the happening of events or occurrences that are against the laws of nature or violate the usual course of things."[63] Ahmad Khan also took a hard, critical look at the traditions of the Prophet. He questioned the historicity and authenticity of many, if not most, traditions, much as the noted scholars Ignaz Goldziher and Joseph Schacht would later do. He advocated a critical reexamination of the *hadith*, including those in the two major collections of Muslim and Bukhari, and the acceptance of only those that could be traced directly to the Prophet himself.

Sayyid Ahmad Khan's approach to Islamic reform was both theoretical and practical. In addition to his prolific writings, which included a multivolume commentary on the Quran, he recognized the need for practical implementation through educational reforms. He established a translation society to make Western scientific thought more accessible, and founded the Anglo-Muhammadan Oriental College at Aligarh (renamed in 1920 Aligarh Muslim University), modeled on Cambridge University. Through these and other educational societies and journals, he promoted Western education in Muslim India. Like al-Afghani and Abduh, he realized that the future of the Muslim community depended on the ability to produce a new generation of leaders equipped to face the challenges and demands of modernity and the West. However, his strong affinity for the West, symbolized by his adoption of a European lifestyle and his acceptance of knighthood from Queen Victoria of England, undermined his influence. Many of the *ulama* and anticolonialists dismissed "Sir" Sayyid's loyalism and reformism as political and cultural capitulation to the British.

While Ahmad Khan did not produce the integrated curriculum to educate his version of the new Muslim leader or the new science of theology he had deemed so necessary for the future survival of the Muslim community, he did contribute to the spirit of reform in the subcontinent. An heir to the heritage of Wali Allah, he expanded and, in the end, took Islamic reform in new directions, extending its scope to include a rationalist reinterpretation of the Quran and a reevaluation of Prophetic traditions and the law. The issues that his work raised regarding the relationship of Islam to modern Western thought, the place and role of reason in interpreting religion, and the relationship of the Muslim community to the Hindu community were real questions that future generations would continue to grapple with. His modernist orientation remained a major alternative influence to that of the more traditional *ulama*, influencing the education and outlook of many Muslim elite leaders in the subcontinent.[64] Ahmad Khan's place and importance in the chain of Indian reformist thought was acknowledged by the man whose name would come to be synonymous with Islamic reform in the twentieth century, Muhammad Iqbal:

[Ahmad Khan was the] first modern Muslim to catch a glimpse of the positive character of the age that was coming. . . . But the real greatness of the man consists in the fact that he was the first Indian Muslim who felt the need for a fresh orientation of Islam and worked for it.[65]

Muhammad Iqbal (1875–1938) represented the next phase in modern Islam. He combined an early Islamic education with advanced degrees from Cambridge and Munich in philosophy and law. In a sense, he represented the best of what Sayyid Ahmad Khan might have wished. Although by the twentieth century the situation in the Indian subcontinent had changed from that of Sir Sayyid Ahmad Khan's age, Muslims, who were now obtaining modern educations, still lived in a society whose *ulama* generally preached an Islam that did not adequately address modern realities.

> No wonder then that the younger generation . . . demand a fresh orientation of their faith. With the reawakening of Islam, therefore, it is necessary to examine, in an independent spirit, what Europe has taught and how far the conclusions reached by her can help us in the revision, and if necessary, reconstruction of theological thought in Islam.[66]

Muslim corporate identity also continued to be an important issue. However, it was not one of loyalty to the British raj, but instead, independence and national identity. The Muslim community was divided over the question of Muslim participation in the Indian independence movement. Many had joined with Hindus in the Congress party and pressed for the creation of a single, secular nation-state. Others increasingly argued that, given strong communal sentiments and politics, India's Muslim minority would face a serious threat to its identity and survival in a predominantly Hindu secular state. As with much of Islamic history, and certainly the history of Islamic revival and reform movements, religious reflection and interpretation were conditioned by and intertwined with the political life of the community.

Muhammad Iqbal's profession was the law; his passion, writing poetry and prose; his lifelong concern, Muslim religious and political survival and reform. From the time he returned from his doctoral studies in Europe, he devoted himself to the revival of Indian Islam. He did this both as a poet-philosopher, and more reluctantly, as a politician. He placed himself within the revivalist tradition of Ahmad Sirhindi, Shah Wali Allah, and Muhammad ibn Abd al-Wahhab, while addressing the questions of Islamic modernism. Islam and the Muslim community were in danger; they remained in decay and decline, were politically powerless, morally corrupted, and culturally backward. All of this, for Iqbal, stood in sharp contrast with the inner nature of Islam, which was dynamic and creative. Drawing on his Islamic heritage and influenced by his study of Western philosophy (Hegel, Bergson, Fichte, Nietzsche), he developed his own synthesis and interpretation of Islam in response to the sociohistorical conditions and events of his time. Nowhere is this synthesis of East and West more evident than in Iqbal's dynamic concept of the self. Rejecting Plato's static universe and those aspects of Sufism that denied the affirmation of the self in the world, Iqbal, utilizing the Quran, developed a dynamic *Weltanschauung* in his theory of selfhood that embraced all reality: individual self, society, and God. For Iqbal, the relationship of God to Islamic society and the Muslim to society incorporates both permanence and change. God, the ultimate or absolute self, has a creative, dynamic life that is both permanent and changing, as creation is the unfolding of the inner possibilities of God in a single and yet continuing act. The individual, the basic unit of Muslim society, is Quranically (2:30) charged as God's vicegerent with the mission of carrying out God's will on earth. Muslims share in this ongoing process of creation, bringing order out of chaos, by endeavoring to produce the model society to be emulated by others. An interdependence exists; the individual is elevated through the community, and the community is organized by the individual.

At the heart of Iqbal's vision of Islam is the unity of God (*tawhid*). The oneness of God applies not only to the nature of God but also to His relationship to the world. As God is the one creator, sustainer, and judge of the universe, so too His will or law governs every aspect of His creation and is to be realized in every area of life. This belief is the basis for Iqbal's view of the community as a religiopolitical state and of the supremacy of Islamic law in Muslim society. Based on the Prophetic tradition that "the whole of this earth is a mosque" and on Muhammad's role as Prophet as well as head of the Medinan state, Iqbal concluded, "All that is secular is therefore sacred in the roots of its being."[67] There is no bifurcation of the spiritual and the temporal. Church and state are not two sides of the same thing, for Islam is a single, unanalyzable reality.[68] Nowhere is this more evident than in Islamic law. Iqbal reasserted the Sharia's role as the comprehensive guideline for a society of believers and the need for it to be reintroduced into Muslim societies. During the nineteenth century, Islamic law, with the exception of family law, had been displaced in many Muslim countries by European codes. In the Indian subcontinent, the interaction of Islamic law and British law had produced Anglo-Muhammadan law, much of which was based on British common law. For Iqbal, Islamic law was central to the unity and life of the Muslim community: "When a community forsakes its Law, its parts are severed, like scattered dust. The being of the Muslim rests alone on Law, which is in truth the inner core of the Apostle's faith."[69]

Convinced that the survival of Islam and the Muslim community's role as a political and moral force in South Asia were dependent on the centrality of Islamic law, Iqbal emphasized to his friend and coworker Muhammad Ali Jinnah, the leader of the Muslim League party and the founder of Pakistan, the need for a Muslim state or states in India. However, Iqbal did not have in mind the simple restoration of law as it was delineated in the doctrines of the law schools. For Iqbal, just as God has a creative, dynamic life that is both permanent and changing, Islam's way of life as interpreted in Islamic law is itself dynamic and open to change: "[T]he early doctors of law taking their cue from this groundwork evolved a number of legal systems. But with all their comprehensiveness, these systems are after all individual interpretations and as such can not claim any finality."[70]

Iqbal distinguished between eternal, immutable principles of the Sharia and those regulations that were the product of human interpretation and thus subject to change. He regarded the condition of Islam as a "dogmatic slumber" that had resulted in five hundred years of immobility due to the blind following of tradition and believed that the restoration of Islamic vitality required the "reconstruction" of the sources of Islamic law. While acknowledging the role of the *ulama* in the past, Iqbal blamed them for the conservatism that had characterized Islam since the fall of Baghdad. With their perpetuation of what he called the fiction of the closing of the door of *ijtihad*, these scholar-guardians of Islam, who were the followers of those who had developed Islamic law, stopped the dynamic process of reinterpretation and reapplication of Islamic principles to new situations. Instead, they were content to simply perpetuate established traditions. Iqbal rejected the centuries-long tendency to regard Islamic law as fixed and sacrosanct. Like other Islamic revivalists and modernists, he believed that Muslims must once again reassert their right to *ijtihad*, to reinterpret and reapply Islam to changing social conditions. This right belonged to all qualified Muslims and not just the *ulama*. He believed that the traditional criteria used to designate one as an interpreter was both self-serving and shortsighted. The failure of the *ulama* to broaden their training left them ill prepared for resolving many new, modern issues. For these reasons, Iqbal extended and redefined *ijtihad* and *ijma*. He suggested that the right to interpret and apply Islam for the community be transferred from the *ulama* to a national assembly or legislature. This collective or corporate *ijtihad* would then constitute the authoritative consensus (*ijma*) of the community. In this way, he also transformed the meaning of consensus of the community from its traditional one, the agreement of the religious leaders and scholars, to the consensus of modern legislative assemblies, the majority of whose members would have a better knowledge of contemporary affairs. In addition, he recommended that, because of the complex nature of many modern problems, the legislature should seek the advice of experts from traditional and modern disciplines. Shortly after its establishment, Pakistan would establish such a council of experts, the Islamic Ideology Council. Iqbal's approach proved attractive to modernists as a way to enhance the legitimacy of parliamentary government and reforms in family law. However, threatened by an outlook that diminished their status and power in society, the *ulama* were resistant.

While Iqbal admired the accomplishments of the West—its dynamic spirit, intellectual tradition, and technology—he was critical of its excesses, such as European imperialism and colonialism, the economic exploitation of capitalism, the atheism of Marxism, and the moral bankruptcy of secularism. Therefore, he turned to the past to "rediscover" principles and values that could be employed to reconstruct an alternative Islamic model for modern Muslim society. This resulted in the discovery of Islamic versions of democracy and parliamentary government, precedents in Islamic belief that, through reinterpretation, could be used to develop Islamic equivalents to Western concepts and institutions. Thus, for example, Iqbal concluded that because of the centrality of such beliefs as the equality and brotherhood of believers, democracy was the most important political ideal in Islam. Though history, after the period of the Rightly Guided Caliphs, had prevented the community from realizing this Islamic ideal, it remains a duty for the Muslim community. That Iqbal did not believe that he was creating an Islamic rationale for simply copying Western values and institutions is strikingly evident in his conclusion that England embodied this "Muslim" quality:

> Democracy has been the great mission of England in modern times . . .
> it is one aspect of our own political ideal that is being worked out in it.
> It is . . . the spirit of the British Empire that makes it the greatest Muhammadan Empire in the world.[71]

The very bases for Islamic democracy—the equality and brotherhood of all Muslims—militated against Iqbal's acceptance of the concept of nationalism. Although as a young man he had been an Indian nationalist, he returned from his studies in Europe committed to pan-Islamism. In addition to considering territorial nationalism as antithetical to the universal brotherhood established by Muhammad and embodied in the caliphate, he regarded nationalism as the tool used by colonialism to dismember the Muslim world. The political ideal of Islam was a transnational community that transcended ethnic, racial, and national ties; it was based on an inner cohesion that stemmed from the unity of the community's religiopolitical ideal. As with al-Afghani and others, Iqbal's pan-Islamic commitment was tempered by political realism. He accepted the need for Muslims to gain national independence, but believed that as a family of nations based on a common spiritual heritage, common ideals, and a common law—the Sharia—they should form their own League of Nations. He applied this rationale to the situation of Indian Muslims and in 1930 reluctantly concluded that internal Hindu–Muslim communal harmony was impossible. Iqbal became convinced that the threat of Hindu dominance in an independent India necessitated the establishment of a separate region or state for the Muslims of India in order to preserve their identity and distinctive way of life:

> The nature of the Prophet's religious experience, as disclosed in the Quran, is wholly different [from that of Christianity]. It is individual experience creative of a social order. Its immediate outcome is the fundamentals of a polity with implicit legal concepts whose civic significance can not be belittled merely because their origin is revelational. The religious ideal of Islam is organically related to the social order which it has created. The rejection of the one will eventually involve the rejection of the other. Therefore the construction of a polity on [Indian] national lines, if it means a displacement of the Islamic principles of solidarity, is simply unthinkable to a Muslim.[72]

If Sayyid Ahmad Khan had been the traditionally educated Muslim who sought to make modern Western liberal thought Islamically acceptable, Muhammad Iqbal was the modern, Western-educated Muslim who reinterpreted Islam in conjunction with Western thought to demonstrate its relevance as a viable alternative to Christian European and Marxist ideologies.

Legacy to Modernity

The legacy of Islamic modernism has been mixed. Islamic modernists were trailblazers who did not simply seek to purify their religion by a return to an Islam that merely reappropriated past solutions. Instead, they wished to chart its future direction through a reinterpretation of Islam in light of modern realities. They were pioneers who planted the seeds for the acceptance of change, a struggle that has continued. While their secular counterparts looked to the West rather uncritically and traditionalists shunned the West rather obstinately, Islamic modernists attempted to establish a continuity between their Islamic heritage and modern change. On the one hand, they identified with premodern revivalist movements and called for the purification of internal deficiencies and deviations. On the other, they borrowed and assimilated new ideas and values from the West. For some, like Sayyid Ahmad Khan, this was accomplished by maintaining that Islam was the religion of reason and nature par excellence. For others, like Afghani and Iqbal, the rubric was the reclaiming of a progressive, creative past whose political and cultural florescence demonstrated that the very qualities associated with the power of the West were already present in Islam and accounted for its past triumphs and accomplishments. Thus, the belief that Muslims already possessed an Islamic rationale and the means for the assimilation of modern science and technology was strengthened. For all, the key was to convince their coreligionists that stagnation and decline were caused by blind imitation of the past and that continued survival and revitalization of the Islamic community required a bold reinterpretation of Islam's religious tradition.

Islamic modernists, like secular modernists, represented a minority position within the community but with less direct influence to implement change at a national level. In general, it would not be unfair to characterize modernism as primarily an intellectual movement, though activist reforms were initiated. Modernists sought to inspire and motivate a vanguard within the leadership or future leadership of their communities and had to contend with the resistance of a more conservative religious majority. The religious establishment was often alienated by the reformers' rejection of their traditional authority as the sole interpreters of Islam. They bridled at modernists' claim to independent interpretation and their attempts to chart the course for modern reforms. Abduh's educational reforms, while welcomed by younger *ulama* and students, were resisted by many of the more established religious leaders. Sayyid Ahmad Khan's favorable evaluation of evolution caused *ulama* to condemn him as an infidel. Though he gave the *ulama* control of Islamic studies at Aligarh University, they proved resistant to his reformism.

As noted earlier, Islamic modernism engaged in a process of interpretation or individual investigation (*ijtihad*) that was qualitatively different in its methodology from that claimed by premodern revivalists, who had wished simply to reclaim and implement authentic teachings of the Quran and Sunna. However, modernists, while agreeing with revivalists about the need to reform Sufism and purge Islam of unIslamic practices in law, also felt free to suggest that many practices acceptable in the past were no longer relevant. Moreover, they claimed the right and necessity to formulate new regulations. Instead of simply engaging in a restoration of the practice of Muhammad and the early community, they advocated an adaptation of Islam to the changing conditions of modern society. In effect, this meant new laws and attitudes toward religious and social reforms. Traditionalists criticized such changes as unwarranted innovations, an accommodationism that permitted alien, un-Islamic, Western Christian practices to infiltrate Islam. Reforms were condemned as deviation from Islam (*bida*). Reformers criticized the *ulama* for being out of touch with the modern world, incapable of adequately leading the community, and for being in need of reform; this deepened the resistance of many, though not all, of the religious establishment to Islamic modernism.

What were the effects and accomplishments of Islamic modernism? First, modernists implanted an outlook or attitude toward the past as well as the future. Pride in an Islamic heritage and the achievements of Islamic history and civilization provided Muslims with a renewed sense of identity and purpose. This countered the sense of religiocultural backwardness and impotence engendered by years of subjugation to the West and by the preaching of Christian missionaries. At the same time, emphasis on the dynamic, progressive, rational character of Islam enabled new generations of Muslims to embrace modern civilization more confidently, to regard change as an opportunity rather than a threat.

Second, the example and writings of modernists inspired many like-minded Muslims in other geographic areas. Belief in the absolute relevance, compatibility, and adaptability of Islam to the twin challenges of colonialism and modern culture influenced modernist movements in many other parts of the Muslim world. In North Africa, the influence of al-Afghani and Abduh on the thought and outlook of reformers like Morocco's Bonchaib al-Doukkali (Abu Shuayb al-Dukkali) and Allal al-Fasi, Tunisia's Abd al-Aziz al-Thalabi, and Algeria's Abd al-Hamid ibn Badis (Ben Badis) was such that Islamic reformism in North Africa is often simply referred to as Salafiyya or neo-Salafiyya movements. Salafiyya reformism extended across the Islamic world to Indonesia, where it influenced the Muhammadiyya and Sarekat Islam movements. While these organizations had significant differences, they were similar in their desire to respond to internal decline and external encroachment. All rejected blind adherence to tradition and un-Islamic popular religious practices, and advocated Sufi reform, modernist reinterpretation (*ijtihad*) of the sources of Islam, and educational and social reforms. Most, like the Muhammadiyya, established schools that combined Islamic studies with a modern curriculum and ran social-welfare programs. They published reform-oriented newspapers and journals, such as *al-Islah* ("The Reform") and *al-Muntqid* ("The Critic") in Algeria. Many modernists were anticolonialist and thus participants, often leaders, in nationalist movements that were rooted in religion and harnessed Islam for mass mobilization. Allal al-Fasi organized the Istiqlal (Independence) party in Morocco, combining Islamic reformism with the organization of Sufi orders. Islamic reformers in Algeria joined with some *ulama* and established the Algerian Association of Ulama, whose motto was "Islam is my religion; Arabic is my language; Algeria is my Fatherland."

Third, reformers' espousal of a process of reinterpretation that adapted traditional concepts and institutions to modern realities resulted in a transformation of their meaning to accommodate and legitimate change. As a result, subsequent generations, whether modernist or traditionalist, have come to speak of Islamic "democracy" and to view traditional concepts of consultation and community consensus as conducive to parliamentary forms of government. Similarly, it became quite common for many, including the religious establishment, to accept the use of *ijtihad.*

Fourth, the holistic approach of al-Afghani, Rida, and Iqbal, which viewed Islam as a comprehensive guide for private as well as public life, became part of the modern understanding or interpretation of Islam. Their emphasis on Islam as an alternative ideology for state and society, coupled with the example of eighteenth-century revivalist movements, has been a major influence on modern Islamic activists and movements throughout the twentieth century.

However, the record of Islamic modernism is mixed. Though it was able to prescribe, it proved less successful in implementation. Al-Afghani, Abduh, Rida, Ahmad Khan, and Iqbal failed to provide a systematic, comprehensive theology or program for legal reform. Conservative Muslims continued to see reformism as less an indigenous Islamic movement than an attempt to accommodate Islam to Western thought and culture. Though they attracted a circle of followers, the reformers were not succeeded by comparable charismatic figures, nor did they create effective organizations to continue and implement their ideas. After their deaths, their followers went in many directions. While Rida continued the work of al-Afghani and Abduh, Abduh's associates Saad Zaghlul and Taha Hussein became secular nationalists. Though Muhammad Ali Jinnah and his Muslim League party rallied mass support for the creation of an independent Pakistan through the appeal to Islam, he did not follow Iqbal and implement Islamic law. Islamic reformism tended to become a legacy that was not developed and applied systematically, but instead employed or manipulated on occasion, in a diffuse and ad hoc fashion, when convenient by individuals, nationalist movements, governments, and Islamic organizations. The influence and limitations of Islamic modernism are evident in the interpretations of Islam employed in Muslim family law reform, which became the primary arena for Islamic modernist reform, and in the creation of major organizations like the Muslim Brotherhood and the Jamaat-i-Islami.

MUSLIM FAMILY LAW REFORM

Muslim family law provides the primary example of the implementation of Islamic reform in the first part of the twentieth century. Reflecting the centrality of the family in Islam and in traditional Muslim society, family law had been the heart of the Sharia and the major area of Islamic law that had remained in force to govern the lives of Muslims throughout the Islamic world.

Modern legal change occurred in many parts of the Muslim world during the nineteenth century, when most areas of Islamic law were replaced by modern codes based on European law. Secular courts were created to handle civil and criminal law, and as a result, the jurisdiction of religious (Sharia) courts was severely restricted. As with educational reform, the modernization of law further eroded the role and authority of the *ulama*, as their tasks were now taken over by Western-educated officials and civil servants. However, the one area that remained essentially untouched and in force was family law, the law governing marriage, divorce, and inheritance. The situation changed in the twentieth century when this important and sensitive area of Islamic tradition was subjected to change. Thus, family law reform constitutes a major example of modern religious reform in Islam.

The rationale for Islamic reform had been established by early modernists, such as Muhammad Abduh and Ahmad Khan. Their disciples, Qasim Amin in Egypt and Mumtaz Ali in India, developed the social dimension of their programs, in particular as it related to women. Both focused on the plight of Muslim women as a primary cause of the deterioration of the family and society. In his *The Emancipation of Women* and *The New Woman*, Qasim Amin criticized lack of education, child marriages, arranged marriages, polygamy, and easy male-initiated divorce as causes of the bondage of Muslim women. Mumtaz Ali took a similar position. Ali refuted the antifeminist Quranic exegesis of some classical legal scholars, maintaining that their interpretations did not reflect the meaning of Quranic texts but the customs and mores of the exegetes' own times. Fundamental reforms were required. These ideas informed the positions of feminist movements and political elites a generation later in the 1920s and 1930s. While the modernization of law in the nineteenth century had been accomplished by simply replacing traditional Islamic law with Western-derived legal codes, change in family law was rendered through a process of reinterpretation that sought to provide an Islamic rationale for reforming tradition. Selective changes were introduced through legislation that modified traditional law in order to improve the status of women and strengthen the rights of the nuclear family. Laws were passed to restrict polygamy (polygyny) and to limit a male's unfettered right to divorce. Women were granted additional grounds for divorce. Child marriages were discouraged by raising the minimum ages of spouses.

To justify their departure from tradition, governments relied on Islamic modernist thought and strategies, employing legal doctrines and methods to establish the Islamic character of their reforms, thus forming a link between legal modernization and traditional jurisprudence. Reforms were proclaimed as resulting from the right to reinterpret (*ijtihad*) Islam. The principle of public interest or social welfare, originally regarded as a subsidiary legal source of law by the Maliki school, was pressed into service to legitimate reforms. Abduh's modernist exegesis of the Quran was used to limit polygamy. Other subsidiary sources of law were used to select a legal doctrine from one school and apply it to another or to patch together laws from different law schools or jurists and create a new regulation. For example, the grounds for divorce were substantially broadened in countries that followed Hanafi law (Egypt, Syria, Jordan, India, Pakistan) by borrowing additional provisions from Maliki law, such as desertion, cruelty, and failure to maintain. Thus, traditional authorities were marshaled or reinterpreted to justify reforms.

Despite the relative success of family law reform, many issues were skirted and remained unresolved. Whereas classical law was the product of the *ulama*, modern reforms were undertaken by governments through the action of parliaments or national assemblies whose members were laymen who lacked the training to qualify as traditional interpreters of law. In most instances, the *ulama* felt disenfranchised and viewed the process of modern legal reform as un-Islamic. They charged that a Western secular elite had used its political power to tamper with Islam and force unwarranted innovations on Muslim society. In some instances, the *ulama* mounted a counterattack. In Pakistan, the *ulama* rejected the findings of the Family Law Commission of 1956, charging that the majority of its members (six out of seven) were not *ulama* and thus were unqualified to exercise *ijtihad*, to reinterpret Islam.

The modernist majority had argued that as the Quran and Sunna could not:

> comprehend the infinite variety of human relations for all occasions and for all epochs, the Prophet of Islam left a very large sphere free for

legislative enactments and judicial decisions. . . . This is the principle of *ijtihad* or interpretive intelligence working within the broad framework of Quran and Sunna.[73]

The modernist majority also denied that the *ulama* had any special role and authority and maintained that all informed Muslims had the right to interpret Islam:

> Islam never developed a church with ordained priests as a class separate from the laity . . . some may be more learned in the Muslim law than others, but that does not constitute them as a separate class; they are not vested with any special authority and enjoy no special privileges.[74]

The *ulama* countered, reaffirming their traditional role as the qualified expert-interpreters of the Sharia and accusing the modernists of wishing to ape the West because they had an inferiority complex and were ashamed of their religious tradition. Although they were not able to prevent the passage of reform legislation, they did limit the extent of the reforms. Similarly, many of the *ulama* in Iran had objected to the Shah's passage of the Family Protection Act and had criticized regulations to prohibit women from wearing the veil. While some *ulama* accepted the reforms, the majority were willing to bide their time until a more favorable period when traditional Islamic law might once more be implemented. Differences regarding the authority of traditional law, the need for social change, and the authority of the *ulama* as the sole official interpreters of Islam remained critical issues for the majority of the *ulama* and their traditionalist followers. Their voices would be heard in the 1970s.

Muslim family law reform underscores the basic issue underlying Islamic reform in general, the authority of tradition vis-à-vis the need for reinterpretation and reform in Islam. For more conservative traditionalist Muslims, the classical interpretations of Islam, preserved in the legal manuals developed by the law schools, constitute the blueprint for society. They provide the revealed pattern or norm to be followed. The extent to which there was a dichotomy between law and society did not indicate a need for legal reform but society's departure from the straight path of Islam. The remedy was not adaptation and change but a return to established, sacrosanct norms.

However, reformers maintained that a good portion of past legal practice, the regulations in legal manuals, represented the understanding and interpretation of early jurists who had applied the principles and values of Islam to their societies. They argued that changing conditions required that Muslims once again respond to the needs of society. While acknowledging the immutability of Sharia principles and laws found in the Quran and Sunna, modernists distinguished between Sharia, God's revealed law, and its extrapolation and delineation in the corpus of classical law (*fiqh*, understanding), emphasizing the contingency and relativity of the latter. Their position rested on the distinction employed by early Islamic modernists between the eternal validity of religious duties and the flexibility of much of social law. Thus, they asserted that Islamic reform was both necessary and possible.

A major factor undermining the credibility of reformers in the eyes of traditionalists is that the prime movers of reform have been Western-educated or -oriented rulers and political elites, a minority in society legislating for the more traditional majority. Similarly, feminist movements were regarded as organizations of upper-class women who wished to discard the veil in order to adopt Western dress and lifestyles. Although modernizing elites skillfully appealed to Islam for their methodology, and hence justification, in fact their approach was often superficial and piecemeal. They did not pursue a systematic review and assessment of Islamic law, fearful of its consequences. Because of the considerable resistance to reforms, compromises were often necessary. Indeed, in most Muslim countries, if a man takes a second wife or divorces his wife contrary to reform laws, the action is illegal but not invalid. This tentative approach toward legal reform was denounced as a manipulation and exploitation of Islam. The significance of these unresolved issues and the hold of tradition will be seen in those Muslim countries where the contemporary resurgence of Islam has led to calls for the implementation of Islamic law and the repeal of family law reforms.

Neorevivalist Movements

Parallel to modernist reforms initiated in the first half of the twentieth century was the emergence of a neorevivalism, new religious societies, in particular Hasan al-Banna's Muslim Brotherhood in Egypt and Mawlana Mawdudi's Jamaat-i-Islami (the Islamic Society) in the Indian subcontinent. These movements saw the Islamic community of the twentieth century at a critical crossroads. Like secular and Islamic modernists, they acknowledged the internal weakness of the community, the external threat of Western imperialism, and the value of science and technology. However, the Brotherhood and the Jamaat were more sweeping in their condemnation of the West and assertion of the total self-sufficiency of Islam. While secularists rejected Western political hegemony, they still looked to the West in charting their present and future. They adopted Western dress, manners, music, and movies, and appropriated Europe's political, economic, educational, and legal institutions. Islamic reformers struggled to provide an Islamic rationale for selective borrowing from the West. However, neorevivalist movements like the Brotherhood and the Jamaat saw their options more clearly and simply. Both capitalism and Marxism represented manmade secular paths that were alien to the God-ordained, straight path of Islam. If Muslims were to remain faithful to God and His divine will, they must reject Western secularism and materialism and return solely to Islam, whose perfection assured guidance in all aspects of life:

> Until recently, writers, intellectuals, scholars and governments glorified the principles of European civilization . . . adopted a Western style and manner. . . . Today, on the contrary, the wind has changed. . . . Voices are raised . . . for a return to the principles of Islam . . . for initiating the reconciliation of modern life with these principles, as a prelude to a final Islamization.[75]

For the Muslim Brotherhood and the Jamaat-i-Islami, Islam was not restricted to personal piety or simply a component in social or political life—it was a comprehensive ideology for personal and public life, the foundation for Muslim state and society.

Hasan al-Banna (1906–1949) of Egypt and Mawlana Abul Ala Mawdudi (1903–1979) of India were both raised in the shadow of British colonialism in societies where anticolonial national independence movements were active. They were pious, committed Muslims whose upbringing and education exposed them to Islamic education, modernist thought, and Western learning. Hasan al-Banna had studied in Cairo, where he came into contact with Rashid Rida and the Salafiyya movement. He was influenced by the reformist thought of al-Afghani and Abduh, but as channeled through the more conservative, revivalist phase of Rida's life and al-Manar in the 1920s, with its emphasis on the dangers of Westernization and the complete self-sufficiency of Islam. He established the Muslim Brotherhood in 1928. Mawlana Mawdudi, on the other hand, had been given a traditional Islamic education in which modern education was assiduously avoided. It was only later that he learned English and taught himself modern subjects. In 1938, at the invitation of Muhammad Iqbal, he moved to Lahore and in 1941 founded the Jamaat-i-Islami. Despite distinctive differences in their movements due to local conditions, both Hasan al-Banna and Mawlana Mawdudi combined religion with social activism. They shared a revivalist ideology and established activist organizations that remain vibrant today and have served as an example for others throughout much of the Muslim world.

Both the organization and the ideological outlook of the Brotherhood and the Jamaat were modeled on the example of the Prophet Muhammad and his first Islamic religiosocial reformation or revolution. The Islamic paradigm was reinterpreted and reapplied by these modern religious societies as it had been by revivalists and reformers in the past. Like Muhammad, they established communities of true believers who were distinguished from the rest of society and were totally committed to the struggle (jihad) to transform society. They did not leave (*hijra*) their societies but instead organized their followers into an Islamically oriented community or party within the broader (un-Islamic) society, forming a group of committed, like-minded Muslims who were to serve as the dynamic nucleus to transform society from within. In a sense, they were the vanguard of a religiously motivated elite. They were not a political party, but an ideological fraternity, as their names, the Society of Muslim Brothers (Jamaat al-Ikhwan al-Muslimin) and the Jamaat-i-Islami (Islamic Society), signified. Each developed a well-knit socioreligious organization with a network of branches and cells. Members were trained and reinforced in their faith and commitment to create a more Islamically oriented state and society; this was their reformist struggle or jihad. They were carefully selected and underwent a period of training and ideological indoctrination that emphasized religious knowledge and moral fitness, and concentrated on moral and social programs. Religious instruction, youth work, schools, hospitals, religious publications, and social-welfare projects were among the activities utilized to create a new generation of leaders in a morally strong society.

The Muslim Brotherhood grew rapidly as a mass movement, soon expanding beyond its rural lower- and lower middle-class background to include many members of the new middle class in urban areas. It attracted a broad following: clerks, policemen, merchants, teachers, lawyers, physicians, civil servants, soldiers, and university students. At its height, its membership was estimated at from five hundred thousand to 1 million. In contrast, the Jamaat had a more restricted membership, focusing on developing a new elite leadership. For Mawdudi, change resulted from a vanguard working within society, and therefore, in contrast to the Brotherhood, the Jamaat was primarily an elite rather than a populist organization, concerned with training a core of well-educated and Islamically committed leaders. Although an activist, Mawdudi focused on a systematic presentation of Islam. A gifted and prolific writer, he attempted to provide a theoretical blueprint for the revival of Islam, or what he termed the process of Islamic revolution. His books and articles discuss such themes as the Islamic way of life, Islam and its relationship to the state, law, marriage, and the family, veiling and the seclusion of women, and economics.

Under the leadership of the Supreme Guide, Hasan al-Banna (and later, its prolific and influential ideologue Sayyid Qutb), and Mawlana Mawdudi, the Muslim Brotherhood and the Jamaat-i-Islami reinterpreted Islamic history and tradition to respond to the sociohistorical conditions of the twentieth century. Both regarded Islam as the all-embracing ideology. The union of religion and society, the relationship of Islam to all aspects of life, followed from the doctrine of God's unity (tawhid) and sovereignty over all creation as embodied in the comprehensive nature of the Sharia: "The sharia is a complete scheme of life and an all embracing social order."[76] As they looked at their societies, and the Muslim world in general, both Hasan al-Banna and Mawlana Mawdudi attributed the impotence of their communities to political disunity, social dislocation, moral laxity, and a growing indifference to religion. Western secularism, with its separation of church and state, and the unbridled materialism of capitalism and Marxism were regarded as the major culprits. In contrast, they argued, Islam's organic relationship among religion, politics, and society distinguished it from the West. The separation of religion from the state represented for the Brotherhood and the Jamaat the inherent fallacy of Western secularism. Withdrawal of divine guidance would be the basis for its moral decline and ultimate downfall. Western culture, and all who do not follow Islam, exist, as did pre-Islamic society, in a state of ignorance and darkness.

Both the Brotherhood and the Jamaat incorporated the ideology, symbols, and language of revivalism within their reformist interpretation of Islam. There were two historic options—ignorance and Islam. Modern Muslim society was compared with that of pre-Islamic Arabia, a period of ignorance (jahiliyya), disunity, exploitation, and superstition. They felt that much of the Muslim world was gripped by factionalism, Sufi excesses, and acculturated, alien European institutions, practices contrary to Islam. The unity of the brotherhood of believers must replace the religious, political, and socioeconomic factions that divided and weakened the umma. Following revivalist logic, they called for a return to the Quran, the Sunna of the Prophet, and the practice of the early community to establish an Islamic system of government. Like Islamic revivalists and modernists, they rejected taqlid and upheld the right of ijtihad. They followed modernists in their acceptance of change through legal reform, though not accepting its application in modern family law reforms, which they regarded as Western in inspiration and intent. Unlike Islamic modernists who looked to the West and provided an Islamic rationale for the appropriation of Western learning, these contemporary revivalists emphasized the perfection and comprehensiveness of Islam and, hence, its self-sufficiency. All that Muslims needed could be found in or derived from the Islamic tradition. While open to science and technology, they denounced Muslim intellectuals and governments for their dependence on the West. They believed that the renewal of Muslim society and its social transformation or modernization must be rooted in Islamic principles and values. Thus, instead of speaking of democracy as such, the Brotherhood and Jamaat accepted the modernist reinterpretation of traditional concepts of consultation and community consensus, but noted that in an Islamic democracy the will of the people remained subordinate to the divine will. Mawlana Mawdudi called this a theo-democracy to distinguish it from a theocracy, or a clergy-run state, which he rejected. In an Islamic state, democracy could never mean that the majority had the power to legislate laws that contradicted religious belief regarding alcohol, gambling, prostitution, and so forth. Emphasizing the universality of the *umma* and its mission, they rejected nationalism and European-inspired legal codes, which they regarded as un-Islamic and a threat to Islamic identity, and called instead for an Islamic state to be governed by the Sharia. However, both Hasan al-Banna and Mawlana Mawdudi tempered their idealism with a realistic pragmatism. Mawdudi had rejected both Hindu and Muslim nationalism in India and initially refused to support the establishment of Pakistan as a separate homeland for Muslims. Like al-Afghani, Rida, and Iqbal, pan-Islamic aspirations gave way to a reluctant acceptance of political reality, and thus al-Banna and Mawdudi focused on Egypt and Pakistan respectively, while remaining committed to the eventual restoration of worldwide unity and involved in the broader concerns of the *umma*.

Although they were not political parties, their holistic vision, their belief that the Islamic community was to exist in a state and society governed by Islamic law, drew the Brotherhood and the Jamaat into the political arena. Both had understood their social revolution or reformation as occurring within society; their paths differed as a result of differences in political conditions. The Muslim Brotherhood's dissatisfaction with the failure of Egypt's government to establish an Islamic state escalated into violence, armed conflict, and the assassination of its founder in 1949. Government repression drove the Brotherhood deeper underground and subsequently led to a series of confrontations, imprisonment, executions, and, finally, its suppression and proscription in Egypt in the mid-1960s. In Pakistan, the Jamaat often found itself in opposition to governments and resorted to political action and participation in elections. Although Mawdudi and his followers were sometimes imprisoned for their activities, by and large they were able to work within the system.

The Muslim Brotherhood and the Jamaat-i-Islami demonstrate the strength and attractiveness of neorevivalist movements. After the Brotherhood was banned in Egypt and apparently crushed as its leaders were executed, imprisoned, or driven into exile, Muslim Brotherhood organizations continued to grow in many other parts of the Muslim world—the Sudan, Syria, Jordan, Palestine, Kuwait. Similarly, the Jamaat-i-Islami established organizations in India, Afghanistan, and Kashmir as well as Pakistan. What was the basis of the appeal of neorevivalists? First, they presented themselves as an indigenous movement. Although similar to modernists in their critique of Sufi excesses, saint worship, and the backwardness of the *ulama* and in their appeal to the process of premodern revivalism, neorevivalists did not seek to address modern life by demonstrating the compatibility of Islam with the West. Instead, they claimed that Muslims could adapt to the demands of modernity by reference to Islam alone. There was no need to go outside Islam's way of life, no need to be dependent on the West and run the danger of Westernizing Islam. Second, the organization and activism of neorevivalists contrasted sharply with the tendency of modernism to consist of a loose circle of intellectuals. Their emphasis on discipline, loyalty, and training as well as social-activist programs resulted in more cohesive and effective organizations. Third, though criticizing blind adherence to medieval Islam and claiming the right to *ijtihad,* neorevivalist condemnation of Western values (Westernization) and insistence on the self-sufficiency of Islam proved more attractive to many of the *ulama* and the more traditional sectors of society. This was more akin to the traditional interpretation of Islam that they had learned and the lifestyle and values they cherished. Quite simply, the degree of change advocated by neorevivalists seemed less radical than that of the modernists, less of a departure from tradition. While neorevivalists and modernists advocated legal change, in practice, in sensitive areas like family law reform, the Brotherhood and the Jamaat made common cause with the majority of the traditionalist-oriented *ulama.* They also tended to agree in their condemnation of the free mingling of the sexes, Western dress and manners, movies, and banking interest. The Islamic credentials of modernists, on the other hand, were eroded by the tendency of many of the colleagues or students of early modernists to follow a liberal, Western secular path.

Neorevivalism blended the worldview that informed the activism of premodern revivalist groups, like the Wahhabi and Mahdi movements, with the holistic vision of Islam articulated in theory by modernists like al-Afghani, Abduh, and Iqbal. The result was an ideology grounded solely on Islam, an Islamic alternative that presented Islam as a timeless, rational, comprehensive faith whose transcendent message was relevant to this life as well as the next. Islam was identified with the everyday lives and concerns of Muslims. Poverty, illiteracy, economic exploitation, education, and health care were all issues to which the Islamic message was relevant. The transcendent was made immanent not by Sufi withdrawal or indifference to the material world but by involvement in it. For the Brotherhood and the Jamaat, Muslim submission to God implied the molding of the individual and society. The Quranic teaching that human beings were God's representatives or vicegerents on earth, charged with realizing and spreading His will for humankind, became the theological basis for the social and moral reformism that characterized the work of the Brotherhood and Jamaat. The preaching of Islam was not just a propagation of the faith among non-Muslims, but a revivalist call or mission to those born Muslim to awaken and become better Muslims. The message or interpretation of Islam that they preached and practiced addressed the totality of the human experience.

The strengths of neorevivalism also implied distinct weaknesses. Establishing the appropriateness, indeed superiority, of Islam often degenerated into a one-sided attack on the ills of Western culture. The worst characteristics or social problems (prostitution, alcoholism, high crime rates, sexual promiscuity) of the West were exploited in a polemic that selectively compared Western realities with Islamic ideals, Western Christendom at its worst with Islam at its best. Secularism was equated with godlessness, an absence or denial of religious values, rather than a separation of church and state in order to guarantee religious freedom in pluralistic societies. Women's emancipation movements were dismissed as Western-inspired, anti-Islamic attacks on the sanctity of the family. Instead of adequately reexamining issues related to the real status of Muslim women (education, employment, divorce), traditional patterns were simply reaffirmed without a serious consideration of changing social realities. The source of these problems goes to the heart of the relationship between faith and history, divine revelation and human interpretation.

Neorevivalists have tended to follow conservative traditionalists in their tendency to equate the historical interpretation they inherited from their elders with revelation. They accept a rather romanticized, static notion of the development of Islamic belief and practice. This posture is understandable, given their perception and experience of modernity as the threat of Western political and cultural domination and assimilation. It resulted from the state of seige posed by both European powers and Muslim secular elites, who were regarded as indigenous domestic colonizers responsible for the Westernization of Muslim society: "The faction which works for the separation of Egypt from Islam is really a shameless, pernicious, and perverse group of puppets and slaves of Europe."[77] The need to respond to this internal and external threat motivated revivalists to assume a defensive posture, to defend Islam and its way of life against Westernization, instead of to adequately reexamine and reinterpret Islam. Both Islamic revivalism and modernism failed to produce an integrated, new synthesis or interpretation of Islam. Yet, this did not mean that the Brotherhood and the Jamaat were not open to change. Nothing could be more mistaken than to stereotype their goals as a simple, literalist return to the seventh century. However, the interpretation of Islam implicit in the ideological worldview of revivalism was limited by its failure to reexamine Islamic history more thoroughly. Lacking an awareness of the actual historical (as distinguished from the idealized) development of their faith, revivalists could not fully appreciate the dynamic, creative process of Islamization that characterized the development of Islamic law and theology. They were unable to realize the extent to which human reasoning and sociohistorical conditions affected the formulation of belief and practice: the role of local customary practice in law, social practice as a source of *hadith*, the influence of political considerations on theological doctrine. The breadth of the process of Islamization by which Muslims had adopted and adapted foreign social and cultural practices, integrating them within a framework of Islamic principles and values, remained forgotten. (In contrast, the failure of modernists to produce a systematic reconstruction of Islam meant that their isolated, ad hoc reforms were not seen as part of an integrated whole, but instead as the result of an eclectic borrowing from the West. Therefore, modernists came to be regarded as Westernizers.) For revivalists, as for traditionalists in general, history provided *the* authoritative interpretation of revelation rather than *an* authoritative interpretation open to subsequent reinterpretation and reform as circumstances change. Although revivalists advocated change through *ijtihad*, they tended to accept past practice and undertake change only in those areas not already covered by Islamic law.

Conclusion

Revival and reform have been dominant themes in Islam since the eighteenth century, as Muslims responded to internal and external forces that challenged their faith and social order. Islam was used effectively in the formation of Islamic sociopolitical reform organizations and Islamic modernist movements. Revivalist movements in the eighteenth and nineteenth centuries demonstrated the power of an appeal to Islam in providing a rationale for community decline and initiating religio-political movements bent on social and moral reform. Despite their differences, premodernist movements left a legacy to modern Islam in their ideological interpretation of Islam and their activist methods and organization. Islam proved a potent force in both the response to internal decline and the reaction to European imperialism. Islamic modernists reinterpreted Islamic sources to obtain new answers and to assimilate some Western ideas and institutions. Islamic modernism influenced attitudes toward Islam regarding both its past significance and its modern relevance. Its emphasis on Islam as a progressive, dynamic, rational religion generated a sense of pride, identity, and conviction that Islam was relevant to modern life. Though Islamic modernism did not produce a systematic reinterpretation of Islam and splintered in many directions, its outlook and modernist vocabulary penetrated Muslim society and enabled a new generation of Muslims to confidently embrace modern civilization with the belief that Islam was compatible and adaptable to the demands and challenges of modernity. However, some of these Muslims—neorevivalists—who grew up during the independence struggles of the post–World War I period rejected the accommodationist spirit of Islamic modernism. They combined a holistic interpretation of Islam and an organizational activism, calling for a social order based not on modernist acculturation but on a self-sufficient Islamic alternative. The struggle to produce viable Islamic responses to the new demands of modernity has continued to preoccupy many Muslims in the latter half of the twentieth century, as evident in the contemporary resurgence of Islam.

5

Contemporary Islam: Religion and Politics

The dominant theme of contemporary Islam has been its resurgence. A more pronounced impact of Islam on Muslim life has been evident in much of the Muslim world throughout the 1970s and 1980s, whether it be in women's dress on the streets of Cairo, Istanbul, and Kuala Lumpur or in Muslim politics from Tunis to Mindanao. Islamic laws, taxes, punishments, and banks have been introduced in many Muslim countries. Islam has reasserted itself more forcefully in both the personal and the public lives of Muslim societies in a striking and sometimes dramatic manner often called the Islamic resurgence, Islamic revivalism, or Islamic fundamentalism.

To speak of an Islamic revival or resurgence neither denies the continued presence of Islam in Muslim societies nor implies that it was dead or irrelevant. However, the contemporary revival has brought a noticeable increase in emphasis on religious identity and practice in individual and corporate life. Islamic revivalism is reflected in an increased emphasis on religious observances (mosque attendance, fasting during Ramadan, abstention from alcohol and gambling), a new vitality in Sufism, the proliferation of religious literature, television and radio programs, and audiocassettes, the growth of new Islamic associations committed to socioreligious reform, and the reassertion of Islam in Muslim politics. Understanding the significance of this phenomenon requires at the outset that certain presuppositions be recognized. The first is the modern Western secular tendency to separate religion and politics or to presume that secularization is the only modern option possible. The second is the realization that, for many Muslims, Islam is a total way of life. It is not correct, according to this viewpoint, to speak of religion *and* politics but instead religio-politics. Islam is believed to be relevant and integral to politics, law, education, social life, and economics. These institutions or areas of life are not viewed as secular but religious (Islamic), based on the belief that Islam is a *way of life,* and thus religion and society are interrelated. For many Muslims, the notion that religion is integral to life is the divinely mandated norm; there is no sharp dichotomy between the sacred and the profane. The question is not whether religion should inform life, but when and how. They believe that religious orthodoxy (or more accurately, orthopraxy) and cultural authenticity require it. For these Muslims, the mixing of religion and politics is not the issue—whether it is done to manipulate or control people or in a capricious, distorted manner is.

Islamic symbols, slogans, ideology, and actors have become prominent fixtures in Muslim politics. Islam has been used by governments and by opposition movements alike. Rulers in Libya, the Sudan, Egypt, Iran, Pakistan, and Malaysia have increasingly used Islam in recent years to enhance their legitimacy and policies. Political coalitions, operating under the banner of Islam, toppled the Shah of Iran in 1978–79 and contributed to the downfall of Zulfikar Ali Bhutto's government in Pakistan in 1977, while resistance and opposition movements operate in Afghanistan, Lebanon, Egypt, Syria, the Persian Gulf, and the southern Philippines. Why and how has Islam reemerged so significantly in Muslim life?

Coping with modernity has remained a major issue facing the Muslim community. However, in the post-1950 period, modernity was no longer a new external force infiltrating or invading Muslim lands but an internal established order present in the institutions of society and the outlook of its leaders. Even a venerable Islamic institution like al-Azhar University in Cairo had incorporated modern courses within its curriculum and had modernist rectors. Most governments had tackled the arduous task of nation building by establishing states with a more secular orientation, circumscribing the role of religion in public life, and fostering various forms of secular nationalism, both local (Egyptian, Sudanese, Tunisian) and regional (Arab and Baath nationalism/socialism). During the 1960s, there appeared to be a retreat from the secular path entered upon under the impact of European colonialism in the nineteenth century and continued by newly emerging nation-states in the postindependence period. Arab socialist regimes that had seized power in Egypt, Syria, Iraq, and Algeria buttressed their appeal for popular support by a deliberate, selective use of religion to legitimate their socialist ideologies and governments. Gamal Abd al-Nasser in Egypt provides a classic case. Determined to emerge as a pan-Arab leader and legitimate his Arab socialist revolution and ideology, Nasser created a state-supported periodical, *Minbar al-Islam* ("The Pulpit of Islam"), in which leading scholars and religious leaders linked Arab socialist policies to the Islamic tradition. The shaykh (rector) of al-Azhar gave *fatwas* reconciling socialism and state policies with Islam. Yet, the general trend in these and in most Muslim countries was to restrict religion to personal matters and laws, with the exception of those instances when regimes found it useful to appeal to religion.

The late 1960s signaled a turning point and the dawn of a new phase in the history of Islam with the growth and spread of religious revivalism. Why did religion again become such a visible force? The causes of the resurgence are many and need to be appreciated within the specific contexts of individual countries and regions. However, several phenomena may be identified as common to the contemporary Muslim experience: (1) an identity crisis precipitated by a sense of failure, loss of identity, and lack of self-esteem; (2) disillusionment with the West; the failure of many Muslim rulers and their Western-inspired governments to respond adequately to the political and socioeconomic needs of their societies; (3) the newfound sense of pride and power that resulted from military (Arab-Israeli war) and economic (oil embargo) success in 1973 and the Iranian revolution of 1978–79; and (4) a quest for a more authentic identity rooted in an Islamic past.

For the Arab world and many in the broader Muslim world, the Six-Day War with Israel in 1967 generated a period of soul-searching and self-criticism as Muslims tried to fathom why and how they had reached this nadir in their history. From its creation in 1948, Israel and its Arab neighbors had been at odds over the issue of a Jewish state in Palestine. However, the 1967 war transformed an Arab and Palestinian problem into an Islamic issue. The decisive rout of the combined forces of Egypt, Syria, and Jordan in just six days and their massive loss of territory (the West Bank, especially East Jerusalem, Gaza, and the Golan Heights) raised serious questions about the force of Arab regimes and their nationalist policies, in particular Nasser's Arab nationalism/socialism. Most important, the loss of Jerusalem—the third holiest city in Islam—and its sacred shrines was a major blow to Muslim pride and faith, precipitating a crisis of confidence and identity. The "liberation of Jerusalem" became not only a regional political problem but also a worldwide (Islamic) religiopolitical slogan and issue.

For many in the Middle East and throughout the Muslim world, the 1967 war, remembered in Arab literature as "the disaster," demonstrated the continued state of decline and the utter impotence of Muslims despite their independence from colonial rule. If Islamic belief and history taught that success and power were signs of a faithful community, many again asked, as they had during the colonial period, "What has gone wrong in Islam? Why has God seemingly abandoned His community?" While some blamed the hold of an outmoded traditional way of life and saw religion as the culprit, religious leaders asserted that Islam had not failed the Muslims. Muslims had failed Islam by relying on the West for their guidance and development. Adopting the discourse of religious revivalism, they called for a return to Islam. Behind this call was the belief that it was Islam that had united the tribes under Muhammad, inspired the early expansion and conquests, informed the glories of Islamic empires and civilizations, and served as a motivating force in revivalist reforms. For these religious leaders, the lessons of faith and history were clear. Muslim strength and success were dependent on faithfulness to God's Word and Prophet. Massive failure could only be a sign of waywardness and faithlessness. Coping with modernity did not require new, foreign-inspired alternatives when the community (*umma*) had a tried and true faith and way of life.

Many Western-oriented intellectuals and elites were particularly disillusioned. They had relied on a process of modernization that borrowed heavily from the West, and their hopes had been shattered. They could not claim to have strengthened their societies or to have built secure bridges with their Western mentors and allies.

The ignominious defeat of Arab forces and Israel's movement of its capital to Jerusalem symbolized both Muslim military failure and that of the West as an ally. Israel was regarded as a Western state in the Arab world, created and sustained by support from Western powers, in particular the United States. The message seemed clear: relying on the West for its models of development or as an ally had not worked. The sense of disenchantment and failure felt by modernists coincided with the criticisms of more traditional religious sectors of society. This disenchantment was reflected in Muslim literature in the late 1960s and early 1970s.[78] Whereas previously the content and concerns of secular and religious literature had generally differed, now popular, intellectual, and religious literature had common themes—a growing criticism and rejection of the West; a quest for identity and authenticity, manifested in a nostalgia for the past golden age of Islam; efforts to recover and incorporate an awareness of native (Islamic) cultural and historical identity; and emphasis on traditional moral values. There was a general consensus that Muslims had failed to produce a viable, authentic cultural synthesis and social order that was both modern and true to indigenous history and values. Western models of political, social, and economic development were criticized as imported transplants that had failed, fostering continued political and cultural dependence on the West and resulting in secularism, materialism, and spiritual bankruptcy. Neither Western liberal nationalism nor the Arab nationalism/socialism of Egypt's Gamal Abd al-Nasser had succeeded.

Behind their democratic parliamentary facades, problems of authoritarianism, legitimacy, and limited political participation plagued most Muslim countries. Government promises and development programs had created rising expectations that often went unfulfilled. Poverty and illiteracy remained unchecked. Modernization seemed to benefit a disproportionate few, the new urban-based middle and upper classes, fostering conspicuous consumption and corruption. The negative impact of modernization on village and family life and traditional religious and social values seemed to threaten the religious and moral fabric of society. The adoption of a Western lifestyle (its institutions, values, dress, music, cinema), once enthusiastically embraced as a symbol of progress and modernity, was now increasingly criticized as responsible for the Westernization and secularization of Muslim societies, a threat to cultural identity, and the cause of moral decline and spiritual malaise. Many revivalist themes reemerged: the need for greater self-reliance and a desire to reclaim the accomplishments of the past and to root individual and national self-identity more indigenously (to find pride and strength inside, not outside, the community) in an Islamic tradition that had once been a dominant world power and civilization. The prevailing mood was reflected in the language of authenticity, religiocultural revival (tajdid), reform (islah), and renaissance.

Events in 1973 and 1979 provided a new source of pride and served as catalysts for Islamic revivalism. The ignominious Arab defeat of 1967 was reversed, in the eyes of many Muslims, by the October War of 1973. While the Israeli army was ultimately victorious, many in the Arab world felt vindicated by Egyptian successes in the war. Most importantly, Anwar Sadat's use of Islamic symbols and rhetoric to mobilize and motivate Egyptian forces gave a decidedly religious character to its battles and led to its being regarded as an Islamic war and moral victory. This was the Ramadan war (named for the sacred month of fasting during which it occurred); its code name was Badr, the first great victory for Islam under the Prophet Muhammad; its battle cry was Allahu Akbar ("God is most great"), the traditional summons to the defense of Islam as well as to prayer; those who died in this holy war were not regarded simply as patriots but as religious martyrs.

The Arab oil embargo of 1973 was a second major catalyst for the resurgence. For the first time since the dawn of colonialism, the West seemed dependent on the Muslim world. The Arabs were no longer client states but a world economic power to be reckoned with. For many, these new signs of wealth and power were a source of enormous pride and a sign of the return of God's blessings. Remembering a once glorious past, the Muslims believed the return of God's favor and a new renaissance seemed at hand. Major oil powers like Saudi Arabia, Libya, and the United Arab Emirates used their petrodollars to foster revivalism both out of conviction and to extend their political influence. They assisted other Muslim governments (on condition that they foster Islamic measures), supported Islamic organizations and movements, and underwrote the publication and distribution of Islamic literature and the building of mosques, hospitals, and schools.

The Iranian revolution of 1978–79 seemed a watershed for Sunni and Shii Muslims alike. The prominence of its Islamic ideology and leadership rendered it an "Islamic revolution." Its success in effectively mobilizing Iranians against a seemingly invincible shah seemed to validate Islamic activist claims that a return to Islam would restore religious identity and vitality and enable Muslims, with God's guidance, to implement a more autonomous and self-reliant way of life despite a regime's military power and Western allies. The initial euphoria of postrevolutionary days sparked an enthusiasm and strong sense of pride among many in the Muslim world. The Ayatollah Khomeini's insistence that Iran's revolution was an Islamic, not just a Shii, revolution and his call for others to follow suit inspired not only Shii militant outbursts in Saudi Arabia and the Gulf but also, initially, admiration among Sunni Muslims and organizations. For many, there were clear lessons to be learned from the Iranian experience. The Islamic (Student) Association of Cairo University, in its flyer "Lessons from Iran," echoed the sentiments of many when it saw in the revolution a clear sign of the power of God, a reminder of the Muslim community's vocation as an example and world leader, a vindication of the true nature of Islam as the sole, comprehensive guide for life and the basis of a just society.

> Say, O God, possessor of all sovereignty, you give sovereignty to whom you wish and take sovereignty from whom you wish (Quran 3:26) . . . the importance of this unique and amazing revolution [is] to awaken Muslims and to restore their confidence in their religion and their adherence to it, so that they may assume the reins of world leadership of mankind once again and place the world under the protection of the esteemed Islamic civilization. "You are the best *umma* given to mankind; you prescribe the good and prohibit evil and you believe in God." (Quran 3:110)

The first lesson is the influence of the creed on the Islamic people. What spirit that was which moved in the being of this people who had appeared servile and submissive to injustice and tyranny. They exploded like a volcano, not fearing death and not concerned about life . . . flesh conquered steel. The spirit is the spirit of faith. This revolution indicates the nature of this religion which refuses to let injustice befall its followers and guarantees strength and dignity for them. . . . The revolution also indicates the nature of this religion from another perspective, namely it is a comprehensive religion which legislates for this world and the next and organizes all of life. It is concerned with the justice of government just as it is concerned with assuring that prayer is performed. It sets up a system of economy of which *zakat* is a part. . . . It sets forth in detail rules for dealings between people just as it details the rules of worship. . . . It is religion and state, governance and politics, economics and social organization, education and morals, worship and holy war.

Based on the foregoing, the Iranian revolution represents the first breach in the wall of secularism. . . . [T]he Islamic peoples . . . rejected it and began to set up the rule of God. . . . Secularism is a call to separate religion from the state and to prohibit Islam from interfering in politics or in the affairs of government. It is the perpetual resort of those idolatrous rulers who transgress God's limits, paralyze his Sharia. . . . This revolution confirmed for us that as long as laws and constitutions are not derived from the Sharia of Islam, they form a counterfeit Sharia. . . . Perhaps the most profound lesson which this revolution embodied was the fruit of working for countries of the East and West. Rulers sold their countries . . . and were transformed into puppets in the hands of rulers of East and West.[79]

The initial impact of the Iranian revolution went far beyond Iran. From Cairo to Kuala Lumpur, it became tangible corroboration for those who sought explanations for the apparent failures of their governments and believed that less dependence on outside forces, greater self-reliance, and the reaffirmation of Islam offered an alternative. It is important to note that there were differences of belief and perspective between those for whom greater cultural autonomy and authenticity meant reclaiming an Islamic cultural heritage and those for whom the foundation and point of departure was Islam, an all-embracing religious tradition. For the former, Islam was an element in national cultural identity. For the latter, it was the basis for community identity and life. The heart of contemporary revivalism is this ideologization of Islam; Islam is interpreted as a total ideology that provides the basic framework of meaning and direction for political, social, and cultural life. This belief is reflected in the tendency to speak of Islam as religion and state, as a system of belief and law that governs both spiritual and temporal affairs.[80]

Ideological Worldview of Revivalism

While there are distinctive differences of interpretation, the general or common ideological framework of Islamic revivalism includes the following beliefs:

1. Islam is a total and comprehensive way of life. Religion is integral to politics, law, and society.
2. The failure of Muslim societies is due to their departure from the straight path of Islam and their following a Western secular path, with its secular, materialistic ideologies and values.
3. The renewal of society requires a return to Islam, an Islamic religiopolitical and social reformation or revolution, that draws its inspiration from the Quran and from the first great Islamic movement led by the Prophet Muhammad.
4. To restore God's rule and inaugurate a true Islamic social order, Western-inspired civil codes must be replaced by Islamic law, which is the only acceptable blueprint for Muslim society.
5. Although the Westernization of society is condemned, modernization as such is not. Science and technology are accepted, but they are to be subordinated to Islamic belief and values in order to guard against the Westernization and secularization of Muslim society.
6. The process of Islamization, or more accurately, re-Islamization, requires organizations or associations of dedicated and trained Muslims, who by their example and activities, call on others to be more observant and who are willing to struggle (jihad) against corruption and social injustice.

Radical activists go beyond these precepts and operate on the following assumptions, believing that theological doctrine and political realism necessitate violent revolution:

1. A Crusader mentality, Western (in particular, the United States) and Eastern (the Soviet Union) neocolonialism, and the power of Zionism pit the West against the Islamic world.
2. Establishment of an Islamic system of government is not simply an alternative but an Islamic imperative, based on God's command or will. Therefore, all Muslims must obey and follow this divine mandate by struggling to implement and follow God's law.
3. Since the legitimacy of Muslim governments is based on the Sharia, governments that do not follow it are illegitimate. Those

who fail to follow Islamic law, governments and individuals, are guilty of unbelief. They are no longer Muslim but atheists whose unbelief demands holy war.

4. Opposition to illegitimate governments extends to the official *ulama*, the religious establishment, and state-supported mosques and preachers who are considered to have been co-opted by the government.

5. Jihad against unbelief and unbelievers is a religious duty. Therefore, all true believers are obliged to combat such governments and their supporters, whether individuals or foreign governments. Like the Kharijites in early Islam, radicals demand total commitment and obedience. One is either a true believer or an infidel, saved or damned, a friend or an enemy of God. The army of God is locked in battle or holy war with the followers of Satan.

6. Christians and Jews are generally regarded as unbelievers rather than "People of the Book" because of their connections with Western (Christian) colonialism and Zionism. They are seen as partners in a Judeo-Christian conspiracy against Islam and the Muslim world. Thus, non-Muslim minorities are often subjected to persecution.

The use of Islam in politics has taken a number of forms or modes of expression conditioned as much by local sociopolitical realities as by Islamic belief. The ideology of Islamic political activists is the product of faith and experience, a religious worldview interpreted and applied within the context of a specific country or region. This then accounts for the diversity of Islamic revivalism, its actors, organizations, ideological approaches, and methods. While the increased emphasis on religion in Muslim societies has meant more widespread attention to such common aspects of worship as prayer and fasting, it has also included a rich and at times confusing agenda as governments and Islamic associations have formulated or implemented policies and programs in the name of Islam. The impetus for the implementation of Islam can come from above, imposed by the state or government, or from below, through the pressure of religious organizations or political parties.

State Islam is government imposed, implemented by ruling regimes often with the cooperation of the religious establishment, state-supported clerical leaders. Rulers as diverse as Libya's Colonal Muammar Qaddafi (1969–   ), Egypt's Anwar Sadat (1970–81), Iran's Ayatollah Khomeini (1979–89), Sudan's Colonel Jafar al-Numayri (1969–85), and Pakistan's General Zia ul-Haq (1977–88) have used Islam to enhance their legitimacy and policies. State Islam reflects a broad spectrum, ranging from the conservative Saudi monarchy to Qaddafi's radical populist "state of the masses," from General Zia ul-Haq's martial law regime to Ayatollah Khomeini's clerically guided governance by the (Islamic) jurist. It has included the contrasting styles of monarchs, the military, and the clergy.

Islamic organizations and movements have reflected an equally pluriform rather than monolithic Islam, ranging from moderates who work within existing political systems to violent revolutionaries who seek to topple governments; from open membership to secret cells; from the relatively democratic to the totalitarian. Contrary to popular stereotypes, most activists are neither uneducated peasants from rural areas minimally exposed to modern education nor seminary students. They are not antimodern reactionaries trying to take refuge in the seventh century. Many combine a traditional upbringing with modern education. The majority are university graduates in engineering, law, medicine, science, or education from major national universities in Muslim countries as well as from centers of learning in Europe and America. They are graduates of Cairo, Khartoum, and Teheran universities as well as MIT, Indiana, Oxford, and the Sorbonne. While the *ulama* and theological faculties have played a more important role among the Shii, Sunni organizations are predominantly lay rather than clerical, their membership drawn heavily from students and young professionals (teachers, lawyers, engineers, doctors) recruited from schools and mosques. They include both city dwellers and villagers, members of the lower middle and middle classes. Many are serious, pious, highly motivated people who have become disaffected with the socioeconomic realities of their societies. These are not Muslims reacting to the introduction of modernization, reflexively rejecting a new and unknown reality. They are, instead, from the modern sector of society. Unlike some of their peers, their experience of modernization has not led them to embrace it but to criticize and reject its excesses and espouse an alternative to the dominant, Western form of modernization prevalent in much of the world.

The moderate majority seek reform through the gradual transformation of Muslim society; a radical minority advocate violent revolution. Organizations like the Muslim Brotherhood of Egypt, the Sudan, and Jordan, the Jamiyyat al-Islah (Islamic Reform Society) of Kuwait, Pakistan's Jamaat-i-Islami, and Malaysia's ABIM (Malaysian Islamic Youth Movement) run educational and social programs, youth camps and centers, legal aid societies and hospitals; participate in government and student campus elections; and have even served in the cabinets of Pakistan, the Sudan, Lebanon, and Malaysia. Extremist groups like Takfir wal Hijra (Excommunication and Emigration), al-Jihad (Holy War), Jund Allah (God's Army), and Hizbullah (Party of God) pursue a policy of violent confrontation, based on their conviction that the political realities of Muslim life require armed struggle or jihad. Radicals view Muslim governments as anti-Islamic regimes that either co-opt and control religion or repress the attempts of authentic Islamic movements to implement Islam. As proof, they point to Anwar Sadat, who fostered Islamic student organizations and yet did not implement Sharia law and suppressed dissent in the last days of his rule. Muammar Qaddafi's silencing of the *ulama* who have opposed his idiosyncratic interpretation of Islam, Habib Bourguiba's crackdown on Tunisia's Islamic Trend Movement in 1981 and 1987, and Hafiz al-Asad's leveling of the city of Hama in 1982 to put down a Brotherhood-led uprising are all regarded as part of a pattern of government suppression of Islamic movements. Radicals believe that the refusal of Muslim governments to implement Islamic law and their repression of Islamic activism necessitate the counteruse of violence and armed struggle against the enemies of God, despotic rulers and their foreign allies. Indeed, it is a religious obligation to resist and fight. In contrast to conservative and modernist leaders who have tended to emphasize nonviolent interpretations of jihad, for example as the struggle to be virtuous, radicals believe that Islam is in danger, locked in a defensive war against repressive anti-Islamic or un-Islamic rulers and states. They regard themselves as the true defenders of Islam, in whose name they have assassinated opponents like Egypt's Anwar Sadat, kidnapped and murdered, and attacked government installations and foreign embassies. While many speak of an Islamic alternative, shared aspiration, when translated into ideology and strategy, often yields differing interpretations and agendas.

A variety of Muslim governments have turned to Islam to enhance their political legitimacy and authority as well as mobilize popular support for programs and policies. A more detailed review of several Muslim countries reveals the multiple uses of Islam by governments and activist organizations in Libya, Egypt, Iran, Lebanon, and Saudi Arabia.[81]

Modern nation building in the Muslim world demonstrates three patterns: secular, Muslim, and Islamic. At one end of the spectrum, Turkey, under the leadership and direction of Mustafa Kemal (Ataturk, Father of the Turks, d. 1938), was the only Muslim country to choose a completely secular path, restricting religion to private life. At the other end of the spectrum, Saudi Arabia is a self-proclaimed Islamic state. The vast majority of countries in the Muslim world fall in between. After independence most pursued a path of political development that was heavily indebted to the West for political, legal, economic, and educational institutions. They are Muslim states in that the majority of the population and their heritage is Muslim. Moreover, most of these states have "Islamic" provisions, such as a requirement that the head of state must be Muslim, a declaration that Islam is the state religion, or state control of religion through a ministry of religious affairs. Yet the prevailing tendency in the post-independence period (post–World War II) was to foster secular forms of national identity and solidarity and to limit religion to private rather than public life. Thus, local (Egyptian, Syrian, Libyan) or regional/linguistic (Arab or Baath) forms of nationalism or socialism prevailed. This secular trend changed almost imperceptibly in the 1960s and became more pronounced in the 1970s, for reasons we will discuss.

Egypt

When Gamal Abd al-Nasser and the Free Officers overthrew the Egyptian monarchy in July 1952, they came to power in a nation that had for more than a century pursued a Western-oriented path of development. Despite the initial support Nasser had received from the Muslim Brotherhood, he continued to steer Egypt on a secular nationalist course. However, by the late 1950s, faced with opposition from the Brotherhood and wishing to establish his leadership in the Arab world as well as Egypt, Nasser broadened Egyptian nationalism into an Arab nationalism/socialism, rooted in the region's common Arab-Islamic heritage. He preached a common Arab unity and identity—based on a shared language, history, and religion—whose concerns and interests transcended national borders. Increasingly, Nasser used religious symbols, language, leaders, and rhetoric to legitimate and win support for his Arab socialist ideology and policies. State control of Al-Azhar University and a state-sponsored Supreme Council of Islamic Affairs were used to legitimate and promote the Islamic character of Arab socialism. Official pronouncements or legal decrees (*fatwas*) were obtained from Islamic scholars at Al-Azhar University, which had been nationalized in 1961, to establish the compatibility of Arab socialism and Islam. The state-sponsored Supreme Council of Islamic Affairs published a journal, *The Pulpit of Islam,* in which articles interpreted traditional Islamic beliefs regarding the equality of believers and social justice to legitimate Nasser's socialist policies and programs of land reform, nationalization, and birth control.

Nasser's use of Islam was challenged internationally and domestically. Saudi Arabia resented this popular and charismatic leader's scathing denunciation of conservative Arab monarchies and his regional influence. The Saudis obtained decrees from their *ulama* condemning socialism and preached a pan-Islamic as well as pan-Arab message. The Egyptian Muslim Brotherhood, which had been disaffected by Nasser's failure to create an Islamic state, stepped up its opposition. In 1965, the Brotherhood was accused of attempting to assassinate Nasser. Their leaders were imprisoned and a number were executed, among them Sayyid Qutb, who is remembered as the martyr of Islamic revivalism. The Brotherhood was ruthlessly suppressed. Although it seemed to be effectively eliminated, the Brotherhood continued to exist in prison, in exile, and underground and reemerged under Nasser's successor, Anwar Sadat.

The shock and grief which Nasser's unexpected death caused in the Arab world was reflected in the millions who took to the streets of Cairo for his funeral. However, the pride that Nasser had fostered and the hopes of his Arab socialism had been shattered by the catastrophe of the Arab defeat in 1967. Yet, Nasser's charismatic personality created a void which few men could have filled. Sadat had been completely eclipsed by Nasser's shadow. Upon Sadat's accession to power, he was careful to see that his picture was displayed alongside that of Nasser. As Sadat sought to emerge as a leader in his own right, enhance his political legitimacy, and counter the opposition of Nasserites and leftists who opposed his pro-Western policies, he relied heavily upon Islam. Sadat appropriated the title "The Believer President," had the mass media cover him praying at the mosque, increased Islamic programming in the media and Islamic courses in schools, built mosques, and employed Islamic symbols and rhetoric in his public statements. Sufi brotherhoods and the Muslim Brotherhood, suppressed by Nasser, were permitted to function publicly. The Sadat government encouraged and supported Islamic student organizations on campuses to offset the influence of Nasserite and Marxist student groups. It was not long before Islamic student groups captured student elections at major Egyptian universities. As previously discussed, Sadat effectively cast the 1973 Egyptian–Israeli war as an Islamic holy war. Subsequently, he marshalled the support of Al-Azhar's religious establishment to legitimate key government policies such as the Camp David Accords, family law reforms, and to denounce as extremists the Islamic activists who increasingly challenged the regime during the latter part of the 1970s.

As Islamic organizations such as the Muslim Brotherhood and student groups gained momentum, they became more independent and critical of Sadat policies: his support for the Shah of Iran and early condemnation of the Ayatollah Khomeini, the Camp David Accords, and Sadat's pro-Western economic and political ties. They were also more vocal in their demands for the implementation of Islamic law. A new crop of secret revolutionary groups, some funded by disaffected and radicalized former Muslim Brothers who had been imprisoned under Nasser, began to challenge both what they regarded as Sadat's hypocritical manipulation of Islam and the moderate posture of the Muslim Brotherhood. Militant groups like Muhammad's Youth (also known as the Islamic Liberation Organization), the Army of God, and Excommunication and Emigration (*Takfir wal Hijra*) resorted to acts of violence in an attempt to overthrow the government.

Springing up in both cities and provincial towns, these groups recruited heavily from schools, universities, and local mosques. Many members were educated and highly motivated:

> The typical profile of members of militant Islamic groups could be summarized as being young (early twenties), of rural or small town background, from middle and lower middle class, with high achievement motivation, upwardly mobile, with science or engineering education, and from a normally cohesive family. It is sometimes assumed in social science that recruits of "radical movements" must be somehow alienated, marginal, anomic, or otherwise abnormal. Most of those we investigated would be considered model Egyptian youth.[82]

Despite their differences, all condemned Sadat and Egyptian society as un-Islamic, politically corrupt, controlled by infidels (that is, people who were not "true believers"), and dominated by alien and decadent Western laws and lifestyles which fostered secularism, materialism (conspicuous consumption), and a spiritually lax and permissive society. They believed that the liberation of Egyptian society required that all true Muslims undertake an armed struggle or holy war against a regime they regarded as oppressive, anti-Islamic, and a puppet of the West. Their concern was not only over Egypt's political and military dependence but also its cultural penetration and acculturation, the more insidious threat. Their grievances erupted into attacks against bars, nightclubs, cinemas, Western tourist hotels, as well as government institutions and personnel.

One radical group, the Jihad Organization, had been formed by some of the remnants of Muhammad's Youth or the Islamic Liberation Organization whose leaders had been executed for their attempt in 1974 to seize the Technical Military Academy in Cairo as part of a coup d'état. Its leadership and members were drawn from a cross section of society: civilian, military, and religious. Among them were members of the presidential guard, military intelligence, civil servants, radio and television workers, university students, and professors. The rationale for their actions was articulated in a tract, *The Forgotten Obligation,* written by its ideologue, an electrician named Muhammad al-Farag. In it he reasserted the belief that jihad was the sixth pillar of Islam and that armed struggle or revolt was an imperative for all true Muslims to rectify the ills of a decadent society:

> [W]e have to establish the Rule of God's Religion in our own country first, and to make the Word of God supreme. . . . There is no doubt that the first battlefield for jihad is the extermination of these infidel leaders and to replace them by a complete Islamic Order. From here we should start.[83]

Islamic activists' criticism and condemnation of Sadat had seemed confirmed when he responded to his religious critics in February 1979 by calling for the separation of religion and politics, a position seen as un-Islamic by Muslim organizations who called for the establishment of an Islamic state and the implementation of Islamic law. University Islamic student organizations were banned. For radicals, Sadat was clearly an apostate who merited the death penalty. Sadat's growing authoritarianism and suppression of any dissent came to a head in 1981, when he imprisoned more than 1,500 people from a cross section of Egyptian society (Islamic activists, lawyers, doctors, journalists, university professors, political opponents, ex-government ministers).

On October 6, 1981, Anwar Sadat was assassinated by members of Tanzim al-Jihad as he reviewed a parade commemorating the 1973 war. Lieutenant Khalid Islambuli, the leader of the assassins, had cried out: "I am Khalid Islambuli, I have killed Pharaoh and I do not fear death." Sadat's popularity in the West and his international image as a flexible, enlightened leader stood in sharp contrast to his growing unpopularity at home, where his secular and religious opposition referred to him as pharaoh. For many in Egypt: "Khalid therefore appeared as a sort of 'right arm' of the popular will, and not merely as a militant exponent of an Islamicist group."[84]

The style of Islamic revivalism changed in the 1980s after the death of Sadat. If Islamic revivalism or fundamentalism in Egypt during the 1970s seemed to be a movement of confrontation and violence, the 1980s witnessed the fruits of the broader-based, quiet revolution that had been overshadowed or eclipsed by the conflict between Sadat's growing authoritarianism and his militant opposition.

In contrast to his predecessor, the new Egyptian president, Hosni Mubarak, pursued a path of greater political liberalization and tolerance while at the same time responding quickly and firmly to those who resorted to violence to challenge the authority of the government.

Mubarak distinguished more carefully between religious and political dissent and direct threats to the state. He has been quick to crush outbursts and riots fomented by Islamic militants, to intervene in clashes between Muslims and Coptic Christians, and to try to execute the assassins of Sadat. At the same time, he did not balk at releasing more than 170 defendants in the Sadat trials acquitted by the courts. Religious critics have been allowed public outlets for their opposition; they can compete in parliamentary elections, publish newspapers, voice their objections in the media. The government has sponsored television debates between Islamic militants and representatives of the religious establishment, religious scholars from al-Azhar University. Government-run television and newspapers have regularly featured religious programs and columns which are often independent in their tone and criticisms.

The most important characteristic of Islamic revivalism in Egypt in the 1980s, as in many parts of the Muslim world when Islam is not controlled or suppressed by governments, is the extent to which revivalism has become part of moderate, mainstream life and society rather than merely a marginal phenomenon. It is no longer simply a lower- or lower middle-class phenomenon. Renewed awareness and concern about leading a more Islamically informed way of life can be found among the middle and upper class, educated and uneducated, peasants and professionals, young and old, women and men. They are active in Quran study groups (run by both women and men), Sufi gatherings, mosques, and private associations. As a result, Islamic identity is expressed not only in formal religious practices but also in the social services offered by psychiatric and drug rehabilitation centers, dental clinics, day-care centers, legal aid societies as well as organizations that provide subsidized housing and food distribution or run banks and investment houses.

The *ulama* and the mosques have also taken on a more prominent role. The popularity of preachers such as Shaykh Muhammad Mitwali al-Shaarawi and Abd al-Hamid Kishk, an outspoken critic often regarded as an extremist and imprisoned by both Nasser and Sadat, has made them religious media stars. Their presence is known not only through television but also from their regular newspaper columns, audiocassettes, pamphlets, and books, which enjoy widespread distribution in bookstores, in airports and hotels, and by street vendors. Their popularity extends beyond Egypt to much of the Arab world. Thus, their voices are heard not only in mosques or religious gatherings but also on cassettes played in taxicabs, on the streets, in shops, and the homes of the poor and middle class alike. Wherever one finds magazines, audiotapes, or books being sold, there amidst the coverage of politicians and movie stars will also be popular religious materials.

Mosques and their *imams* (leaders) are also part of the mainstreaming of revivalist activities. The private nongovernment mosques had for some time been a source of independent criticism and opposition to the government. However, the tendency in most Sunni Muslim countries had been for the laity (non-*ulama*), through modern Islamic organizations such as the Muslim Brotherhood, to exercise leadership in relating Islam to the demands and needs of modern society. While this has continued, more and more mosques and their religious officials have also become involved in providing much needed social services.

Egypt has long been regarded as a leader in the Arab world—politically, militarily, and religiously. Among the most modern of Muslim countries, it has experienced the full array of Islamic revivalist activities. Once a barometer for a modernization that was predominantly Western and somewhat secular in orientation, today it provides a full-blown example of the more complex, and at times volatile, experience of many Muslim societies attempting in a variety of ways to integrate their Islamic heritage and values with their sociopolitical development.

Libya

During the late 1960s revolutionary regimes came to power in military coup d'états in Libya and the Sudan. Both colonels Muammar Qaddafi of Libya and Jafar al-Numayri of the Sudan were admirers of Egypt's Gamal Abd al-Nasser, patterned their revolutions on Nasser's model, and justified their coups in the name of Arab socialism. However, by the 1970s, both had found it necessary to buttress their secular nationalist ideology with an appeal to religion.

Libya was the site of one of the earliest and most controversial state implementations of Islam. Although Qaddafi had emulated the policies of his hero, Nasser, regarding religion, by the 1970s Qaddafi was reinforcing nationalist slogans and ideology with an espousal of Islam. Qaddafi embarked upon a series of reforms aimed at eradicating the vestiges of European colonialism and reaffirming Libya's Arab-Islamic heritage. He declared that Libya's Arab socialist path was the socialism of Islam, "a socialism emanating from the true religion of Islam and its Noble Book."[85] Churches were closed and missionary activities curtailed. Arabic replaced European languages in official transactions, names of localities, and street signs. In the early 1970s, Qaddafi announced the introduction of Islamic law. A commission was established to review all Libyan laws to assure that they were in conformity with Islam. In fact, however, Islamic law was never fully implemented. Instead, Qaddafi introduced Islamic penal laws and punishments for gambling, alcohol, theft, and adultery. Full implementation of Islamic law was replaced by his grand design, the Third Way or Third Universal Theory, in which he provided an Islamic alternative to capitalism and Marxism for Libya and the world. The blueprint was delineated in *The Green Book*. The symbolism and significance of this title was not lost upon a Muslim audience. The Quran is the Noble Book; Jews and Christians are "people of the book," possessors of revelation; green is the color of the Prophet Muhammad. The Chinese in mainland China at that time were followers of Mao Tse Tung's *Red Book*. This then was an alternative to prevailing ideologies and blueprints for society, whether Western European (Judaeo-Christian) capitalism, Soviet or Chinese Marxism.

Publication of *The Green Book* (it appeared in three installments—in 1975, 1977, 1979) signaled Qaddafi's own modern and idiosyncratic interpretation of Islam. He claimed *The Green Book* replaced the traditional position of Islamic law as the blueprint for society. He radically redefined Islam and Arab nationalism, stamping them with his own interpretation. *The Green Book* was to be the theoretical framework for the new Libyan society as well as the basis for sociopolitical order and cultural revolution at home and abroad: "*The Green Book* is the guide to the emancipation of man . . . the new gospel. The gospel of the new era . . . the era of the masses."[86] Qaddafi's ideological approach and actions often proved as controversial Islamically as they did in international politics. He had asserted a relationship between the social revolution espoused in *The Green Book* and the Quran and Islamic tradition. The first volume of *The Green Book* does contain references to Islam and the Quran, and Qaddafi's ideological outlook does incorporate the major themes of Islamic renewal and reform similar to those found in eighteenth- and nineteenth-century Islamic revivalism. For example, the backwardness of the Arab world is likened to the "pagan" pre-Islamic period; it is a time of social injustice due to exploitation and moral corruption; Muslims have strayed from the straight path of Islam by blindly following the dictates of Western imperialism. Torn between capitalism with its unbridled emphasis on wealth and power and communism's violent urge to uproot and reshape everything, Muslims must espouse a pattern that is neither West nor East. Instead, Qaddafi maintained, they must once again reclaim, reassert, and follow their divinely mandated mission: "The time has come to manifest the truth of Islam as a force to move mankind, to make progress, and to change the course of history as we changed it formerly."[87] However, the bulk of *The Green Book* does not refer explicitly to Islam. Qaddafi defended himself against his Islamic critics by maintaining that the Third Universal Theory of *The Green Book* is meant to bring about social justice and equality for the entire world, not just Muslims.

When speaking to the Muslim world, Qaddafi has specifically linked his brand of revolutionary socialism and its agenda for change to the revolutionary spirit of Islam. Islam in Qaddafi's hands is transformed into a form of Islamic revolutionary socialism. Muhammad is portrayed as a revolutionary leader whose battle with the power and wealth of the Arab political establishment is likened to the modern-day struggle against kings and princes. For Qaddafi, the principal cause of Muslim backwardness is not Islam but the legacy of European colonialism and the forces of modern political and economic imperialism. Islam is a progressive, socialist movement which stands for a worldwide political and social revolution against these forces of oppression:

> We here in Libya are not ashamed of championing a progressive and highly leftist revolution! But we shall never compromise Islam, in order to supposedly demonstrate to the world that the backwardness which has afflicted Muslims has no relation to Islam. On the contrary, Islam leads people to progress.[88]

Qaddafi's linkage of Islam with a "progressive, leftist revolutionary universalism" can be seen in his assertion that to achieve their God-ordained goal, Muslim nations must support liberation movements wherever they occur, whether or not they are Islamically inspired.[89]

The ire of many of the *ulama,* and indeed many Muslims, across the Islamic world was particularly aroused by Qaddafi's methodology and interpretations of Islam. He challenged the status and role of the *ulama* by emphasizing that all Muslims had a right to interpret Islam and by interpreting Islam himself in a rather sweeping style whose innovations broke with traditional belief and practice. Raising his *Green Book* to the status of the Sharia, interpreting Islam for state and society, encouraging others to do so—all these actions flew in the face of the traditional role of the *ulama.* Qaddafi also encouraged Muslims to break with the centuries-long Islamic practice of dating the Muslim calendar from the emigration (*hijra*) of Muhammad and his followers from Mecca to Medina. Instead he introduced a new Muslim calendar, which begins with the death of the Prophet. For many, the proof of Qaddafi's hubris and unorthodoxy was his position regarding the authenticity and binding nature of the corpus of Prophetic traditions, the *hadith.* Like some Muslim scholars and much of Western scholarship, Qaddafi questioned the authenticity of the traditions of the Prophet, given alterations, interpolations, and fabrication. He concluded that due to this lack of certitude regarding the Sunna of the Prophet, only the Quran should be regarded as binding and as an infallible guide. Many of his critics charged that Qaddafi was merely clearing the way for the authority of his own statements and teachings. Indeed, Qaddafi rejected the binding nature of the Sunna, the schools of Islamic law (which he regarded as sectarian movements), and the traditional religious establishment. Moreover, in a direct assault upon the authority of the *ulama,* he had encouraged his youthful followers to take over the mosques.

In addition to those alienated in the international political arena, Muammar Qaddafi's radical reinterpretation of traditional Islam and Arab socialism earned the opposition of the religious establishment and many Islamic activists at home and abroad. Thus, among those opposition leaders whom he has executed have been members of the Libyan Muslim Brotherhood. Mixing populist rhetoric with political, social, and economic experimentation, Qaddafi attempted to implement an ideological revolution in Libya and to export it internationally. His use of *The Green Book* to displace the Sharia's governance of the political and social order substantially reinterpreted Islam. In the final analysis, Qaddafi devised an ideology and system of government based less on revelation than his own guidance and dictates.

Iran

For many in the West, Islam and events in the Muslim world have been viewed primarily through the prism of the Iranian revolution and Ayatollah Khomeini's Iran: the fall of the Shah, long regarded by the Western media as an enlightened, modernizing monarch and a staunch ally of the United States; the wrenching spectacle of the seizure of the American embassy in Teheran and of "America Held Hostage" by Islamic militants, shown nightly on television and in the press shouting "Death to America"; the kidnapping of Americans and bombings of American embassies and Marines in Lebanon, attributed to Iranian-inspired and supported Islamic radicals; Salman Rushdie's condemnation to death for blaspheming in his novel *The Satanic Verses.* The Iranian experience exemplifies a publicly proclaimed "Islamic" revolution and government as well as the clash of interpretations of Islam that accompany the politicization of Shii Islam.

During the 1960s and 1970s, the Shah of Iran's White Revolution had attempted to implement a wide-ranging modernization program. Despite noteworthy gains, the real impact and advantages of modernization had primarily benefited urban areas and a new modern middle class of technocrats and professionals. Most important, modernization had not included significant political reform. Many sectors of Iranian society had become increasingly critical of the Shah's growing autocratic rule and the rapid, uncritical pace of modernization, which posed a threat to Iranian national autonomy, identity, and culture.

In the face of the regime's refusal to grant broader political participation and its suppression of dissent, an alliance evolved between the traditional, religiously oriented classes (religious leaders, merchants, and artisans), who felt many of the Shah's modern reforms to be an assault on both their religion and livelihood, and many modern, Western-educated intellectuals and professionals. Both shared common concerns about political freedom, the dangers of military and economic dependence on the United States, and the threat of cultural alienation due to the Westernization of Iranian education and society—what one secular intellectual termed "Westoxification" or "Weststruckness," that is, indiscriminate borrowing from and dependence upon the West. Although all shared the goals of overthrowing the Shah and creating a more indigenously rooted government and society, their religious and political outlooks and agendas were in reality quite diverse. For many, the Islamic alternative meant a return to Islam, the establishment of an Islamic state and society. Others wished to restore national pride and identity through a conscious preservation and incorporation of Iran's Persian/Shii identity and cultural heritage. Their differences would emerge once the Shah was overthrown and Iran's new leaders moved from opposition to a common foe to the implementation of an Islamic republic.

As opposition to the Shah mounted, the reinterpretation and politicization of Shii Islam emerged as the most viable and effective vehicle for articulating national concerns, legitimating demands for reforms, and for gaining popular support. Islam provided an indigenous, non-Western alternative—a sense of identity, a common set of religiocultural symbols and values and thus an ideological framework within which a variety of factions could co-exist. The ideological worldview of Shii Islam, in particular its religious history, gave meaning and legitimacy to a mushrooming opposition movement. Indeed, early Shii religious history and belief lent itself to the interpretation of Shiism as a religion of protest and revolution: the disinheritance of Ali, Husayn, and the early Imams by Sunni caliphs; Shii revolts against Umayyad and Abbasid Sunni rulers; and especially the martyrdom of the Imam Husayn at Karbala. All these events offered inspirational examples and symbols for the ensuing battle against oppression and injustice, and the legitimacy of protest, martyrdom, and, if necessary, revolution.

Modern Iranian history had also provided selective examples or precedents for the use of Islam in protest movements to preserve Iranian independence and national interests. In the Tobacco Protest (1891–92) to prevent the selling of tobacco concessions to Europeans and the Constitutional Revolt (1905–11), which set some limits on the Shah's power by instituting liberal reforms, a modern constitution, and parliamentary form of government, local religious leaders (mullahs) were pressed into service, joining with other sectors of society in the protests. In both cases, religious leaders and institutions were part of broad-based movements to safeguard Iranian identity and autonomy and check an autocratic Shah. Similarly, during the 1970s the mullah-mosque network offered a ready-made system of organization and mobilization. The imprisonment of many key secular leaders and the imposition of martial law accentuated the more independent status and role of religious leaders, who represented a vast reservoir of grass roots leadership. Their mosques, situated throughout Iran's cities, towns, and villages, became centers for political organization and agitation. Government regulations could not restrict the functioning of mosques, the economic support which religious leaders received from wealthy merchants and others who paid their Islamic tithes or taxes (the annual tithe on wealth for the poor, *zakat*, and the Shii religious tax on income, *khums*, which is paid directly to religious authorities), or the sermons at Friday community prayer which drew upon Shii religious history to excoriate the evils of imperial oppression. The battlefield at Karbala in the seventh century became the streets of Teheran and other Iranian cities in the twentieth century; the confrontation between the armies of Caliph Yazid and the martyred Husayn was transformed into the contemporary confrontation between the Shah (the new Yazid) and the modern-day forces of Husayn, the Iranian people. Thus, the classic Shii myth of good and evil, the army of God versus that of Satan, with its lessons of sacrifice and martyrdom, had its modern-day meanings and application. Similarly, traditional Shii belief in the return of the hidden Twelfth Imam, its promise of ultimate victory and a reign of perfect social justice, could be drawn upon to inspire and motivate.

The Islamic component in Iran's revolution had many sources, drawing on a variety of Islamically oriented leaders and their ideological interpretations of Islam. Among the more prominent and influential were Mehdi Bazargan, Dr. Ali Shariati, and the Ayatollah Khomeini. Bazargan (b. 1907), who would become the provisional prime minister of the Islamic Republic of Iran in 1979, is a French-trained engineer and Islamically inspired political activist who had been a long-time critic of the Shah and had been imprisoned for his beliefs. In 1961, he and the Ayatollah Taleqani (1910–78) established the Liberation Movement of Iran, which sought to bridge the gap between religious and secularly oriented Iranians to create a more Islamic state and society. Bazargan was particularly effective because he combined a traditional religious outlook and vocabulary with modern concerns, and was thus able to speak to the *ulama* as well as modern, educated students and professionals. Using the doctrine of God's unity or oneness and citing as examples Muhammad's joint role as prophet-statesman and the status and activities of the Imams as religiopolitical leaders, Bazargan argued for a process of Iranian reform based on the integral relationship of Islam to politics and society.

Ali Shariati (1933–77), the son of a preacher-scholar, was a Sorbonne-educated intellectual and teacher. As a young man, he and his father had belonged to the Movement of God-Worshipping Socialists, which tried to combine Shii Islam with European socialism. He had been active in Bazargan's Liberation Movement of Iran in the 1960s and influenced by the example of the Algerian and Cuban revolutions. Shariati combined the Islamic reformist spirit of Bazargan and Taleqani, the ideas of sociologists such as Emile Durkheim and Max Weber, and the revolutionary Third World socialist ideals of Franz Fanon and Che Guevera. He synthesized Shii Islam and Western social scientific language to develop a thoroughgoing reinterpretation of traditional Islam, a kind of liberation theology. He denounced "world imperialism, including multinational corporations and cultural imperialism, racism, class exploitation, class oppression, class inequality, and *gharbzadegi* [Weststruckness]."[90] His goal was to reverse what he regarded as the retrogressive state of Shii Islam and to construct a revolutionary Islamic ideology for sociopolitical reform. For Shariati, Shii Islam provided the symbols for a much-needed social and cultural revolution. Nowhere was this more evident than in his reinterpretation of Shii belief in the hidden Imam's return. Shariati believed that the real meaning and significance of this doctrine had been distorted into a political quietism, with believers passively awaiting the return of the Imam, the future coming of a messianic Mahdi or rightly guided leader. In the interim, a depoliticized Shiism accepted the legitimacy of temporal rulers during the absence of the Imam. Instead, he believed the period of expectation or awaiting should be marked by active striving to usher in the age of social justice and equity because, as he noted, this messianic doctrine included promise of ultimate victory:

> Contrary to what Beckett says in *Waiting for Godot, intizar* [expectation or waiting for the return of the Imam] is not a futile idea. . . .

Oppression, crime, injustice, all are unfinished stories and events in human history. . . . The story shall end with Justice and Truth triumphing over oppression and corruption. . . . Belief in the final Saviour, in the Shii Imams and the Twelfth Imam, means that this universal Revolution and final victory is the conclusion of the one great continual justice seeking movement of revolt against oppression.[91]

Shariati's teachings disturbed both the political and the religious establishments. The Shah regarded Shariati as an Islamic Marxist and revolutionary, while many of the *ulama* condemned his innovative reinterpretation of traditional Shii beliefs, which was critical of the *ulama*'s role in Iranian history. Shariati distinguished between original Islam (the Islam of Ali and his early followers)—which he claimed was dynamic, progressive, scientific, and revolutionary—and the scholastic, institutionalized, bureaucratic Islam (Safavid Islam) of the *ulama*, who had been co-opted by the Safavid rulers. The *ulama* produced a rigid, passive and retrogressive religion of the establishment. For Shariati, both Western imperialism and a retrogressive religious leadership were responsible for the decline of Muslim society. The *ulama* had too often become government advisers or fallen into quietism rather than asserting their true role as protectors of Islam against oppressive governments. Thus Shariati believed that reform must come primarily from lay intelligentsia rather than from the traditional religious leaders. His dynamic revolutionary Islam, which preached a more indigenous ideology—Iranian/Islamic rather than Western/imperialist—proved very effective among many of Iran's modern, educated professionals and students. More than 100,000 copies of his lectures were published and distributed, and thousands flocked regularly to hear him speak. For them, Shariati demonstrated the relevance of Shii Islam to modern life and to serve as the basis for a much-needed social revolution.

In sharp contrast to Shariati stands the champion of clerical rule, the Ayatollah Ruhollah Khomeini (d. 1989). If Shariati was the ideologue of the Iranian revolution, Khomeini was its living symbol and guide. An early, outspoken critic of the Shah, he had been forced to live in exile from the 1960s until his triumphant return from France in 1979. The freedom and independence he enjoyed in exile enabled him to remain vociferous in his call for reform and to cultivate his image and role as the symbol of opposition to the Shah, the outspoken voice and conscience of Islam and the Iranian people. From exile, he continued to guide his followers in Iran; his speeches and writings were smuggled into Iran on audiocassettes and pamphlets and widely distributed through the mullah-mosque network.

Khomeini, like many others in Iran and throughout the Islamic world, condemned Western imperialism, the Westernization of Muslim societies with its threat to Islamic identity and culture, and Israel, which he regarded as an outpost of American neocolonialism:

> The foul claws of imperialism have clutched at the heart of the lands of the people of the Quran, with our national wealth and resources being devoured by imperialism . . . with the poisonous culture of imperialism penetrating to the depths of towns and villages throughout the Muslim world, displacing the culture of the Quran. The sinister influence of imperialism is especially evident in Iran. Israel, the universally recognized enemy of Islam and the Muslims, at war with the Muslim peoples for years, has, with the assistance of the despicable government of Iran, penetrated the economic, political, and military affairs of the country; it must be said that Iran has become a military base for Israel which means, by extension, for America.[92]

In contrast to Bazargan and Shariati, Khomeini remained religiously conservative in his education, vocation, worldview, and lifestyle. While all three shared common national and religious concerns—the experience of government repression, opposition to the Shah, rejection of political quietism, and the struggle for Islamically oriented sociopolitical reforms—Khomeini's outlook was shaped by his clerical background and interests. For Khomeini, the comprehensiveness of Islam and its integral relationship to society were inseparably linked to clerical dominance:

> Islam has a system and a program for all the different affairs of society: the form of government and administration, the regulation of people's dealings with each other, the relations of state and people, relations with foreign states and all other political and economic matters. . . . The mosque has always been the center of leadership and command, of examination and analysis of social problems.[93]

However, religious traditionalism did not preclude change and development in his interpretation of Islam. His qualified acceptance of monarchy during the 1940s was replaced in the 1970s by his unequivocal declaration that Islam is fundamentally opposed to monarchy. Khomeini's lectures in 1970 on Islamic government not only reiterated the inseparability of Islam and politics and clerical involvement in politics, as advocated by Bazargan and a number of Shii ayatollahs, but also argued that in the absence of the Imam, the clergy should not only advise the government on Islamic matters but rule directly. His doctrine of jurist rule asserted that since an Islamic government is one based upon Islamic law, the most qualified to rule would be an expert (*faqih*) or group of experts in Islamic law. However, Khomeini's opinions would have remained academic if the political situation had not deteriorated so badly in the mid-1970s. The increasingly repressive measures of the Shah transformed an opposition movement demanding reform into a resistance movement, organized under the umbrella of Islam, calling for a new political and social order. This movement comprised diverse groups in the Iranian political and ideological spectrum: from secularists to Islamic activists, from liberal democrats to Marxists. In 1970, the Ayatollah had spoken of an Islamic revolution that might take centuries; he could not foresee that events in 1979 would lead to his triumphant return to Iran and the establishment of the Islamic Republic of Iran.

While the Shah provided a common foe and Islam a unifying symbol, the sharp differences among revolutionary factions came to the surface shortly after the downfall of the Pahlavi dynasty. The rupture occurred as Iran's new leaders turned to the task of implementing its Islamic identity and ideology—establishing the Islamic republic and drafting its first constitution. A sharp division existed over the role of the clergy and the implementation of Islamic law. Liberal constitutionalists, among whom were secularists, Islamic modernists like Mehdi Bazargan, and religious authorities like the Ayatollah Shariatmadari, believed that the clergy should have an indirect role in government as members of a committee who could veto any law judged contrary to Islam. The second camp, led by the Ayatollah Khomeini and supported by a majority of the mullahs, advocated direct rule by religious leaders and the full implementation of traditional Islamic law.

After an initial struggle, Khomeini and his clerical followers prevailed. They consolidated their power and dominated Iran's government, parliament, judiciary, military, Revolutionary Guards, the press, and media. Censorship of news and publishing, ideological control of university curricula and professors, prohibitions on alcohol, gambling, drug use, and sexual offenses were all enforced in the name of Islam. Islamic courts and judges sentenced and punished those convicted of offenses ranging from drug smuggling and homosexuality to political dissent. Dissent, both Islamic and secular, was silenced. Competing interpretations of Islam were often no longer tolerated but eclipsed or displaced by a doctrinaire ideology which left little place for the followers of Islamically oriented laity like Shariati and Bazargan or for dissenting clerics. Many were driven out of office, fled the country, imprisoned, or executed. The Ayatollah Shariatmadari was defrocked and other clerics silenced.

During the first decade of Iran's existence, Khomeini and his clerical cohorts defined the nature and limits of Iran's Islamic identity and ideology and oversaw its implementation. Even then, sharp differences in Islamic domestic and foreign policy often existed. Postrevolutionary attempts to articulate and implement an Islamic alternative to the Shah's modernization program revealed deep divisions between those who advocated private sector freedom and those who favor radical socioeconomic reforms through state control of the economy. The clerically dominated Council of Guardians, influenced by merchants (*bazaaris*) who had been the financial backbone of the *ulama* and the revolution, consistently vetoed reform legislation as contrary to Islamic law.

Strong differences of interpretation have also occurred over the meaning of export of the revolution, which is rooted in the Quranic mandate to realize and propagate God's message. This principle is embodied in the first constitution of the Islamic Republic's commitment "to perpetuate the revolution both at home and abroad." Khomeini's espousal of a nonsectarian, universalist Islam, transcending Sunni–Shii differences, informed Iran's advocacy of a universal Islamic revolution to liberate all the oppressed and justified Khomeini's outspoken leadership on Islamic issues internationally. This doctrine was used to justify the incitement of revolts in Saudi Arabia, Bahrain, and Iraq; to support the Moro in the southern Philippines; to legitimate Iranian intervention in Lebanon; and to justify Khomeini's condemnation of Salman Rushdie.

Lebanon

The dominant reality of Lebanon for the past fourteen years has been its civil war. Lebanon also offers the second major example of militant Shii politics. Ironically, the two Middle Eastern countries most torn by violence and civil strife, Iran and Lebanon, were once regarded as the most stable, modern, and Western-oriented. It was not uncommon for Lebanon to be referred to as the Switzerland of the Middle East or for Beirut to be described as the Paris of the Middle East (reflecting the influence of French culture and fashions). Moreover, Beirut's banks, shops, boutiques, cinemas, and leading universities (the French Jesuit Université St. Joseph and the American University of Beirut) reflected Western influence and offered the best that was available in the United States and Europe.

Shii organizations such as AMAL, Hizbullah, and al-Jihad, which have mobilized Shii Muslim in protest and revolutionary activities, have been major actors in the Lebanese civil war. Since the late 1970s, a Shii community, long a distant third in political and economic power in a state dominated by Maronite Christians and Sunni Muslims, has become a formidable force. Domestic political developments in Lebanon reflect a situation in which one could conclude that:

> Without question, the most important development in Lebanon during the 1980's has been the emergence of an assertive, politicized, but riven Shiite community.[94]

The Shii of Lebanon existed in a confessional or sectarian state whose government was based on the balancing of several major religio-political communities or confessional groups' interests.

Historically, with the division of the Ottoman Empire after World War I, Lebanon had been placed under French rule, known as the French Mandate. The French subsequently oversaw the creation of modern Lebanon, whose government was based on an informal agreement, the National Pact of 1943, designed to assure the dominance of France's Christian Lebanese allies. A sectarian system of government, based on the census of 1932 which identified the Maronite Christians as the largest community, institutionalized the relative population strengths of Lebanon's major religious communities: Maronites, Sunni Muslims, Shii Muslims, and Druze. Thus, the president was to be a Maronite, the prime minister a Sunni Muslim, and the speaker of the chamber of deputies a Shii. Key positions in the government, cabinet, parliament, ministries, and military were apportioned along confessional, or sectarian, lines. Within this system, the Shii minority were a distant third to the more numerous and prosperous Christian and Sunni Muslim communities. However, Shii prominence in political affairs increased in the 1970s, and a major catalyst for this turn of events was an Iranian-born and -educated Shii cleric, Imam Musa Sadr. As the Ayatollah Khomeini had come to symbolize the hopes and aspirations of Iran's dispossessed, so too the charismatic Musa Sadr came to represent the reinvigorated and mobilized Lebanese Shii community.

Musa Sadr had come from Iran to Lebanon in 1959. The Lebanese Shii were primarily rural, poor, and disorganized. By the early 1970s, he had become the leading Shii cleric in Lebanon, a major force in organizing a weak, disparate community. Musa Sadr appealed to Shii identity and community solidarity to sustain a populist movement for social and political reform, and in 1974 he organized the Movement of the Disinherited. Musa Sadr reinterpreted Shii religious history and belief. Early Shii suffering at the hands of Sunni rulers was likened to the tyranny, discrimination, and exploitation suffered under the Christian-dominated Lebanese political system. He identified AMAL ("Hope": the militia which had evolved from this movement) with the liberation of

Lebanon's oppressed and disinherited. Demonstrations and strikes were utilized to press the government to modify the Lebanese political system to better reflect the new social realities of a Lebanon in which Muslims, not Christians, were now the dominant population. AMAL organized the Shii and led rallies and marches to protest socioeconomic injustice and the Israeli military threat in south Lebanon. Although he had initially rejected force and insisted on nonviolent means to protest social injustices, the political realities of Lebanon led him to alter his position. In a land of militias and escalating sectarian warfare, AMAL, originally organized to provide the Shii community with protection, to defend the rights of a community who had now grown in numbers to become Lebanon's largest confessional group, became radicalized.

Five events precipitated a radicalization of Shii politics: the Lebanese Civil War of 1975, the disappearance of Musa Sadr in 1978, the Iranian revolution of 1978–79, and the Israeli invasions of Lebanon in 1978 and 1982. The failure of Lebanon's Christian-dominated government to acknowledge the changed demographics (no census was taken after 1932!) and redistribute power more equitably to reflect a Muslim (Sunni and Shii combined) majority and of the Christian and Sunni Muslim leadership to respond to the needs of a Shii community that had grown from 18 percent in 1968 to 30 percent, or approximately one million, of the population, plus the presence of significant numbers of Palestinians in the south had exacerbated an already fragile and volatile political situation.

The mysterious disappearance of Musa Sadr while visiting Muammar Qaddafi in Libya in 1978 transformed Musa Sadr from a symbol of Shii protest to a cult hero and breathed new life into AMAL. Like the Ayatollah Khomeini, Musa Sadr had cultivated his religious persona, often identifying himself with the early Imams, in particular Ali and the martyred Husayn. Also like Khomeini, he did not try to prevent his followers from calling him Imam. Indeed, many came to call him "Imam of the Disinherited." Musa Sadr's disappearance fit nicely into the Shii paradigm of martyrdom and the occultation of the Hidden Twelfth Imam. He was transformed into a religious hero, a worthy descendant of Husayn. Many maintained that Imam Musa Sadr had not died; he had merely disappeared and would return.

The Iranian revolution and the Israeli invasions of 1978 and 1982 significantly contributed to the further deterioration of Lebanon's war-torn politics and the radicalization of the Shii. The impact of the Iranian revolution, with its heightened sense of Shii pride and identity, testified to the power of Shii faith and ideology and verified the politicized Shii model of resistance and its promise of ultimate triumph. However, by

1982, AMAL, under Musa Sadr's lay successor, Nabih Berri, had increasingly pursued a moderate, pragmatic policy, maintaining relations with Lebanon's Christian-dominated government and Western powers. Its leadership, rhetoric, and agenda were less Islamic and more that of a nationalist organization, pursuing full Shii political and socioeconomic parity within Lebanon's pluralistic, multiconfessional state. AMAL did not call for a Shii-dominated state, an Islamic state, or the introduction of Islamic law. The Israeli invasion of Lebanon and the massacres at Shatilla and Sabra in 1982, attributed to a Christian militia, discredited Berri in the eyes of more alienated and radicalized Shii youth and Iranian-influenced militants. They rejected AMAL's accommodationist attitude, charging that Berri had collaborated with the Christian government, Israel, and the United States, which has long been regarded as an ally and sponsor of both the Lebanese and Israeli governments.

With the assistance of Iran, radical Islamic organizations like Islamic AMAL, Hizbullah, and Islamic Jihad emerged in Baalbek, a Shii center in the Beqaaa Valley. Calling for an "Islamic revolution," Iran offered a more militant, confrontational, and explicitly Islamic alternative to the Shii of Lebanon. Like Islamic AMAL, which broke with Berri and opted for a more explicit Islamic identification, all rejected AMAL's secular nationalism and, influenced by the example of Iran, called for an Islamic republic for Lebanon and the implementation of a more Islamic way of life. The groundwork had been well prepared. Politically, many Shiites had come to perceive or experience a seemingly endless deterioration of their position and the failure of moderation to achieve a more equitable situation. Ideologically, like the Ayatollah Khomeini, Lebanese Shii religious leaders such as Musa Sadr and Shaykh Muhammad Husayn Fadlallah (Hizbullah's ideologue and adviser) had been engaged in a powerful reinterpretation of Shii Islam which supported a populist, militant, political activist movement of resistance and protest.

Hizbullah, the Party of God, had sprung up in the wake of the Iranian revolution with the support of Iranian Revolutionary Guards ostensibly sent to Lebanon to fight Israel. Its motto ("the Party of God will surely be the victors") was taken from Quran (58:22), for they perceived their battle as that of the Party of God against the Party of Satan (Quran 58:19–20)—whether Christian militias, Israeli forces, Western imperialism, or even AMAL. Members of Hizbullah regarded the Iranian revolution as tangible proof of God's guidance and assistance in the battle against tyranny and injustice. Thus, Iran and Khomeini provided a model to be emulated. Posters of the Ayatollah Khomeini, who was often referred to as leader of the faith, adorned the houses and streets of Shii areas; his words were often reported and quoted. Indeed, Khomeini's politicized interpretation of Islam, emphasis on the special role of the clergy as the elite vanguard for reform, and condemnation of foreign imperialists, especially the United States, are essential principles of Hizbullah's ideological worldview. Quoting Khomeini, Hizbullah ideologues maintained that "the original objective of the imperialist countries is to destroy the Holy Koran and to obliterate it, and to destroy Islam and the Muslim ulama (leadership) . . . and their plan is to keep [Islamic countries] backward, and in the name of encouraging education . . . they have suppressed religious schools."[95]

Pro-Iranian Shii clerics provided leadership and guidance for Hizbullah. Their mosques became centers for recruitment, training, and mobilization. The clerics attracted students and young professionals, who regarded their situation as so desperate as to justify armed struggle (jihad) in their defense against political oppression, imperialism, and social injustice. Iran provided training, arms, and substantial financial aid to Hizbullah, supported its military operations as well as such religio-social activities as the building of mosques and the reconstruction of war-torn homes, hospitals, clinics, schools, and farms.

Throughout the 1980s Hizbullah grew to be an umbrella group with which a variety of smaller groups, such as the shadowy Islamic Jihad, allied themselves. Within the shifting alliances of Lebanon's Civil War, the various groups have fought Christian militias, Israeli and Syrian troops, and AMAL, and engaged in kidnappings, hijackings, and bombings such as those of the American and French embassies as well as the barracks of multinational forces in Beirut in 1983.

Despite Iranian influence among the Shii, Islamic movements in Lebanon are Lebanese in leadership, ideology, politics, and direction. They are run by Lebanese and possess agendas which reflect their constituency and are tailored to the Lebanese reality. In present-day Lebanon, as in Northern Ireland or Israel, membership in a (religious) communal group or organization may simply designate political affiliation or identification and have little to say about whether a person is a practicing Muslim, Christian, or Druze. The motivations and ideological orientations of individuals and organizations vary widely, and the resurgence of the Shii community encompasses a diversity of religious viewpoints. Thus, AMAL and Hizbullah have represented quite different applications of Shii identity and belief in Lebanon. Although inspired by the memory of an Iranian-born charismatic cleric, AMAL has stood for a more pluralistic, multiconfessional state and lay-dominated organization and has carefully eschewed a primarily Islamic path for Lebanon. Hizbullah and its associated groups have more rigorously espoused an Islamic identity, ideology, clerical leadership, and goal.

Saudi Arabia

A visitor to Saudi Arabia is initially struck by a host of images that seem to confirm the Islamic character of the state—a seemingly endless number of mosques; a society that seems to stop at prayer time as shops close and the faithful, wherever they are, face Mecca to pray; prohibition of alcohol; women veiled and segregated in public life. Saudi Arabia provides a striking and at times paradoxical example of a traditional yet modern self-styled Islamic state. The Saudis proudly proclaim their Islamic heritage and traditions. Religion is the basis of Saudi Arabia's national identity, society, law, and politics. The House of Saud has relied on Islam to unite and rule its tribal society, to legitimate its authority and institutions, and to assert its leadership in the Islamic world. Saudi Arabia encompasses an area that is the original birthplace of Muhammad and the homeland of Islam. The Saudis are the keepers of the holy cities of Mecca and Medina and guardians of the annual pilgrimage to Mecca.

Although the modern Kingdom of Saudi Arabia was officially established as a nation-state in 1932, its roots date back to the eighteenth-century Islamic revivalist Wahhabi movement, with the alliance of religion and political power under Muhammad ibn Abd al-Wahhab and Muhammad ibn Saud. The Saudi flag, which combines the Muslim confession of faith ("There is no god but the God . . .") and the crossed swords of the House of Saud and ibn Abd al-Wahhab, reflects this union of faith and politics. The Wahhabi spirit and strict interpretation of Islam have remained a prominent force in Saudi politics and society.

Islam provides the ideological basis for Saudi rule. The Quran is its constitution, and the state is governed by Islamic law, applied by a Sharia court system whose judges and legal advisers are *ulama*. The House of Saud has been careful to cultivate its relationship with the *ulama*, the guardians of Islamic law, through intermarriage and state patronage. The monarchy itself has been justified or rationalized by maintaining that the king himself is subject to the Sharia, God's law. For example, the removal of an inept ruler, King Saud ibn Abd al-Aziz, in 1964, and the transfer of power to his brother, King Faisal, were legitimized by a ruling from the *ulama* which cited the Islamic legal principle of "public interest." Thus, the ruler, government, law, and judiciary are in principle Islamically rooted and accountable.

The Saudis have utilized other traditional but informal Islamic institutions, such as religious officials or police, who in the early Islamic era supervised public markets and morals, to support their rule. Today, Committees for the Enforcement of Good and the Prohibition of Evil monitor proper "Islamic" public behavior; making sure that shops close during prayer times, the fast of Ramadan is observed, alcohol is not consumed, men and women dress and act modestly.

Islam has been employed by the House of Saud both domestically and internationally. Religious interpretations and justifications have been used to outlaw political parties and trade unions as un-Islamic while at the same time to justify the infusion of modern technology and social change. Thus, while tradition has been source of strict separation of the sexes in public life and the veiling of women, the limits of revelation and the application of the rather rigid and strict Hanbali interpretation of Islamic law have paradoxically proven quite flexible. Islam has been utilized to demonstrate the compatibility of religion and modernization. The Quran and the traditions of the Prophet have been interpreted to justify using foreign workers and to gain acceptance of everything from television and automobiles to women's education. Precedents in Islamic history, such as a caliph's use of complaint or grievance courts, have provided the basis for the Saudis to expand their judiciary and to create civil or complaint courts to handle matters not covered by Islamic law in the past. While the Quran and Islamic law are strictly enforced, reforms have been implemented where revelation is silent. In these areas, the Saudi government has claimed the right to interpret (ijtihad) and apply Islam. In the name of Islamic legal principles, such as public interest, regulations or royal decrees (as distinguished from human legislation, which is technically proscribed) can introduce modern commercial regulations or laws.

Internationally, Islam has been a factor in Saudi Arabia's diplomacy and foreign policy. When Egypt's Gamal Abd al-Nasser sought to extend his influence in the Arab world as the leader of a pan-Arab nationalist movement in the 1960s and to present Arab socialism as an "Islamic socialism," King Faisal responded to the challenge of pan-Arabism by invoking Islam as a counterideology and placing himself at the head of an alternative pan-Islamic movement. Saudi–Egyptian rivalry for leadership in the Arab world became an occasion for the king to reinforce Saudi leadership in the broader Islamic world as well. If Nasser spoke of the Arab nation, Faisal countered with the Islamic nation. Faisal stressed the transnational nature of the Islamic community or "Islamic nation," calling for a pan-Islamic alliance based upon common faith, doctrine, and unity which transcended all nationalism:

> It is in these moments, when Islam is facing many undercurrents that are pulling Muslims left and right, east and west, that we need time for more co-operation and closer ties to enable us to face all problems and

difficulties that obstruct our way as an Islamic nation, believing in God, His Prophet, and His Laws.[96]

King Faisal set Saudi Arabia on a course of Islamic leadership which has lasted to the present day. The king emphasized his role and that of Saudi Arabia as protectors of the holy sites and, by extension, of Islam and the interests of the Islamic world. Ideologically, Saudi Arabia has cultivated its image as the defender of Islam against Arab and Islamic radicalism (whether it be the brand of Nasser, Qaddafi, or Khomeini), Zionism, and atheistic communism. A host of international Islamic organizations, such as the Muslim World League, the Organization of the Islamic Conference (OIC), and the Islamic Development Bank (IDB), have been established, based in and funded in large part by Saudi Arabia. The Muslim World League, based in Mecca but with branches throughout the world, seeks to promote Saudi Arabia's interpretation of Islam; it funds programs, conferences, and other Islamic activities and projects. The OIC fosters intergovernment cooperation among Islamic governments, and the IDB supports economic development projects in Muslim countries. Over the years the Saudis have used their oil wealth to support and spread Islam and in the process assert their Islamic credentials and leadership, often in contention with leaders of other Muslim countries like Nasser, Qaddafi, or the Ayatollah Khomeini. Substantial amounts of money have been dispersed to governments and organizations throughout the Muslim world to build mosques, schools, and clinics, to subsidize the salaries of mosque officials and promote missionary activities worldwide, to translate and distribute Islamic literature, to encourage and provide financial incentives to Muslim governments to further Islamize their societies, and to support Islamic organizations like the Muslim Brotherhood and the Jamaat-i-Islami.

The Saudi appeal to Islam has proven to be a two-edged sword. Islam has been used as a yardstick by which opponents of the House of Saud have attacked the government. This happened twice dramatically in 1979, when Saudi Arabia was rocked by two explosive events. First, on November 20 the Grand Mosque in Mecca was seized for two weeks by several hundred militants who denounced the Saudi monarchy, repudiated the kingdom's modernization program as contrary to Islam, condemned the *ulama* for collaborating with the government, and declared the advent of a true Islamic state. The royal family was careful to obtain an Islamic legal ruling from the *ulama* requesting that government forces rescue the mosque and restore order. Second, while still reeling from the seizure of the Grand Mosque, riots broke out on November 27 among some of the 250,000 Shii in Saudi Arabia's oil-rich Eastern Province, where they constitute 35 percent of the population. Inspired by the Iranian revolution, the pent-up emotions and grievances of members of Saudi Arabia's Shii minority, who felt discriminated against by their Sunni rulers and called for a fairer distribution of oil wealth and services, had exploded earlier in the year when Khomeini had returned triumphant to Iran. Khomeini's denunciation of Saudi Arabia and the Gulf governments as un-Islamic, and of their military and economic ties with the United States as "American Islam," were persistent:

> The ruling regime in Saudi Arabia wears Muslim clothing, but it actually represents a luxurious, frivolous, shameless way of life, robbing funds from the people and squandering them, engaging in gambling, drinking parties, and orgies. Would it be surprising if people follow the path of revolution . . . ?[97]

Throughout the 1980s, Saudi Arabia found itself in contention with Iran—two competing interpretations of Islam and two competitors for leadership in the Islamic world. The situation was exacerbated by Saudi support of Iraq in the Iran–Iraq war. Iran used the pilgrimage to Mecca to propagate its revolutionary message and to reject the Saudi claim to be keepers of the holy sites. Iranian pilgrims, carrying posters of Khomeini and chanting anti-U.S., -Soviet, and -Israel slogans, clashed with Saudi security forces in 1982. Tensions climaxed in 1987, when more than four hundred people were killed in a confrontation between Iranian pilgrims and Saudi security forces.

As a result of the Islamic revival, the Iranian revolution, and Saudi domestic politics, the Saudi monarchy became even more attentive to its Islamic image in the 1980s. Religious symbolism and social values were reemphasized. Sensitive to criticisms of the un-Islamic character of monarchies, King Fahd replaced the title "Royal Majesty" with "Servant of the Holy Places." Greater assurances were given that the pace of Saudi development would be controlled and selective so there would be no compromise of Islamic social values. The influx of foreigners was more strictly controlled, as was their observance of prohibitions on alcohol and modest dress and behavior in public. At times the religious police became more assertive in their enforcement of public morality.

Despite Saudi Arabia's creation as an Islamic state and its deliberate Islamic profile, the House of Saud has not been immune to challenges to its legitimacy and leadership domestically and internationally. Like most contemporary Muslim governments and societies, it has experienced the impact of the resurgence of Islam.

Conclusion

The hopes and euphoria engendered by the Arab oil boycott of 1973 and reinforced by the success of the Iranian revolution in 1979 have been challenged by the sobering realities of the 1980s: the dramatic drop of oil revenues and its socioeconomic impact on Muslim societies, the devastating consequences of the Iran–Iraq war, the disintegration of war-torn Lebanon, the all too common specter of Muslim fighting Muslim. Islamic revivalism has often meant government manipulation of Islam to delay or control elections, to ban or restrict political parties, to impose press and media censorship, or to suppress political and religious dissent. The vast moderate majority of Islamic activists, despite their growth and achievements, have often been overshadowed by a radical minority who assassinate, kidnap, and bomb in the name of Islamic political and social justice.

Yet, several important points must be remembered when viewing developments in the Muslim world. The process of modernization in the West extended over several centuries. The establishment of modern states, the creation of a sense of national identity and political legitimacy, the development of appropriate economic and social institutions took time and experimentation. The process was accompanied by heated debates, riots, and revolutions (the American, French, and Russian). Similarly, the accommodation of religion and modernity (religion and science, revelation and reason) and the resolution of issues of modernization (the changing family, role of women in religion and society, sexual, corporate, and medical ethics) continue to challange the faith and unity of modern Judaeo-Christian communities. Issues of political and cultural identity and of religious values remain important concerns in the West today, inspiring a variety of religious reform and revivalist movements: among them, Christian and Jewish revivalism in the United States and liberation theology and Christian-based communities in Central America.

The political and economic realities of the post–World War II independence period have hampered the process of self-determination in many parts of the Muslim world that have had only decades, rather than the several centuries enjoyed by the West, to cope with the challenges of modernity. Until political and educational reforms permit a more broad-based, consensual approach to the development of indigenously rooted national political systems and the resolution of issues of Islamic reform and change, Muslim governments and societies, like much of Middle East politics, will remain fragile, precarious, and potentially volatile.

6

Islam and Change: Issues of Authority and Interpretation

Modern Islam exhibits a rich, and at times bewildering, array of interpretations. Indeed, some observers maintain that there is not one but many Islams. Many devout Muslims take issue with this, and instead assert that there is only one Islam and that the distinction must be made between the one Islam and the many Muslims. Perhaps it is more useful to say that Islam, like most religious traditions, has been mediated through many interpretations and applications throughout its history. This continues to be the case today. The many interpretations and uses of Islam by governments, movements, and individuals have produced a diversity of ideologies, actors, organizations, and programs. Islam in recent years has been used to legitimate monarchies (Morocco and Saudi Arabia), military regimes (Pakistan, Libya, the Sudan), and a theocracy (Iran). Self-styled Islamic regimes have spanned the political spectrum, from radical socialism in Libya to the conservative Saudi monarchy. Islamic movements display a similar diversity; composition is clerical and lay, traditionalist and modernist, educated and illiterate, political activist and Sufi mystic, moderate and extremist. The many faces and forms of Islam raise two fundamental questions: Whose Islam? and What Islam?

Whose Islam? Who is to interpret, formulate, and implement Islam? In the past, the traditional Sunni religious leadership (*ulama*) claimed the prerogative to interpret Islam, while the caliph was to ensure its implementation. In Shii Islam, the *ulama* were sources of guidance and emulation in the absence of the Imam. In contemporary times, Muslim governments and individual rulers like Egypt's Anwar Sadat, Libya's Colonel Muammar Qaddafi, the Sudan's Colonel Jafar al-Numayri, Pakistan's General Zia ul-Haq, and the Ayatollah Khomeini have themselves interpreted Islam in order to enhance their legitimacy and policies. At the same time, they have been criticized by others as using Islam to justify authoritarian rule, suppress political parties, and impose censorship. Their Muslim critics regard this as a manipulation of religion through the selective use of a "negative Islam" of punishments, taxes, and restrictions. One can see this problem in the suppression of dissent in postrevolutionary Iran, where the clergy routed not only the Shah but also fellow Islamic revolutionaries, such as Mehdi Bazargan, the first prime minister of the Islamic republic, and Abol-Hasan Bani Sadr, its first president. Although questions of power precipitated the clashes, underlying the confrontation were distinctively different traditionalist and modernist visions. Pakistan offers another example. While General Zia ul-Haq's coup d'état in 1977 and pledge to introduce an Islamic system of government were initially welcomed, many came to decry his "negative Islam," exemplified by the postponement of elections, banning of political parties, and martial law regulations—all in the name of Islam. Similarly, the introduction of Islamic laws (the September laws of 1983) and military courts, the punishment of non-Muslims for violating the ban on alcohol, and the execution of the leader of the Republican Brothers for apostasy by the Sudan's Jafar al-Numayri brought criticism from Muslims and non-Muslims alike.

Self-proclaimed Muslim leaders have been opposed by others in the name of Islam. These organizations have offered their own programs for Islamic reform. Some have resorted to violence to achieve their goals. Their critics often charge that, like political leaders, they are manipulating religion for political ends. Since Islam lacks a centralized teaching authority or organized hierarchy, there is no obvious answer to the question, "Whose Islam?"

What Islam? What interpretation(s) of Islam is normative and appropriate? A central issue here is the relationship of tradition to modernization. Does a return to Islam mean the reclamation and implementation of the traditional legal blueprint of Muslim society in all its details, or does it mean a return to the sources of Islam, to those principles and values on which new laws and institutions may be constructed? In classical terms, is the implementation of Islam in state and society simply to be a process of imitation of the past (*taqlid*) or of reinterpretation (*ijtihad*) and reform of tradition? Is there one classical Islamic model, or are there many possible models for development? If a new synthesis that provides continuity with the past is to be achieved, how will this be accomplished? Who will formulate it—the head of state, the *ulama,* lay experts? How will the new forms be approved and implemented: by a ruler, a clerical leader like the Ayatollah Khomeini or committee of *ulama,* an elected national assembly?

Varying attitudes toward modernization continue to exist, but the reality of modern change has been accepted. Radio, television, oil technology, computers are part and parcel of Muslim life. Even conservative religious leaders freely utilize loudspeakers to call the faithful to prayer, and cassette recordings are used for religious education or political agitation. The key questions are: What change, and how much change, is possible? What is the Islamic rationale for change? Whose interpretation of Islam should prevail?

The history of modern Islam has challenged many presuppositions and expectations. The prevailing wisdom was that modernization required the separation of religion from public life, as modernizing societies progressively and inevitably became secularized. The very process of modernization, which includes the impact of reason, science, and technology, was seen as encouraging and enhancing this secularization process. For many, the survival of religion in the post-Enlightenment world required that faith come to grips with reason and, through a process of reform, yield some ground. As the more rationalist approach of modern biblical criticism and critical theological scholarship resulted in a substantial reformulation of faith and belief in Christianity and Judaism, many predicted that if Islam did not follow suit, it could not hope to remain relevant to modern generations of Muslims. Islamic revivalism, like some forms of Christian revivalism, has countered and discredited such a uniform, evolutionary view of historical change and development. Revivalism has been most visible in countries where modernism had been strongest. Moreover, technology and modern education have often been used to reinforce rather than undermine belief and practice. Whereas in the past, religious leaders might reject radio and television, today they harness the media and the cassette to preach and disseminate, to educate and proselytize. The message of Islam is no longer mediated solely through local religious leaders. As any visitor to the Muslim world is quick to observe, Islamic teachings are now transmitted through both the government-controlled mass media and the cassettes, books, and pamphlets available in markets and mosques or, where necessary, secretly printed and distributed by underground organizations. The writings of such ideologues and activists as Hasan al-Banna, Sayyid Qutb, Mawlana Mawdudi, Yusuf Qardawi, Ali Shariati, Ayatollah Khomeini, and many others are now available in inexpensive translations or in pamphlets that summarize and popularize their ideas. Similarly, the sermons and speeches of popular preachers are transmitted across the Muslim world via audio and videocassettes so that their influence is not restricted to a particular locale or nation. Because of the mass media and modern technology, Muslims in villages, towns, and cities are no longer solely dependent on their local imams and *ulama* or the state-run media for their understanding of Islam. Instead, they are exposed to a diversity of interpretations. There are a variety of voices available internationally through official and unofficial channels, above and below ground.

Moreover, although most Muslim countries adopted Western models of political, economic, educational, and legal development, their citizens have not fully appropriated intellectually and psychologically their implicit values. While an elite minority has accepted and become fully acculturated to a Western secular worldview and system of values, the majority has not internalized a secular, rationalist outlook. The hold of tradition cuts across the spectrum of classes and occupations, encompassing a cross section of society: craftsmen and merchants, bureaucrats and teachers, judges and physicians, professors and lawyers. An appreciation of those factors that have reinforced and indeed sacralized tradition in Islam is important to understand both the continued strength of tradition and its impact on change.

A series of developments during the early formative centuries produced a sacralized tradition in which the line between revelation and human interpretation is often blurred. Time-honored tribal tradition, the accumulated wisdom and practice (*sunna*) of Arabia, was Islamized and sacralized. Its authority was attributed not to a human community but to God's revelation. In particular the notion of tribal *sunna* gave way to that of Prophetic Sunna, the practice of Muhammad; the authoritative basis for the Muslim community's practice was grounded in what the Prophet said, did, or permitted. Tribal tradition was replaced by "Islamic" tradition. The development of Islamic law and the notion that it was the product of God's revelation (Scripture and Prophetic tradition) and not human wisdom further reinforced the belief that Islamic tradition was an expression and source of God's divinely revealed law. The tendency of some pious Muslims to seek approbation for their beliefs and practices by attributing them to Prophetic traditions obscured the human dimension or source of certain beliefs and practices. For many, Islamic law was no longer viewed as the product of God's revelation and human interpretation. Instead, it was regarded by the majority of the *ulama* as the divinely revealed, perfect blueprint for society. By the tenth century most Sunni jurists had come to believe that since the guidelines for individual and community life were established, personal interpretation (*ijtihad*) was no longer necessary or permitted. Society was simply to emulate or follow (*taqlid*) the guidelines of sacred tradition as delineated and preserved in Islamic law. Thus, tradition was effectively standardized and sanctified by grounding it in revelation and sacred law. As such, it became a strong source of community identity and cohesion, providing an underlying sense of unity, certitude, and guidance amid the diversity of local cultures and popular religious practices that characterized the lands of Islam. However, these benefits were obtained at a cost, a tendency to forget the dynamism, diversity, and human creativity that had contributed to the development of Islam. The human input into the formation of Islamic tradition and law (the role of reason, local customs, the selective assimilation and Islamization of non-Muslim beliefs and institutions) became obscured as later generations preserved and transmitted a more static, romanticized sense of Islamic history. Islamic tradition became relatively fixed and sacrosanct; future generations were simply to follow Islam's way of life, the straight path of Islam, as authoritatively and comprehensively set forth in Islamic law. Substantive change or innovation (*bida*) was regarded as heresy, departure from the revealed law or practice of the community.

The sacrosanct nature of tradition in Islam is of primary significance; it serves as a bedrock of faith, an inspirational reality for traditionalists, and a major hurdle for modern reformers. Two general approaches or attitudes to Islamic renewal and reform can be identified: (1) a traditionalist desire to restore an early Islamic ideal; and (2) a reformist call for renovation or reconstruction through Islamic, as distinct from Western, reform. Both approaches emphasize reliance on Islamic sources. A key difference between traditionalist and reformers is their understanding and use of Islamic history and tradition as well as the nature and degree of change they advocate. All may agree on the desirability of renewal and reform; however, they part ways when they turn to such considerations as the direction, method, and degree of change as well as who can legitimize that change. For the sake of greater precision and clarity, it is useful to speak of four orientations or attitudes toward change, while recognizing that such categorization is arbitrary and that individuals and groups may overlap from one category to another. They are secularist, conservative, neotraditionalist (or neofundamentalist), and reformist (neomodernist).

Secularists advocate the restriction of religion to private affairs and its exclusion from public life. Sometimes dismissed as nonbelievers, most counter that they are religious but believe that religion should be restricted to private life (i.e., to prayer, fasting, pilgrimage, personal morality). They believe that mixing religion with politics is inappropriate and regard those who do so as manipulating Islam for political rather than religious ends.

The three religiously oriented positions, while differing in important ways, will be seen to overlap. All advocate a return to Islam; however, their meanings and methods vary. The conservative position is represented by the majority of the *ulama,* for whom Islam is expressed quite adequately and completely in the classical formulation of Islam, developed by the law schools during the early Islamic centuries, and embodied and preserved in the manuals and commentaries on Islamic law. When conservatives accept *ijtihad* in principle, they mean in practice the interpretation or application of traditional Islamic laws, not a reinterpretation that is open to change in law. Thus, they are not concerned with a process of reformulation that alters or replaces traditional Islamic law with new prescriptions. They see little need to go back directly to the Quran and Sunna to develop new answers. Islam is a closed cultural system fully articulated in the past. This interpretation of Islam, they say, governed the Muslim community down through the centuries and remains valid for today and for all ages. Therefore, conservatives emphasize following past tradition (*taqlid*) and are wary of innovation or deviation from it. Since Islamic law is the divinely revealed path, it is not the law that must change or modernize, but society that must conform to God's will. To the extent that there is a dichotomy between law and society, society has departed from the straight path of Islam. The remedy is not adaptation and change but a return to established norms. Though many of the *ulama* reluctantly accepted the imposition of modern legal reforms, they did so as an interim measure, since it left their own "ideal blueprint" intact to be reimplemented at a later time. Thus, in recent years, a major index of the revival has been renewed demands for the implementation of Islamic law in Iran, Pakistan, the Sudan, Egypt, and other areas. However, conservatives are prone to accept the established order and bide their time. They are followers, rather than activists, who often function as part of the religious establishment. The attitude of conservatives can be seen in countries like Pakistan and Egypt, where the majority of the *ulama* and their followers, though they may have voiced their objections from time to time, were willing to compromise, to cooperate, or to remain quiescent. When the climate changed in the late 1970s and 1980s, they were willing to join with those who called for the abrogation of modern family law reforms and the implementation of Islamic law. However, they did not wish or see the need for a reformulation of law; instead they advocated the restoration of traditional law. Similarly, when the mullahs who now dominate the Iranian parliament came to power, they abrogated Iran's Family Protection Act and implemented the Islamic laws found in medieval manuals. Where change does occur, it is gradual and by way of exception and in areas not covered by traditional law.

Neotraditionalists (or neofundamentalists) resemble conservatives in many respects. They, too, advocate a return to Islam and the Sharia. Neotraditionalists, however, while respecting the classical formulations of Islamic law, are not wedded to them. Instead, they claim the right to go back to the fundamental sources of Islam to reinterpret (ijtihad) and reapply them to contemporary needs and conditions. Movements like the Muslim Brotherhood and the Jamaat-i-Islami represent this approach. Like eighteenth-century revivalists, they believe that the law historically came to incorporate many un-Islamic practices. Thus, theirs is a movement to revitalize the community by a return to Islam's revealed sources. Neotraditionalists are more apt to become political activists, challenging the political and religious establishments. They are also more flexible than conservatives in their ability to adapt to change. Their leadership is often lay rather than clerical, as in the case of men like Hasan al-Banna, Sayyid Qutb, and Omar Telmasani of Egypt's Muslim Brotherhood, and Mawlana Mawdudi and Khurshid Ahmad of the Jamaat-i-Islami. Both neotraditionalists and conservatives reject Muslim secularism and Islamic modernism. Secularizers are regarded as agents of Western imperialism, native Westernizers who undermine Islam. Modernists are seen as well intentioned, but as having Westernized Islam and thus sacrificed its authentic vision and voice. Neotraditionalists insist that their reinterpretation of Islam is based solely on Islamic sources, which can provide the answers for Islamic society today. In contrast to Islamic modernism, neotraditionalism claims Islamic self-sufficiency rather than compatibility with the West. It seeks to emphasize those areas that distinguish Islam from the West: traditional prohibitions and punishments regarded as Quranically mandated (hudud, the "limits" set by God) for drinking alcohol, gambling, theft, fornication, adultery as well as the banning of banking interest, the payment of the zakat as a social welfare tax, and public separation of the sexes. While Westernization is rejected, selective modernization is not. Science and technology are cautiously appropriated and "Islamized," that is, subordinated to Islamic values and purposes. Western values and mores are rejected outright, since Islam is regarded as totally self-sufficient. This attitude is exemplified by the slogan for an international conference on Islamic economics held in Pakistan in 1982: "Islamic economics = economics minus Western values plus Islamic values." It is the neotraditionalists, rather than the conservatives, who have in recent decades ideologized Islam, attempting to interpret Islam as an alternative system for politics, law, education, and banking. Because of the variety that exists in human interpretation, a variety of interpretations of Islam are represented in neotraditionalist thought. Moreover, over a period of time, changes in leadership and circumstances have also led to differing Islamic positions on the same issue. While Muslim Brotherhood leaders like Sayyid Qutb and Mustapha al-Sibaii advanced Islamic socialism as a means to social justice in the late 1950s and early 1960s, today the Brotherhood tends to emphasize private ownership as the Islamic norm. In addition, the Brotherhood's original tendency to regard Arab nationalism and unity as a necessary stage in the revival of Islam has given way to an emphasis today on Islamic solidarity rather than Arab unity. Similarly, while Mawlana Mawdudi originally maintained that a ruler might regard *shura* (consultation) as simply informative and nonbinding, regardless of the number of its supporters, in later years he taught that such advice was binding.

Finally, the most adaptable group are Islamic reformers or neomodernists. They, too, are activists who look to the early Islamic period as embodying the normative ideal. Although they overlap with neotraditionalists, with whom they are often grouped, reformers distinguish more sharply between substance and form, between the principles and values of Islam's immutable revelation and the historically and socially conditioned institutions and practices that can and should be changed to meet contemporary conditions. They maintain that the regulations enshrined in the law books represent the understanding and interpretation of early jurists who applied the principles and values of Islam to their societies. They distinguish between the revealed immutable Sharia principles and laws contained in the corpus of traditional law from those regulations in Islamic law that are contingent and relative. The latter need to be reformulated in light of the needs of modern society. Many reformers, after an early traditional education, obtained advanced degrees at Western-oriented national universities or major universities in the United States, Great Britain, and France. Reformers include Iran's Sorbonne-educated Dr. Ali Shariati; Tunisia's Raschid Ghannoushi, leader of the Islamic Tendency Movement, renamed the Renaissance; Saudi Arabia's Dr. Abd al-Hamid Abu Sulayman, a University of Pennsylvania graduate and former secretary general of the World Assembly of Muslim Youth (WAMY); the Sudan's Sorbonne-trained Dr. Hassan al-Turabi, leader of the Muslim Brotherhood; the Oxford-educated great-grandson of the Mahdi of the Sudan, ex-Prime Minister Sadiq al-Mahdi; and Malaysia's Anwar Ibrahim, a graduate of the University of Malaya, former leader of ABIM (Malaysian Islamic Youth Movement), and currently minister of education. They neither opt for a Western secular orientation nor, in their view, are as Western-oriented as earlier generations of Islamic modernists. Unlike Muhammad Abduh and Sayyid Ahmad Khan, current Islamic reformers do not see themselves as responding to the West but instead as seeking in a more independent, authentic manner to meet the changing needs of their societies. They have learned from the West but do not wish to Westernize Muslim society. They remain Islamically oriented and emphasize commitment to "Islamic modernization," a future in which political and social development are more firmly rooted in past history and traditional values. But in contrast to many neotraditionalists, their rhetoric is not as critical of the West, and they are open to a selective process of assimilation. Reformers emphasize Islamization, a process by which Islamic principles and values are reapplied to meet the conditions of a new social milieu. Like neotraditionalists, they interpret Islam as a total ideology and seek to implement Islamic laws and establish Islamic banks. Compared to the neotraditionalists, they are more creative and wide-ranging in their reinterpretation and less tied to the traditional interpretations of the *ulama*. For this reason, the more conservative members of the *ulama* regard them as a threat to their authority. The *ulama* attack their "deviationism" and challenge reformers' qualifications as reinterpreters, maintaining that they alone are the qualified guardians of Islam.

The Ulama and Legal Reform

For the *ulama*, the modern period has brought a serious erosion of their traditional power and authority. Educational and legal reforms have greatly curtailed the dominant role of the *ulama* in education and law, restricted their sources of revenue, and raised serious questions about their competence and relevance. In most Muslim countries, modern secular educational systems have been set up alongside the traditional religious (*madrasa*) schools. Governments have tended to favor national schools, as have students who wish to be trained for and compete for jobs as modern professionals. More often than not, the *madrasas* have attracted less state support and fewer of the talented students. They are regarded as seminaries rather than as universities; their diplomas have a more limited value and usefulness. Similarly, the introduction of modern law has seen the rise of a new class of civil lawyers and judges, as the expertise of the *ulama* was restricted to family law courts. Whereas Islamic law was determined by religious scholars, modern legal reform has been accomplished through the action of rulers or parliamentary bodies, most of whose members were laymen, and enforced by civil courts. The *ulama*'s sense of disenfranchisement has been heightened by the abolition of religious endowments or their administration by government agencies, further reducing the economic independence and social role of the *ulama*. The state, by controlling revenues and paying salaries, has increased its control of religious institutions and social-welfare programs. Moreover, the greater value placed on modern education has also contributed to the general tendency to hold the *ulama* responsible for the ills of Muslim societies. Among Sunni Muslims in particular, secularists, Islamic modernists, and many neotraditionalists alike, the *ulama* have been regarded throughout much of the twentieth century as ignorant and obscurantist religious leaders incapable of providing necessary leadership. Like Sufism, the *ulama* are often regarded as a major cause of Muslim weakness and decline:

> [If] we ask ouselves how it was that a movement which at the beginning was revolutionary, progressive, and modern, could be turned into an agent of intellectual petrification and social stagnation, our reflection will lead us to two factors which were not present in Islam orginally, but which appeared together during the ages of the decline of Islamic civilization and became so firmly rooted that people imagined them to be among the fundamental principles of Islamic religion. The first was the appearance of a caste [the *ulama*] which monopolized the explanation of religion, claiming that it alone had the right to speak in the name of religion. . . . The second factor was the conviction of this caste that any laws, decisions, and solutions found in earlier religious sources were binding doctrines whose observance was obligatory, and which could not be modified or changed in any respects, whether they dealt with matters of doctrine or touched on affairs of daily life.[98]

The majority of *ulama* continue to maintain that they alone possess the requisite religious learning and thus ought to be the ultimate authority in determining what the law is or should be. The Ayatollah Khomeini has taken this argument one step further. He has asserted that since an Islamic state is one that is governed by the Sharia and since the *ulama* are the experts in law, government by the jurist-scholar is the best form of government, prior to the return of the Hidden Imam. Other religious leaders believe that national assemblies or parliaments should rely on a committee of *ulama* to advise them on matters of law. However, increasingly one finds Muslim voices who, while not directly challenging the existence of the *ulama* as an institution, do attempt to redefine their role and areas of competence. In order to limit the scope of *ulama* authority and justify lay input, they remind their followers that Islam knows no clergy and that all Muslims are equal and responsible before God. They argue that the title *alim* (pl. *ulama*) simply means "learned," one who has knowledge or is an expert. Thus, the title belongs properly not to a specific clerical group or class but to any Muslim who is qualified. This point is made subtly by Dr. Hassan al-Turabi, leader of the Sudan's Muslim Brotherhood and a former attorney general, in discussing the role of the *ulama* in parliamentary deliberations regarding legislation in an Islamic state:

> [T]he ulama should have a role in this procedure . . . not as the ultimate authority determining what the law is, but as advisors in the *shura* [assembly] to enlighten the Muslims as to the options which are open to them. What do I mean by ulama? The word historically has come to mean those versed in the legacy of religious [revealed] knowledge [*ilm*]. However, *ilm* does not mean that alone. It means anyone who knows anything well enough to relate it to God. Because all knowledge is divine and religious, a chemist, an engineer, an economist, or a jurist are all ulama. So the ulama in the broad sense, whether they are social or natural scientists, public opinion leaders, or philosophers, should enlighten society.[99]

However, for the majority of the *ulama*, any attempt to limit the area of their competence is to be resisted. Thus, the authority of the *ulama*, along with the nature of Islamic law and the question of legal reform, remain pivotal issues facing the Muslim community.

Revivalism has brought in its wake a widespread debate over the role of Islamic law in society today. Whatever the differences in orientation and agenda, central to Islamic revivalism throughout the Muslim world has been the demand for more Sharia law. The rule of thumb employed to judge the Islamic commitment and character of Muslim society has been the presence or absence of Islamic law. Moderates and radicals alike see the un-Islamic nature of their societies, as epitomized by Western-inspired legal codes, and clamor for implementation of Islamic law. Countries as different in degree of modernization and Westernization as Egypt, the Sudan, Libya, Iran, Pakistan, Nigeria, Malaysia, and Mauritania have had to face this issue. Many, out of conviction or political expediency, have declared the Sharia as *the* source of law even if such a claim has merely amounted to a constitutional provision rather than substantive change. Some, like Iran, Pakistan, Libya, and the Sudan, have enacted legislation to enforce traditional Islamic penalties for theft, fornication, and adultery. Even more have curbed gambling, night clubs, and alcohol consumption, and have intensified censorship of television and the cinema. Khomeini's Islamic republic has repudiated Iran's Family Protection Act, and conservative *ulama* in Pakistan have called for the repeal of Pakistan's Muslim Family Laws Ordinance. In both cases, past reforms have been deemed the work of Westernized governments and elites. Such actions frustrate Islamic reformers and confirm secularist fears that a return to the Sharia will mean a regressive enactment of traditional law. In fact, more often than not the introduction of Islamic laws has consisted of a restoration of traditional laws instead of a reinterpretation and reformulation of fresh laws and regulations. This is due to the predominance of traditional Islam and the continued failure to distinguish between Sharia, God's law in revelation, and *fiqh*, the understanding and elaboration of law by early jurists that produced the corpus of Islamic law. The former is believed to be divine in origin, while the latter is the product of revelation and human reasoning or interpretation. What are Muslim attitudes toward change? Must the implementation of Islamic law mean simply the restoration of traditional law? Does a "return to Islam" mean a replication of past norms, or can it be a process of reform informed by the Islamic legal tradition but not restricted to it? If legal change is to occur, who should oversee the process?

The real issue in law, as in sociopolitical change in general, is the question of change. How much change in the Islamic tradition is necessary; how much departure from tradition is legitimate? Conservatives see little need or justification for substantive change. Neotraditionalists, who accept *ijtihad* in principle, reinterpret sparingly in practice. They exhibit a "*taqlid* mentality." Though they accept the need and possiblity for change in principle, they so revere traditional law that they are loath to support substantive changes. The majority of Muslims tend to share these attitudes, and thus the resurgence of Islam has often tended to be a process of revivalism or restoration instead of reform through the reinterpretation and reformulation of tradition. Two important areas that reflect this attitude or outlook are the status of women and the rights of non-Muslims.

Women's Rights

During the twentieth century, significant changes have occurred in the lives of many Muslim women. Influenced by the West and the rationales of Islamic modernism, legal reforms, voting rights, and educational and employment opportunities have altered and broadened women's role in society. In addition to being wives and mothers, women have played a more prominent role in public life as teachers, lawyers, physicians, and cabinet ministers. Admittedly, many of these changes have affected a small proportion of the population and vary from one country or region to another. There is a world of difference between the impact of modernization (Westernization) on women in Egypt, Syria, Iran, and

Malaysia and that experienced by women in Saudi Arabia and the United Arab Emirates. Moreover, there is often a sharp contrast between urban and rural areas within the same country. Contemporary Islamic revivalism has fostered new changes and concerns that Islam will be used to justify a return to the veil, separation of the sexes, and the restriction of women's role in public life. The record and options have been more nuanced than that conjured up by images of women accustomed to Western dress being forced to wear the *chador* (veil) and live in *purdah* (seclusion). Here again, though, the force of a sacrosanct tradition continues to play an important role.

As discussed earlier, despite the interpretation of some Muslims, the veiling and seclusion of women is not based on a clear text of the Quran, but instead is borrowed from non-Islamic sources. The Quran itself does not mandate that women should be completely veiled or separated from men, but speaks of their participation in the life of the community and common religious responsibility with men to worship God, live virtuous lives, and to cover themselves or dress modestly. Influenced by the practices of conquered peoples in Syria and Persia, upper-class urban women adopted the veil, and during the early centuries of Islam the separation of women became more common. Although there are no clear Quranic texts, Muslim exegetes interpreted verses of the Quran to justify these practices. These interpretations and practices became so embedded in tradition that, although the practices of veiling and seclusion have varied over time and from one region to another, the veiling and seclusion of women have come to be regarded by many as integral to Islam. (This despite the fact that veiling was less common among village women who had to work in the fields and less visible in Africa and Southeast Asia as compared with the Middle East and South Asia.) As a result, any attempt to change these customs is simply dismissed as an attack on the Islamic ideal under the influence of the West. Mawlana Mawdudi reflects the traditionalist position:

> People have tried their very best to prove that the present form of Purdah was a custom in pre-Islamic communities, and that the Muslims adopted this custom of ignorance long after the time of the Holy Prophet. The question is: Where was the necessity of carrying out this historical research in the presence of a clear verse of the Quran, the established practice of the time of the Holy Prophet, and the explanations given by the Companions and their pupils? Obviously this trouble was taken in order to justify the objective of life prevalent in the West. For without this, it was not possible to advocate the Western concepts of "progress" and "civilization" that have got deeply fixed in the minds.[100]

One result of the contemporary revival of Islam has been a refocusing on the Muslim family, in particular, a reexamination of the status of women in Islam. Women and the family have traditionally been regarded as the heart of society; as wives and mothers, women have been regarded as the culture bearers, exemplars, and teachers of family values.

Islamic law and practice provided a centuries-long tradition and institution for fostering an Islamically oriented society. However complicated and difficult it might be to define and implement specific models for modern Islamic states, since the early Islamic ideal quickly gave way to usurpers and kingdoms, the traditional Muslim family offered a clear and easily identifiable starting point for implanting a strong sense of faith, identity, and values. In modern times, Muslim women had two distinct models before them: the modern Westernized lifestyle common among an elite minority of women and the traditional "Islamic" lifestyle of the majority of women, who lived much the same as previous generations had. The social impact of revivalism has left some Muslim women grappling anew with a desire to develop an alternative lifestyle that is both modern and compatible with their Islamic faith and identity (a lifestyle that integrates modern life and Islamic identity and values). The debate over Islamic identity and women's role in society has been most visible in matters of dress and personal conduct. A return to Islamic dress and behavior refers not only to renewed calls for the donning of traditional clothing and debates over such issues as the proximity of, or contact between, the sexes, but also to the appearance, among the urban middle class in particular, of new forms of nontraditional "modest" Islamic dress. This apparel is worn by students and professional women from Cairo to Kuala Lumpur. For some it is the wearing of a veil (*hijab*) or scarf that covers the head. For others, it is a modest form of Islamic dress, which consists of a head covering and a long dress with sleeves covering the arms. Thus, only the hands and face are uncovered.

The return to some form of Islamic dress reflects the sense of concern for what is viewed as the social and moral decline in many Muslim societies as well as the tension between modernity and authenticity, a concern to subordinate social change to indigenous, Islamic values and ideals. For many women, it is an attempt to combine traditional values and ideals with contemporary levels of education and employment, and thus produce a more integrated lifestyle, one that is both modern and Islamic. Moreover, in societies where it has become increasingly common to blame the ills and failures of society on Westernization and to associate Western dress and values with cultural imperialism, an undermining of Islamic life, license, and immorality, the donning of Islamic dress represents an attempt to make things right, to attain true progress and success, by returning to God's law:

> Once we thought that western society had all the answers for successful, fruitful living. If we followed the lead of the West we would have progress. Now we see that this isn't true; they [the West] are sick societies; even their material prosperity is breaking down. America is full of crime and promiscuity. Russia is worse. Who wants to be like that? We have to remember God. Look how God has blessed Saudi Arabia. That is because they have tried to follow the Law. And America, with all its loose society, is all problems.[101]

Such women are not critical of progress in education, technology, and science because many are professionals. They reject what they regard as the false progress of uncritical acculturation, or Westernization, which is blamed for social disintegration and a loss of values. Islamic dress also has the practical advantage of enabling some women to assert their modesty, dignity, and self-esteem in a public manner in societies where Islamic dress represents female modesty and respectability, whereas Western dress often symbolizes a more modern (Westernized), permissive lifestyle. It creates a protected, private space of respectability in the midst of the permissive atmosphere and sexual harassment that many experience in crowded, urban settings.[102]

For many women, the Western lifestyles of the upper class are both out of touch with the socioeconomic realities of life and often a new source of exploitation rather than emancipation. The following description of the impact of modernization—as Westernization—on Iranian women epitomizes a critique offered by many in the Muslim world:

> Iran adopted the worst of the West, including the exploitation of women's bodies to sell modern merchandise. Because we didn't tackle the real feminist issues, we just went from sex objects Oriental style to being sex objects Occidental style. Worse yet, we often get squeezed in between. Under such circumstances, the chador could be a tool for reasserting a woman's human dignity by forcing people to respond to her talents and personality rather than to her body alone.[103]

New experiments by educated Muslim women to orient their lives more Islamically have also resulted in more women "returning to the mosque." In the past, the restriction of women to the home and their limited educations had resulted in their not participating in observances in the mosque. While some, separated from the men, might attend the Friday congregational prayer, it was more common for women to pray at home and to leave religious learning to men. Today, in many Muslim countries, particularly those that have been regarded as among the more modernized, such as Egypt, Tunisia, Jordan, and Malaysia, women are forming their own prayer and Quran study groups, which, in some cases, are led by women. They cite the example of Muslim women in early Islam who fought and prayed alongside their men and of women who were held in high repute for their knowledge and sanctity as justification for their present activities.

While a return to some form of modest Islamic dress goes hand in hand with modern professional life for some, other more traditional voices increasingly emphasize that women's chastity and modesty require a more limited social role, if not withdrawal from public life. Traditionalists stress that while men and women are equal before God, they have complementary, not identical, roles in society. Thus, while education and new social responsibilities are recognized, there is also growing pressure to emphasize a woman's primary duty as wife and mother and to permit her to work only if necessary. Finally, more conservative forces call for the total covering of women, including the face and hands, as well as their complete segregation from, instead of participation in, public life. The diversity of Muslim perspectives on these issues is evident among neotraditionalist organizations, such as the Muslim Brotherhood and the Jamaat-i-Islami. It is common to equate these organizations in terms of their ideological goals and methods. Yet, their interpretations of Islam regarding the role of women have remained quite different. Following their founder, Mawlana Mawdudi, the Jamaat-i-Islami teach that the modesty of women, the sanctity of the Muslim family, and the strength of Muslim society require that women be completely covered by the *burqa* or *chador* and that they live in seclusion (*purdah*), that is, separated from male (nonfamily members) society. For the Muslim Brotherhood, Islamic dress does not require covering the face; women are permitted to work, provided it does not seriously conflict with their first duty to husband and family.

For feminists and secularists in the Muslim world today, the renewed public debate over the role of women in Islam and the increased wearing of Islamic forms of dress raise fears that the hold of tradition will reassert itself by reversing modern reforms in law, education, and employment. The examples of Iran and Pakistan fuel such fears. After the Iranian revolution, women who had donned the *chador* as a symbol of opposition to the Shah and for the sake of anonymity in public antigovernment demonstrations, suddenly found themselves demonstrating in March 1979 against a law that would have made the *chador* compulsory. Though the regulation was rescinded, veiling was made compulsory in government and public offices in the summer of 1980. In addition, coeducation was banned, and women were barred from the judiciary and legal professions.

In Pakistan, Islamization under General Zia ul-Haq (1977–88) led to pressures from more conservative sectors, especially the *ulama,* for a return to mandatory veiling and seclusion and the repeal of family law reforms that restrict polygamy and a male's unilateral, unfettered right to divorce. Religious leaders gave *fatwas* maintaining that women should be prohibited from holding political office. A government-appointed commission recommended that only women over fifty years of age be permitted to hold political office and then only with the permission of their husbands or male relatives. Bitter debates occurred over legislation that would adopt traditional laws that assign the value of women's testimony or evidence in court as half that of men and provide less compensation for a crime committed against a woman than a man.

Modern women's rights organizations in Pakistan and many Muslim countries found themselves increasingly on the defensive. Their critics charge that they contributed to the ills of Muslim society by fostering the Westernization rather than the true, authentic (Islamic) liberation of women and that they did not represent the majority of women but only a minority Westernized elite class. Traditionalists made their point by organizing counterdemonstrations of women who support the reimplementation of traditional Islamic laws and practices. Despite these developments, in 1989 after the death of General Zia ul-Haq, Benazir Bhutto (the Radcliff-Oxford educated daughter of former Prime Minister Zulfikar Ali Bhutto) was elected Pakistan's first woman prime minister. Her election as the first woman head of state in the Muslim world was the cause of some debate among religious leaders not only in Pakistan but also in many other Muslim countries.

The social impact of revivalism has witnessed a variety of Muslim responses in attempts to formulate more Islamically oriented models for women, ranging from experimentation with new forms of Islamic dress and lifestyles to reversion to more traditional ways. This phenomenon reflects an emphasis on both authenticity and traditionalism. However, the predominant tendency has been to equate authenticity with a reassertion of traditionalist interpretations of Islam (traditional ideals and norms of dress and behavior), demonstrating the pervasive presence and force of traditional Islam. This is understandable, since most Muslims were raised on these traditional interpretations. It is the Islam of their local religious leaders and scholars. Therefore, traditional Islam constitutes the norm that most turn to for guidance, manipulate for political gain, reject as outdated, or selectively follow. Today, only a relatively few reformers maintain that the real, dynamic history of Islam, hidden by *ulama*-inspired historical romanticism, legitimates substantive change and reforms. Even these few, if they are political leaders or heads of Islamic organizations that seek popular support, must be sensitive to the religious understanding of a more conservative constituency. Since most are political activists, they have not had the leisure to produce a systematic interpretation or reformulation of Islam. Few have had the charismatic authority and organizational structure to widely disseminate their ideas, in particular to penetrate and influence the *ulama*-controlled religious educational system and thus affect significant numbers of religious teachers and scholars.

Non-Muslim Minorities

The revivalist mood and orientation of resurgent Islam has also affected the status and rights of non-Muslims. In recent years, tensions and clashes between Muslim and non-Muslim communities have increased: the Copts in Egypt, Bahai in Iran, Chinese in Malaysia, and Christians in the Sudan, Pakistan, and Nigeria. The creation of more Islamically oriented societies, especially the introduction of Islamic laws, has resulted in varying degrees of tension, conflict, violence, and killing in the name of religion. For militant Muslims, Christian minorities are often seen as those who cooperated with colonial powers, benefited from their protection, and were the fruit of Christian missions. The Bahai of Iran and the Ahmadiyya of Pakistan, on the other hand, are regarded as apostates or heretics who rejected and broke away from Islam. Minorities who have enjoyed relative equality and freedom in modern nation-states now fear that Islamization will mean a reversion to the tolerated, "protected" status of religious minorities under traditional Islamic law. Non-Muslims belonged to a separate class of citizens who constituted their own community. In exchange for their allegiance to the state and payment of a poll tax, they were free to practice their faith and be governed by their religious leaders and laws in private life in such areas as worship, education, and family law. However advanced such laws may have been relative to their times, today minorities regard such treatment as second-class citizenship. Moreover, protected status was extended only to those communities regarded as "People of the Book," not to apostates or heretics. Events in Egypt, Iran, Pakistan, and the Sudan merely reinforce their fears. In Egypt, there have been attempts to make apostasy (and hence a Muslim's conversion to Christianity) subject to the death penalty. Moreover, clashes between militant Muslims and militant Christians in Egypt in the late 1970s and the 1980s have resulted in stonings, church bombings, disruption of Christian services, and death. In Iran, the *ulama* in the 1950s mounted an unsuccessful campaign to persuade the government to pass legislation to suppress the Bahai, whom they regarded as apostates from Islam, and dismiss them from public office. In the aftermath of the Iranian revolution, the Bahai religion was declared illegal, many were imprisoned and executed, and their property was seized. The Iranian government's insistence that the Bahai be punished for political reasons did little to silence its critics. In Pakistan and the Sudan, the imposition of Islamic law resulted in the subjection of non-Muslims to the ban on alcohol and the suppression of sects that proclaim themselves Muslims. In Pakistan, the Ahmad-iyya were declared a non-Muslim minority, and in the Sudan, Mahmud Taha, leader of the Republican Brothers, was executed for apostasy.

Non-Muslim minorities face another potential restriction on their rights. If states become more Islamically oriented, will this prevent non-Muslims from holding key government positions? With the exception of the head of state or prime minister, in most Muslim states citizens may hold any office, regardless of their faith. This Western, liberal, secular approach is increasingly contested by those who argue that non-Muslims should not hold key government, military, judicial, or legislative positions responsible for formulating and implementing the Islamic ideology of the state, since non-Muslims could not be fully committed to that ideology. Thus, while the constitutions of many modern Muslim states grant equality of citizenship and opportunity, the contemporary resurgence has resurrected pressures to reassert legally the traditional attitude toward non-Muslims, which has remained unchanged in Islamic law and is operative in the minds and outlook of many Muslims. This is reflected in the religious communalism evident in social life, if not in the workplace, the continued presence of communal villages or neighborhoods, and the tendency of most religious leaders and organizations, despite constitutional reforms, to teach and preach a restricted role for non-Muslims. As with the question of women's status, the tendency to legislate change from above, without adequately addressing traditional ideals and values that remain a part of faith and religious history, creates a dichotomy between modern practices and traditional ideals that must be resolved. The unresolved contradictions between the two are like a smoldering fire, barely visible until a strong change in the direction of the wind causes it to ignite and erupt.

Islamization

While both traditionalists and reformers speak of Islamization, their meaning and use of the term differ. For traditionalists, Islamization is primarily the reintroduction of past institutions and practices with little substantive change, for example, reinstituting traditional Islamic laws and punishments, the veiling of women, separate facilities for men and women, and the "protected" status for non-Muslims. They are literalist in approach and concerned with the letter of the law. This does not mean that they are opposed to science and technology. Indeed, one could argue that a significant proportion of those who join both moderate and radical religious movements are trained in the sciences, engineering, and medicine. Reformers view the process of Islamization in a far more dynamic and creative fashion, based on a more historical understanding of the dynamics of Islam's development. They regard themselves as undertaking once again the very process of interpretation and assimilation that characterized the early formation and development of Islamic law and tradition. It is a twofold process of deriving laws and practices from Islamic sources and adopting and adapting ideas and institutions from foreign sources, provided they are not contrary to Islam. Just as Islamic law and Muslim governments were not based solely on Quranic and Prophetic guidelines, but instead borrowed and incorporated freely from preexisting practices in Arabia, Byzantium, and Persia, reformers feel free to interpret, adopt, and modify as they see fit, staying within the limits set by God's revelation. While traditionalists take great pains to emphasize the total self-sufficiency and comprehensiveness of Islam, reformers insist that while much of past law and practice may be useful, new circumstances and problems require new solutions, formulated in the light of Quranic principles and selective borrowing from the international community. Reformers, while critical of the West, tend to be less anti-Western and polemical in their rhetoric and approach. They feel free to borrow from other cultures, insisting that their goal is "Islamic modernization," not simply wholesale Westernization. Sadiq al-Mahdi of the Sudan and Dr. Ali Shariati of Iran are representative of this approach. Both regard traditionalist Islam as a historically conditioned understanding of the Quran and Sunna, based on *ulama*-produced medieval formulations of Islamic belief and law. Shariati, a Shii Muslim, went further when he distinguished between the true dynamic, revolutionary spirit of pristine Islam (Alid Islam, the Islam of Ali's time) and the prevailing interpretation of Islam, a static, quiescent, retrogressive

Islam of the *ulama* (Safavid Islam), who were co-opted by the Safavid rulers of Iran: "Original Islam was an intellectually progressive Islamic movement as well as a militant social force, the most committed, most revolutionary Islamic sect."[104]

For Sadiq al-Mahdi, the descendant of the Sudanese Mahdi and former Prime Minister of the Sudan, the current Muslim dilemma is the product of a regime of "internal and indigenous colonialism," formed by elites who restructured their societies in the image of the West and under the threat of communism, and the traditionalist response to these threats in defense of Islam. He advocates a response that repeats a process as old as Islam itself—Islamization—which in the current context would mean the separation of Islam from the traditionalist formulation of it and the separation of modernization from Westernization in order to produce a new, modern, Islamically oriented synthesis:

> Along with these two responses: rejection of traditionalism in favor of the acculturating designs and rejection of acculturation in favor of the traditionalist thesis, there was a third response, namely: separating Islam from the traditionalist thesis, separating modernization from the acculturation syndrome, and establishing a synthesis which is both Islamic and modern. Westernization is the West's version of modernization. It is embedded in Western culture and interests. Sovietization (or for that matter sinicization) are Soviet and Chinese versions of late-comers to modernization and are embedded in Russian and Chinese cultural views and interests. Modernization can and must be divorced from those cultural and historical expressions of it.[105]

Dr. Hassan al-Turabi, the leader of the Sudanese Muslim Brotherhood, summarizes the historical interpretation and Islamic rationale of many reformers:

> Any form or procedure for the organization of public life that can ultimately be related to God and put to his service in the furtherance of the aims of Islamic government can be adopted unless expressly excluded by the Shariah. Once so received, it is an integral part of Islam whatever its source may be. Through the process of Islamization, the Muslims were always very open to expansion and change. Thus, Muslims can incorporate any experience whatever if not contrary to their ideals. Muslims took much of their bureaucratic forms from Roman and Persian models. Now much can be borrowed from contemporary sources, critically appreciated in the light of Shariah values and norms, and integrated into the Islamic framework of government.[106]

Despite the writings and activities of reformers, given the traditionalist backgrounds of the majority of religious leaders and the Muslim masses, the Islamic experiments and ideology of governments and religious organizations have been predominantly traditional in orientation.

Thus, when religious forces gain power (Iran) or influence (Pakistan) or become more vocal in calling for the Islamization of society (Egypt, the Sudan, Malaysia, Tunisia, Lebanon), the Islam many advocate or introduce is predominantly that of the past, not simply in its revealed principles but often in its derivative prescriptions and forms. Central to the failure of secular and Islamic reformers to produce a coherent, systematic modern synthesis capable of legitimating substantive change and that of traditionalist leaders to break the bonds of their "*taqlid* mentality" is the split mentality which has plagued modern Muslim societies.

The story of modern Islam has been that of two groups of Muslims who possess two quite different outlooks on life: an elite, Western-oriented minority convinced that they must forge ahead regardless of the obscurantist opposition of religious leaders; and a religious leadership who, believing Islam and its authority are under siege, are suspicious of and resistant to modernization programs, identifying them with a Western, secularist, materialist, godless drift in their societies. While the religious leadership is dismissed as an obstacle to change, Western secular elites are conveniently blamed for the spiritual and social ills of society.

This division in Muslim society has been caused by the existence of two parallel systems of education: traditional religious and modern secular. The bifurcation of education has been a product of the process of modernization in most Muslim countries. Traditional religious schools, despite some modern curriculum reform, produce graduates with predominantly traditional educations who continue to serve as local religious leaders, teachers, and scholars. They are often ill-prepared to appreciate and respond creatively to the demands of modernity. They see little need for a fresh reinterpretation of traditional ideals and values and thus fail to provide the kind of religious leadership required in modern society. Modern secular schools often enjoy better government funding and support, providing the "new" training and academic credentials for prestige positions in modern society (medicine, law, engineering, government service). Their graduates are well-versed in modern disciplines but have often lacked the solid knowledge of their religious and cultural tradition necessary to formulate changes with sufficient sensitivity to the history and values of their cultural milieu. Too often, Western systems and presuppositions were adopted uncritically by modern elites. Opportunities to render change with some continuity with the past went unrecognized and unrealized. Where such change was attempted, it was carried out in an ad hoc, unsystematic fashion that made reforms vulnerable to charges of cultural manipulation in the interest of Westernization. Both traditional and modern elites failed to provide a new religiocultural synthesis capable of providing continuity in the midst of modern change. The diffusion of the Islamic modernist movement and the rise of Islamic activist organizations like the Muslim Brotherhood and the Jamaat-i-Islami attest to this failure. Many of the younger generation, in particular those coming from traditional backgrounds but now studying at state schools and universities, find themselves caught in the middle. Islamic activist organizations offer guidance, a sense of community, and a program for harnessing faith and action to achieve social justice through sociopolitical reform. Therein lies the appeal of Islamic activism.

The bifurcation of education and society and the consequent training of two distinct mind-sets or outlooks—traditional and modern—is clearly illustrated in contemporary revivalism. The demand for more Islamically oriented states requires a reinterpretation of Islam that combines a reexamination of political, social, legal, and economic institutions and the values that inform these institutions. If secularists have denied the necessity and feasibility of undertaking such a task, the religious leadership has generally proven incapable of it. Conservative religious leaders tend to be fixated on the past. For them tradition is not so much a source of inspiration and direction as a literal map to be followed in all its details. This perfect blueprint for Muslim society, contained in the traditional (classical) legal manuals, is not seen as a response to a specific sociohistorical period—a conditioned product hammered out by jurists in light of Islamic principles and values—but as a final, comprehensive guide. Conservatives fail to distinguish between revealed, immutable principles and historically conditioned laws and institutions that were the product of the early jurists' fallible human reasoning and the assimilation of foreign influences and practices. Moreover, the hold of tradition can be found in a more hidden form among those who advocate reinterpretation (*ijtihad*) and change in principle, but who, when pressed on specific changes, often exhibit a "*taqlid* mentality," a tendency to reflexively follow past practice whether out of intellectual conviction or a pragmatism that defers to the dominant traditionalist culture.

Yet, we must avoid an oversimplified distinction between intransigent traditionalists and reform-minded modernists. The tendency of the more tradition-bound to view their understanding of Islam as definitive has not precluded actual change. The very process of preserving and passing on a tradition requires interpretation of tradition and judgment regarding its application to specific problems and situations. The study, preaching, and interpreting of Islam by individual religious scholars and teachers, as well as its implementation, occur in changing historical and social contexts. A diversity of readings or understandings of texts and situations is inherent in this process. Thus, normative Islamic ideologies, espoused in a particular time and place, are themselves the product of both the carriers and interpreters of culture and their contexts.[107] The very diversity found in the schools and manuals of Islamic law reflect the influence of reason, differing cultural contexts, and changes in the history of the community. So today, traditional beliefs, practices, and institutions take on new meanings in the teachings of even those who regard themselves as the most orthodox of believers. The Ayatollah Khomeini's interpretation of Islamic government as governance by the jurist has been criticized by some traditionalists and modernists alike, laity and clergy. Iran's official description of itself as an Islamic "Republic," much of its constitution, and many of its institutions (e.g., parliament and ministries) are clearly adaptations of modern (Western) institutions. Zia ul-Haq's implementation of Islamic laws, while sometimes dismissed by his critics as fundamentalist, has often been quite innovative. Pakistan's Federal Sharia Court is not the traditional Islamic law court but an appeals court system, unknown in the past.

While some Islamic political activist organizations wish to restore the caliphate, the majority opt for more modern interpretations of traditional concepts and institutions. The application of Islamic history and values to modern conditions has produced fresh interpretations. In the name of Islam, constitutionalism, democracy, and parliamentary forms of government have been adopted and rendered Islamic. The parliaments or national assemblies of the Islamic republics of Iran and Pakistan as well as those of less religiously oriented states are called *majlis-i-shura* (consultative assemblies), a modern reinterpretation of the assembly of notables charged with the selection of the early caliphs. The legal principle of community consensus (*ijma*), which was in fact the retrospective agreement of the *ulama* on matters of law, is often transferred to or equated with the activity of modern parliaments. A variety of Muslims, drawing on a rich and diverse tradition, reconstruct an Islamic ideology to inform politics, economics, law, education, and social affairs. Past Islamic teachings are reinterpreted and applied to modern banking to produce Islamic banks, which now exist in many Muslim countries. Curriculum reform, sometimes referred to as the Islamization of education, retains modern disciplines but seeks to replace those Western values regarded as contrary to Islam with Islamic ones. These activities have resulted in a variety of interpretations and conclusions. Whether their orientations are traditionalist or modernist, moderate or radical, most Muslim leaders have been engaged to varying degrees in a process of development and change.

Contemporary Islamic revivalism is a complex and multifaceted phenomenon that has demonstrated its strength, diversity, and staying power for almost two decades. Many Muslims have been disillusioned with the abuses or manipulation of religion by some governments and radical organizations. At the same time, revivalism continues to grow as a broad-based socioreligious (dawa) movement, functioning today within virtually every Muslim country and internationally. Dawa traditionally meant "the call" to Islam, propagation of the faith among nonbelievers. Today, Islamic "Call" societies represent a rapidly growing and diversified socioreligious movement consisting of many organizations aimed not simply at non-Muslims but at calling upon Muslims themselves to return to Islam, to more fully and self-consciously reappropriate their Islamic identity and be more observant in the practice of their faith. Focusing on the individual and the community at the grass-roots level, these movements emphasize the transformation of society through religious education, and moral and social reform. Thus, in addition to propagation of the faith, *dawa* organizations engage in education (schools, child-care centers, youth camps), religious publication and broadcasting, economic programs (Islamic banks, investment houses, insurance companies), and social services (hospitals, clinics, legal aid societies). Although their programs are aimed at young and old alike, the youth movement represents the thrust of *dawa* organizations. Muslim student associations exist in most Muslim countries. Active in schools and universities, they are dedicated to producing a new modern generation of leaders in government, the bureaucracy, the professions—Islamically, not secularly, oriented. In this way, they work for social change *within* the existing state system.

The growth, proliferation, and increasing sophistication of the *dawa* movement will continue to foster a religious revivalism focused primarily on producing better Muslims and a better society. However, Islamic organizations, as history has shown, can move easily from the social to the political, from lobbyists for social and moral reform to militant political activists and revolutionaries, when circumstances warrant.

Conclusion

The history of Islam in the twentieth century reflects the realities of Muslim politics, a record of Muslim societies struggling to assert their independence and define themselves in the modern world. While religion remained an important force in the religious life and culture of many Muslims, its public and political role was progressively circumscribed. Most modern states pursued a more secular path, which, while sensitive to religious sensibilities, tended to limit the public role of religion. Despite institutional and intellectual changes and reforms in public life, the Islamic belief and practice of most Muslims remained relatively untouched. The significance and strength of tradition's hold on Muslim society and its lack of effective leadership may be seen in the paucity of systematic attempts at reinterpretation and reform. Many Muslim countries found it easier to continue along parallel paths of religion and secularity, as in law and education. Secular leaders were content to mandate or legislate change from above and, when necessary, to use Islam on occasion. The systematic reconstruction advocated by early Islamic modernists like Muhammad Abduh and Muhammad Iqbal never occurred. The majority of religious leaders preferred to bide their time until a "restoration" of Islam might take place. Many cooperated with governments that increasingly took over the administration of religious education, law, and religious endowments. Others were content to preach a moralistic Islam devoid of social activism. In the 1930s and 1940s, new Islamic societies, the Muslim Brotherhood and the Jamaat-i-Islami, attempted to fill this vacuum with organizations that reasserted the relevance of Islam to all areas of life, diagnosed the ills of Muslim society, and offered an Islamic activism aimed at redressing issues of religious identity and social justice.

Since the late 1960s, Islamic revivalism has progressively come to dominate religious and political discourse in much of the Muslim world. Both the political and religious establishments have found it necessary to respond through co-option, cooperation, repression, or rejection. Often the more conservative, nonactivist *ulama* have been on the defensive. Some have cooperated in government efforts to control and contain; others have become more outspoken and militant in their teachings and actions. Just as the violent actions of a minority of radicals should not obscure the moderate activities of the majority, so too the breadth of the personal dimension of Islamic revivalism should not be overshadowed by its political dimensions.

For many Muslims a "return to Islam" means greater awareness and observance of their faith: study of the Quran, prayer, fasting, dress, Sufism, following the Sharia. For some of these, the greater affirmation of Islam in personal and community life implies recognition that Islam knows no clear separation of the sacred and profane, the spiritual and the mundane. They believe that the restoration of Islam to its rightful place in Muslim life requires bridging the secular gap between religion and society through the implementation of Islamic law and that the Islamic reorientation (Islamization) of the state and its institutions requires organization and political action in order to persuade, pressure, or coerce the political and religious establishments to comply. In divergent ways, a variety of Muslims continue to grapple with the task of defining (or redefining) more clearly a framework of meaning within which they can understand, interpret, and respond to the modern experience.

There is indeed an Islamic revolution occurring in many parts of the Muslim world. However, the most significant and pervasive revolution is not that of bombs and hostages, but of clinics and schools. It is dominated by social activists (teachers, doctors, lawyers, dentists) and preachers rather than warriors. The battle is often one of the pen, tongue, and heart rather than the sword. Radicalism and terrorism, though capturing the headlines, are a very small though at times deadly part of a phenomenon characterized more by a broad-based religiosocial revolution which has affected most Muslim societies.

Like their Abrahamic cousins, Jews and Christians, many Muslims today are deeply concerned about the secular drift and outlook of their societies and its impact on faith and values. Similarly, the application of centuries-old religious traditions to modern life provides new challenges and has resulted in a variety of responses or schools of thought. Restoration of the Sharia, the pivotal link between faith and action, has become the common agenda of all Muslims who wish to counter the dangers of secularization, preserve a strong sense of faith and identity, modernize without Westernizing, and foster an economic development that avoids the excesses of materialism by remaining attentive to the requirements of social justice. Differing and competing interpretations of Islam have resulted not only in an enriching diversity of faith but also in divisive conflicts within the community of believers.

As the history of Islam has shown, belief in one God, one revelation, and one final Prophet has been the basis for a strong, vibrant monotheistic faith. However, monotheistic has not meant monolithic. The unity of Islam, from its early formation to contemporary developments, has encompassed a diversity of interpretations and expressions of faith. So too today, one-fifth of the world's population testifies to the dynamism of Islam and the continued commitment of Muslims to follow "the straight path, the way of God, to whom belongs all that is in the heavens and all that is on earth" (42:52–53).

GLOSSARY

ashura   the "tenth" of the Muslim month of Muharram when Shii Muslims commemorate the martyrdom of Imam Husayn at Karbala

ayatollah (ayatullah)   "Sign of God," title of a high ranking Shii religious leader

baqa   to rest or abide in God; Sufi experience that follows the annihilation (*fana*) of the ego-self

bida   innovation; deviation from Islamic tradition

caliph   for Sunni Muslims, successor of Muhammad as leader of the Islamic community

chador   traditional garment, worn in public, covering a woman from head to foot

dar al-harb   "abode of war"; non-Islamic territory

dar al-Islam   "abode of peace"; Islamic territory, i.e., where Islamic law is in force

dawah (dakwah)   "call to Islam," propagation of the faith; more broadly, social welfare and missionary activities

dhikr   "remembrance," Sufi practice of repeating or remembering God's name to become more conscious of God's presence

dhimmi   "protected" or covenanted people; non-Muslim citizen who is subject to poll tax (*jizya*)

din   religion

fana   annihilation or extinction of the ego-centered self in Sufism to experience unity of God

faqih (pl. fuqaha)   legal expert; jurisprudent

faqir   "poor" or mendicant; a follower of Sufism who has embraced poverty or detachment from worldly goods

fatwa   formal legal opinion or decision of a mufti on a matter of Islamic law

fiqh   "understanding"; Islamic jurisprudence, religious law

hadd: (pl. hudud)   "limits"; Quranically prescribed penalty or punishment for theft, adultery, fornication, false witness, drinking intoxicants

hadith   narrative report of the Prophet Muhammad's sayings and actions

hajj   annual pilgrimage to Mecca required of all Muslims at least once in their lifetime

halal   permitted, lawful activities

hanif   Quranic term for a pure or true monotheist; used for Abraham and for those in pre-Islamic Arabia who before the revelation of the Quran remained monotheists despite the paganism and polytheism of their times

haram   prohibited, unlawful activities

hijab   veil or head covering worn by Muslim women in public

hijra emigration of Muhammad from Mecca to Medina in A.D. 622 where he established rule of Muslim community-state

hizbullah party of God

ibadat "worship"; regulations in Islamic law governing religious observances

Id al-Adha "festival of sacrifice," the last day of the *hajj*

Id al-Fitra "festival of the breaking of the fast," the end of Ramadan

ijma consensus, or agreement of the community, a source of Islamic law

ijtihad independent analysis or interpretation of Islamic law

ikhwan brotherhood

iman "faith," religious belief or conviction in the fundamental doctrines of Islam

islah reform or revitalization of the Muslim community through return to the Quran and example of the Prophet

islam submission or surrender to the will of God

jahiliyyah period of ignorance, i.e., pre-Islamic Arabia; used by contemporary revivalists to refer to un-Islamic behavior in society

jihad "strive, effort, struggle" to follow Islam; can include defense of the faith, armed struggle, holy war

jinn intelligent beings, usually invisible spirits, who can sin as well as be sacred; the Western word "genies" is derived from this term

jizya poll-tax on *dhimmi* (non-Muslims) which entitled them to protection and to practice their faith

kaba cube-shaped shrine located in the center of the Grand Mosque in Mecca, the focal point for daily prayer and the pilgrimage

kafir "unbeliever" or infidel, one who is "ungrateful" and rejects the message of Islam

kalam "speech," theology

khalifah "successor" of Muhammad, caliph in Sunni Islam

khutba sermon delivered in a mosque at the Friday congregational prayer

madrasa religious college or university, seminary

mahdi divinely guided leader who is to come in the future to establish God's rule on earth, a socially just society

marja-i-taqlid "source of emulation"; supreme authority on law in Shii Islam whose interpretation should be followed; title is conferred by the people on the most distinguished clergymen of the period

masjid "place of prostration," mosque, center for Muslim worship

mihrab "niche" in the wall of a mosque, indicating the direction of Mecca, which Muslims face when performing their daily prayers (*salat*)

millet system non-Muslim religious communities living within the Islamic domain; distinctive system used by Ottoman rulers to recognize and regulate the rights and duties of non-Muslims

minbar pulpit from which a sermon is delivered at the Friday prayer

mosque (masjid) see *masjid*

muamalat human relationships; Islamic laws (e.g., civil, criminal, family) governing social relations

mufti specialist on Islamic law competent to deliver a *fatwa* or legal interpretation/brief

muhtasib originally an inspector of markets who supervised or policed business transactions and practices; the office was later expanded to include the monitoring of public morality in general

mujaddid "renewer," one who brings about the renewal (*tajdid*) of Islam: a widely held Muslim belief based on Prophetic tradition teaches that God sends a *mujaddid* (renewer) at the beginning of each century to restore or strengthen Islam

mujahid (pl. mujahidin)   soldier of God

mujtahid   one who practices *ijtihad* or interprets Islamic law

mullah   a local religious leader

mumin   believer, one who possesses faith (*iman*)

muslim   one who submits (*islam*) to God's will

nizam   system, e.g., nizam al-Islam, Islamic system of government

pir   Sufi master

purdah   seclusion and covering of women in public

qadi   judge who administers Shariah law

qibla   direction of the Kaba at Mecca which Muslims face when performing their daily prayers (*salat*)

qiyas   juristic reasoning by analogy, source of Islamic law

ray   personal opinion or judgment in interpreting Islamic law

riba   usury

salaf   "ancestors," the first generations of the Muslim community; because of their proximity to the Prophet Muhammad, their beliefs and practice are considered authoritative

salat   official prayer or worship observed five times daily

sawm   fasting, the fourth pillar of Islam which requires abstention from food and drink from dawn to sunset during the month of Ramadan

shahadah   confession or profession of faith: "there is no god but Allah and Muhammad is His Prophet/Messenger."

shahid   martyr ("witness" to faith)

shariah   "path"; Islamic law

shaykh   head of a tribe or Sufi order; term applied to a ruler, religious teacher, or tribal leader

shia   "party or faction" of Ali, those Muslims who believe that Muhammad designated Ali and his rightful descendants the true leaders of the Muslim community

shirk   idolatry, polytheism or associationism; to associate any other deity, person, or thing with God

shura   consultation

Sufi   follower of Sufism, Islamic mysticism

sultan   ruler, military commander in medieval Islamic states

sunnah   normative practice or exemplary behavior of Muhammad

tajdid   revival, renewal of Islam through return to its sources, the Quran and example of the Prophet

talaq   pronouncement of divorce or repudiation by husband

taqiyya   resort to dissimulation in the face of danger, especially among Shii

taqlid   unquestioned imitation or following of tradition, past legal or doctrinal precedents; the opposite of *ijtihad*

tariqa   "way or path," the teachings and devotional practice of mystical brotherhoods; also used to refer to Sufi brotherhoods

tasawwuf   Sufi way or path

tawhid   unity of God (absolute monotheism), Allah's absolute sovereignty over the universe

taziyyah   Shii passion play depicting the martyrdom of Husayn

ulama   religious scholars or clergy

ummah   Islamic community, refers to the worldwide Muslim community

umra "visitation," lesser pilgrimage to Mecca which can be performed any time of the year.

usul al-fiqh principles of Islamic jurisprudence, sources of Islamic law (Quran, Sunnah of Prophet, consensus [*ijma*], analogical reasoning [*qiyas*]).

vilayat-i-faqih guardianship or government by an expert in Islamic law

wali friend or protégé of God, Sufi saint

waqf (pl. awqaf) endowment of property for religious purposes such as building of mosques, schools, hospitals

wisaya "testament," designation of Ali as executor of Muhammad's will and testament

zakat annual alms tax or tithe of 2 1/2 percent levied on wealth and distributed to the poor

zawiyya Sufi residence or center

zina illegal sexual intercourse, includes both adultery and fornication

zulm oppression; sin

NOTES

1. W. Montgomery Watt. *Muhammad at Mecca* (Oxford: Oxford University Press, 1953), p. 24.

2. *The Life of Muhammad*, A. Guillaume, trans. (London: Oxford University Press, 1955), p. 107.

3. Ibn Hisham, as quoted in Philip K. Hitti, *History of the Arabs*, 9th ed. (New York: St. Martin's Press, 1966), p. 120.

4. 1 Samuel 17:45, *The Oxford Annotated Bible: Revised Standard Version* (New York: Oxford University Press, 1962). See also Exodus 14:14, Deuteronomy 20:4, 1 Samuel 15:33, 1 Kings 18:36–40, and 2 Kings 10:25–31.

5. Geoffrey Parrinder, *Mysticism in the World's Religions* (New York: Oxford University Press, 1976), p. 121.

6. Rachel Biale, *Women and Jewish Law* (New York: Schocken Books, 1984), pp. 49–51.

7. Philip K. Hitti, *Islam: A Way of Life* (New York: Henry Regnery, 1971), p. 27.

8. Marshall S. G. Hodgson, *The Venture of Islam* (Chicago: University of Chicago Press, 1974), vol. 1, p. 185.

9. Francis E. Peters, "The Early Muslim Empires: Umayyads, Abbasids, Fatimids," in *Islam: The Religious and Political Life of a World Community*, Marjorie Kelly, ed. (New York: Praeger, 1984), p. 79.

10. See Bernard Lewis, *The Origins of Ismailism* (Cambridge: Cambridge University Press, 1940); W. Madelung, "Ismailiyya," in *The Encyclopedia of Islam*, 2nd ed., vol. 4, H. A. R. Gibb et al., eds. (Leiden: E. J. Brill, 1960), S. M. Stern, "Ismailis and Qarmatians," in *L'Elaboration de l'Islam*, Claude Cahen, ed. (Paris: Paul Geuthner, 1961), pp. 99–108.

11. Bernard Lewis, *The Arabs in History* (New York: Harper & Row, 1966), p. 149.

12. Laura Vecca Vaglieri, "The Patriarchal and Umayyad Caliphates," in *The Cambridge History of Islam*, P. M. Holt, Ann K. S. Lambton, and Bernard Lewis, eds. (Cambridge: Cambridge University Press, 1977), 1A, p. 103.

13. Lewis, *Arabs in History*, p. 131.

14. *Islam: from the Prophet Muhammad to the Capture of Constantinople*, Bernard Lewis, ed. and trans. (New York: Harper & Row, 1974), pp. 179–81.

15. Bernard G. Weiss and Arnold H. Green, *A Survey of Arab History* (Cairo: The American University in Cairo Press, 1985), p. 187.

16. Seyyed Hossein Nasr, as quoted in Weiss and Green, p. 187.

17. Lewis, *Arabs in History*, p. 133.

18. Hodgson, *Venture of Islam*, vol. 1, p. 236.

19. Peters, "Early Muslim Empires," p. 85.

20. Roger Savory, "Christendom vs. Islam: Interaction and Co-existence," in *Introduction to Islamic Civilization*, Roger Savory, ed. (Cambridge: Cambridge University Press, 1976), p. 133.

21. Ira Lapidus, *A History of Islamic Societies* (Cambridge: Cambridge University Press, 1988), p. 315. For an authoritative discussion of the Ottoman, Safavid, and Mughal empires, see Lapidus, chaps. 17–19.

22. Fazlur Rahman, "The Mesage and the Messenger," in *Islam: The Religious and Political Life*, Kelly, ed., p. 43.

23. Morris S. Seale, *Muslim Theology*, 2nd ed. (London: Luzac and Company, 1980), pp. 67–68.

24. Fazlur Rahman, *Islam*, 2nd ed. (Chicago: University of Chicago Press, 1979), p. 91.

25. N. J. Coulson, *A History of Islamic Law* (Edinburgh: Edinburgh University Press, 1964), p. 12.

26. I. Goldziher, *Muslim Studies* (London: Allen & Unwin, 1967), vol. II, pp. 17–254; D. S. Margoliouth, *The Early Development of Mohammedanism* (London: William Norgate, 1914), pp. 65–98; C. Snouch Hurgronje, *Selected Works of C. Snouch Hurgronje*, C. H. Bousquet and Joseph Schacht, eds. (Leiden: E. J. Brill, 1957); Joseph Schacht, *Origins of Muhammadan Jurisprudence* (Oxford: Oxford University Press, 1950), especially pp. 138–76.

27. See, for example, Fazlur Rahman, "Sunna and Hadith," *Islamic Studies* 1 (June: 1962), and *Islam*, chapt. 3.

28. Rahman, "Sunna and Hadith," p. 4.

29. H. A. R. Gibb, *Mohammedanism* (New York: Oxford University Press, 1962), p. 86.

30. For a more thorough analysis of Muslim family law, see John L. Esposito, *Women in Muslim Family Law* (Syracuse, N.Y.: Syracuse University Press, 1982).

31. Abu Dawud, *Sunan* (Kanpur, India: Matba Majidi, 1346 A.H.) I: 296.

32. *The Hedaya*, Charles Hamilton, trans., 2nd ed. (Lahore, Pakistan: Premier Book House, 1957), p. 73.

33. R. Levy, *The Social Structure of Islam* (Cambridge: Cambridge University Press, 1955), p. 126.

34. Muhammad al-Ghazzali, *Our Beginning in Wisdom*, Ismail R. al-Faruqi, trans. (Washington, D.C.: American Council of Learned Societies, 1953), p. 111.

35. *Islam*, John Alden Williams, ed. (New York: George Braziller, 1962), pp. 138–39.

36. Margaret Smith, *Rabia the Mystic and Her Fellow-Saints in Islam* (Cambridge: Cambridge University Press, 1928), p. 30.

37. W. Montgomery Watt, *Muslim Intellectual: A Study of al-Ghazali* (Edinburgh: Edinburgh University Press, 1963), p. 136. See also W. Montgomery Watt, *The Faith and Practice of al-Ghazali* (London: George Allen & Unwin, 1953).

38. Watt, *Muslim Intellectual*, p. 135.

39. John O. Voll, "Renewal and Reform in Islamic History: *Tajdid* and *Islah*," in *Voices of Resurgent Islam*, John L. Esposito, ed. (New York: Oxford University Press, 1983), p. 33.

40. Reynold A. Nicholson, *Studies in Islamic Mysticism* (Cambridge: Cambridge University Press, 1967), p. 46.

41. Seyyed Hossein Nasr, *Ideals and Realities of Islam* (London: George Allen & Unwin, 1966), p. 162.

42. Hamadi ibn Abdullah al-Buhri, *Utenzi wa Sayedina Huseni*, as quoted in *Textual Sources for the Study of Islam*, Andrew Rippon and Jan Knappert, eds. and trans. (New York: Barnes & Noble, 1987), p. 140.

43. Ibid.

44. Ibid., p. 142.

45. Ali Shariati, *Fatima is Fatima*, Layleh Bakhtiar, trans. (New York: Muslim Students Council, n.d.), p. 136.

46. Peter Chelkowski, *Taziyeh: Ritual and Drama in Iran* (New York: New York University Press, 1979), p. 3.

47. Hamid Enayat, *Modern Islamic Political Thought* (Austin: University of Texas Press, 1982), pp. 182–83.

48. For an excellent discussion of revivalism in the eighteenth century, see John O. Voll, *Islam: Continuity and Change in the Modern World* (Boulder, Colo: Westview Press, 1982), chapt. 2.

49. John O. Voll, "Renewal and Reform in Islamic History," in *Voices of Resurgent Islam*, chapt. 2.

50. A. Merad, *"Islah,"* in *The Encyclopedia of Islam*, new ed., vol. 4, p. 141.

51. Voll, "Renewal and Reform," p. 33.

52. John O. Voll, "The Sudanese Mahdi: Frontier Fundamentalist," *International Journal of Middle East Studies* 10 (1979): 159.

53. Jamal al-Din al-Afghani, "Islamic Solidarity," in *Islam in Transition: Muslim Perspectives*, John J. Donohue and John L. Esposito, eds. (New York: Oxford University Press, 1982), pp. 21, 23.

54. Jamal al-Din al-Afghani, "An Islamic Response to Imperialism," in *Islam in Transition*, pp. 17–19.

55. Muhammad Abduh, *The Theology of Unity*, Ishaq Musaad and Kenneth Cragg, trans. (London: George Allen & Unwin, 1966).

56. Ibid., pp. 39–40.

57. Albert Hourani, *Arabic Thought in the Liberal Age: 1798–1939* (Oxford: Oxford University Press, 1970), p. 227.

58. Malcolm H. Kerr, *Islamic Reform: The Political and Legal Theories of Muhammad Abduh and Rashid Rida* (Berkeley: University of California Press, 1966), p. 190.

59. Rashid Rida, *al-Wahabiyyun wal Hijaz* (Cairo: Manar Press, 1926), p. 47.

60. Ahmad Khan, "Lecture on Islam," in *Islam in Transition*, p. 42.

61. Ibid.

62. *Majmua*, I, 213–14, as quoted in J. M. S. Baljon, *The Reforms and Religious Ideas of Sir Sayyid Ahmad Khan* (Lahore, Pakistan: Sh. Muhammad Ashraf, 1964), p. 78.

63. *Tafsir al-Quran*, Vol. III, p. 32, as quoted in B. A. Dar, *Religious Thought of Sayyid Ahmad Khan* (Lahore, Pakistan: Sh. Muhammad Ashraf, 1957), p. 182.

64. See, for example, Kemal A. Faruki, "Pakistan: Islamic Government and Society," in *Islam in Asia: Religion, Politics, & Society*, John L. Esposito, ed. (New York: Oxford University Press, 1987), pp. 54, 75.

65. Muhammad Iqbal, *Thoughts and Reflections of Iqbal*, S. A. Vahid, ed. (Lahore, Pakistan: Sh. Muhammad Ashraf, 1964), p. 277.

66. Muhammad Iqbal, *The Reconstruction of Religious Thought in Islam*, rev. ed. (Lahore, Pakistan: Sh. Muhammad Ashraf, 1968), p. 8.

67. Iqbal, *Reconstruction*, p. 155.

68. Ibid., p. 154.

69. Muhammad Iqbal, *The Mysteries of Selflessness* (London: Oxford University Press, 1953), p. 37.

70. Iqbal, *Reconstruction*, p. 168.

71. Muhammad Iqbal, "Islam as a Political and Moral Ideal," in *Thoughts and Reflections of Iqbal*, p. 52.

72. Muhammad Iqbal, as quoted in "A Separate Muslim State in the Subcontinent," in *Islam in Transition*, pp. 91–92.

73. *Report of the Commission on Marriage and Family Laws*, as excerpted in *Islam in Transition*, pp. 201–02.

74. Ibid., p. 202.

75. Hasan al-Banna, "The New Renaissance," in *Islam in Transition*, p. 78.

76. Mawlana Abul Ala Mawdudi, *The Islamic Law and Constitution*, edited by Khurshid Ahmad, 6th ed. (Lahore, Pakistan: Islamic Publications, 1977), p. 5.

77. Muhammad al-Ghazzali, *Our Beginning in Wisdom*, p. 54.

78. See, for example, John J. Donohue, "Islam and the Search for Identity in the Arab World," in *Voices of Resurgent Islam*, chapt. 3; and Ali Merad, "The Ideoligisation of Islam," in *Islam and Power*, Alexander S. Cudsi and Ali E. Hillal Dessouki, eds. (Baltimore: Johns Hopkins University Press, 1981), chapt. 3.

79. "Lessons from Iran," in *Islam in Transition*, pp. 246–49.

80. Ali Merad, "The Ideologisation of Islam," in *Islam and Power*, p. 38.

81. For a more extended analysis of the roles of Islam in politics, see John L. Esposito, *Islam and Politics*, 2nd ed. (Syracuse, N.Y.: Syracuse University Press, 1987), which has been a source for this discussion.

82. Saad Eddin Ibrahim, "Egypt's Islamic Militants," *MERIP Reports* 103, (February 1982), p. 11.

83. Johannes J. G. Jansen, *The Neglected Duty* (New York: Macmillan, 1986), p. 193.

84. Gilles Kepel, *Muslim Extremism in Egypt: The Prophet and the Pharaoh* (Berkeley: University of California Press, 1986), p. 192.

85. "The Libyan Revolution in the Words of its Leaders," *The Middle East Journal* 24 (1978), p. 208.

86. As quoted in *Islam and Politics*, p. 158.

87. Muammar al-Qaddafi, *The Green Book*, as excerpted and translated in Donohue and Esposito, eds. *Islam in Transition*, p. 105.

88. As quoted in Mahmoud Mustafa Ayoub, *Islam and the Third Universal Theory: The Religious Thought of Muammar al-Qadhdhafi* (London: KPI, 1987), p. 90.

89. Ibid., p. 88.

90. As quoted in Ervand Abrahamian, "Ali Shariati: Ideologue of the Iranian Revolution," *MERIP Reports* 102 (January 1982), p. 26.

91. Donohue and Esposito, *Islam in Transition*, p. 303.

92. *Islam and Revolution: Writings and Declarations of Imam Khomeini*, Hamid Algar, trans. (Berkeley: Mizan Press, 1981), p. 185.

93. Ibid., pp. 249–50.

94. Augustus Richard Norton, "Estrangement and Fragmentation in Lebanon," *Current History* (February 1986), p. 62.

95. Marius Deeb, "Shia movements in Lebanon: their formation, ideology, social

basis, and links with Iran and Syria," *Third World Quarterly*, vol 10, no. 2 (April 1988), p. 694.

96. As quoted in Abdullah M. Sindhi, "King Faisal and Pan-Islamism," in Willard A. Beling, ed. *King Faisal and the Modernization of Saudi Arabia* (London: Croom Helm, 1980), p. 188.

97. Jacob Goldberg, "Shii Minority in Saudi Arabia," Juan R. I. Cole and Nikki R. Keddie, eds. *Shiism and Social Protest* (New Haven: Yale University Press, 1986), p. 243.

98. Muhammad Nuwayhi, "A Revolution in Religious Thought," in *Islam in Transition*, p. 161.

99. Hassan al-Turabi, "The Islamic State," in *Voices of Resurgent Islam*, p. 245.

100. Abul Ala Mawdudi, *Purdah and the Status of Women in Islam*, translated and edited by al-Ashari (Lahore, Pakistan: Islamic Publications, 1972), pp. 200–01.

101. John Alden Williams, "Veiling in Egypt as a Political and Social Phenomenon," in *Islam and Development: Religion and Sociopolitical Change*, John L. Esposito, ed. (Syracuse, N.Y.: Syracuse University Press, 1980), p. 83.

102. Valerie J. Hoffman-Ladd, "Polemics on the Modesty and Segregation of Women in Comtemporary Egypt," *The International Journal of Middle East Studies* 19 (1987), pp. 23–50.

103. Naila Minai, *Women in Islam: Tradition and Transition in the Middle East* (New York: Seaview Books, 1981), pp. 228–29.

104. Ali Shariati, "Intizar, the Religion of Protest," in *Islam in Transition*, p. 297.

105. Al-Sadiq al-Mahdi, "Islam—Society and Change," in *Voices of Resurgent Islam*, p. 239.

106. Hassan al-Turabi, "The Islamic State," in *Voices of Resurgent Islam*, pp. 249–50.

107. Dale F. Eickelman, "The Study of Islam in Local Contexts," *Asian Studies* Vol. XVII (1982), p. 12.

SELECT BIBLIOGRAPHY

Reference Works

Adams, Charles J. "Islam," in *A Reader's Guide to the Great Religions*, 2nd ed. Charles J. Adams, ed. (New York: Free Press, 1977).

Ali, Muhammad. *A Manual of Hadith*, 2nd ed. (Lahore, Pakistan: Ahmadiyyah Anjuman Ishaat Islam, n.d.).

Gibb, H. A. R., and J. H. Kramers, *Shorter Encyclopedia of Islam* (Ithaca, N.Y.: Cornell University Press, 1953).

Gibb, H. A. R., and J. H. Kramers, et al. *The Encyclopedia of Islam*, 2nd ed. (Leiden: E. J. Brill, 1954–).

Holt, P. M., Ann K. S. Lambton, and Bernard Lewis, eds. *Cambridge History of Islam* (Cambridge: Cambridge University Press, 1970).

Hughes, Thomas Patrick. *A Dictionary of Islam* (London: W. H. Allen, 1953).

Khan, Muhammad Muhsin. *The Translation of the Meanings of Sahih al-Bukhari*, 9 vols, 3rd rev. ed. (Chicago: Kazi Publications, 1979).

Littlefield, David W. *The Islamic Near East and North Africa: An Annotated Guide to Books in English for Non-Specialists* (Littleton, Col.: Libraries Unlimited, 1977).

Mishkat al-Masabih, 4 vols., James Robson, trans. (Lahore, Pakistan: Sh. Muhammad Ashraf, 1964–1966).

Pearson, J. D., comp. *Index Islamicus* (Cambridge: W. Heffer, 1958–).

Sahih Muslim, Abdul Hamid Siddiqi, trans. (Lahore, Pakistan: Sh. Muhammad Ashraf, 1971–1973).

Weekes, Richard V., ed. *Muslim Peoples: A World Ethnographic Survey* (Westport, Conn.: Greenwood Press, 1978).

Translations of the Quran

Ali, A. Yusuf. *The Koran: Text, Translation and Commentary* (Washington, D.C.: American International Printing Company, 1946).

Arberry, A. J. *The Koran Interpreted* (London: Allen & Unwin, 1955; New York: Macmillan, 1964).

Asad, Muhammad, *The Message of the Quran* (Gilbraltar: Dar al-Andalus, 1980).

Bell, Richard. *The Quran, Translated with a Critical Rearrangement of the Surahs*, 2 vols. (Edinburgh: T. T. Clark, 1937–1939).

Dawood, N. J. *The Koran* (Baltimore: Penguin Books, 1961).

Irving, T. B. *The Quran* (Brattleboro, Vt.: Amana Books, 1985).

Pickthall, Mohammed Marmaduke. *The Meaning of the Glorious Koran* (New York: New American Library and Mentor Books, n.d.).

Secondary Sources

Abdalati, Hammudah. *Islam in Focus* (Indianapolis: Islamic Trust Publications, 1977).

Abduh, Muhammad. *The Theology of Unity*, Kenneth Cragg and Ishaq Musa'ad, trans. (New York: Humanities Press, 1966).

Ahmad, Mumtaz, ed. *State Politics and Islam* (Indianapolis: American Trust Publications, 1988).

Anwar, Zainah. *Islamic Revivalism in Malaysia: Dakwah Among the Student* (Selangor, Malaysia: Pelanduk Publications, 1987).

Arberry, A. J. *An Introduction to the History of Sufism* (London: Longman, 1942).

———. *Sufism: An Account of the Mystics of Islam* (New York: Harper Torchbooks, 1970).

Arjomand, Said Amir, ed. *Authority and Political Culture in Shi'ism* (Albany: State University of New York, 1988).

Azami, Muhammad Mustafa. *Studies in Early Hadith Literature*, 2nd ed. (Indianapolis: American Trust Publications, 1978).

Bakhash, Shaul. *The Reign of the Ayatollahs: Iran and the Islamic Revolution* (New York: Basic Books, 1986).

Baljon, John. *Modern Muslim Koran Interpretation* (Leiden: E. J. Brill, 1961).

Bannerman, Patrick. *Islam in Perspective: An Introduction to Islamic Society, Politics and Law* (London: Routledge, 1988).

Beck, Lois Grant, and Nikkie R. Keddie, eds. *Women in the Muslim World* (Cambridge, Mass.: Harvard University Press, 1973).

Bell, Richard. *Bell's Introduction to the Qur'an*, revised and edited by W. Montgomery Watt (Edinburgh: Edinburgh University Press, 1970).

Burckhardt, Titus. *An Introduction to Sufi Doctrine*, D. M. Matheson, trans. (Lahore, Pakistan: Sh. Muhammad Ashraf, 1959).

Chittick, William C., ed. and trans. *A Shiite Anthology* (Albany: State University of New York Press, 1981).

Cole, Juan R.I., and Nikki R. Keddie, eds. *Shi'ism and Social Protest* (New Haven: Yale University Press, 1986).

Coulson, Noel J. *A History of Islamic Law* (Edinburgh: Edinburgh University Press, 1964).

Cragg, Kenneth. *Counsels in Contemporary Islam* (Edinburgh: Edinburgh University Press, 1965).

———. *The Event of the Qur'an: Islam in Its Scripture* (London: Allen & Unwin, 1971).

———. *The Mind of the Qur'an: Chapters in Reflection* (London: Allen & Unwin, 1973).

———. *The House of Islam* (Belmont, Calif.: Wadsworth, 1975).

———. *Readings in the Quran* (London: Collins, 1988).

Cragg, Kenneth, and R. Marston Speight, eds. *Islam from Within: Anthology of a Religion* (Belmont, Calif.: Wadsworth, 1980).

Denny, Frederick M. *An Introduction to Islam* (New York: Macmillan, 1985).

Donohue, John J., and John L. Esposito, eds. *Islam in Transition: Muslim Perspectives* (New York: Oxford University Press, 1982).

Donner, Fred McGraw. *The Early Islamic Conquests* (Princeton, N.J.: Princeton University Press, 1981).

Enayat, Hamid. *Modern Islamic Political Thought* (Austin, Tex.: The University of Texas Press, 1982).

Esposito, John L. *Women in Muslim Family Law* (Syracuse, N.Y.: Syracuse University Press, 1982).

_____, ed. *Voices of Resurgent Islam* (New York: Oxford University Press, 1983).

_____, ed. *Islam in Asia: Religion, Politics, and Society* (New York: Oxford University Press, 1987).

_____. *Islam and Politics*, 2nd ed. (Syracuse, N.Y.: Syracuse University Press, 1987).

Fernea, Elizabeth Warnock, and Basima Qattan Bezirgan, eds. *Middle Eastern Women Speak* (Austin: University of Texas Press, 1987).

Fyzee, Asaf Ali Asghar. *Outlines of Muhammadan Law*, 3rd ed. (London: Oxford University Press, 1964).

Gatje, Helmut. *The Qur'an and Its Exegesis*, Alford T. Welch, trans. (London: Routledge and Kegan Paul, 1976).

Gibb, H. A. R. *Modern Trends in Islam* (Chicago: University of Chicago Press, 1947).

_____. *Mohammedanism: An Historical Survey*, 2nd ed. (New York: Oxford University Press, 1962).

Gilsenan, Michael. *Saint and Sufi in Modern Egypt: An Essay in the Sociology of Religion* (Oxford: Clarendon Press, 1973).

Goldziher, Ignaz. *Muslim Studies Muhammedanische Studien*, S. M. Stern and C. R. Barber, trans. (Chicago: Aldine, 1966).

_____. *Introduction to Islamic Theology and Law*, Andras and Ruth Hamori, trans. (Princeton, N.J.: Princeton University Press, 1981).

Graham, William A. *Divine Word and Prophetic Word in Early Islam* (The Hague and Paris: Mouton, 1977).

Haddad, Yvonne Yazbeck. *Contemporary Islam and the Challenge of History* (Albany: State University of New York Press, 1982).

Haddad, Yvonne Y., Byron Haines, and Ellison Findly, eds. *The Islamic Impact* (Syracuse: Syracuse University Press, 1984).

Haddad, Yvonne Yazbeck, and Adair T. Lummis. *Islamic Values in the U.S.: A Comparative Study* (New York: Oxford University Press, 1986).

Hamidullah, Muhammad. *Muslim Conduct of State*, 7th ed. (Lahore, Pakistan: Sh. Muhammad Ashraf, 1977).

Haneef, Suzanne. *What Everyone Should Know About Islam and Muslims* (Chicago: Kazi Publications, 1982).

Haykal, Muhammad Husayn. *The Life of Muhammad*, Ismail R. al-Faruqi, trans. (Indianapolis: American Trust Publications, 1976).

Hiro, Dilip. *Islamic Fundamentalism* (London: Paladin Grafton Books, 1988).

Hitti, Philip K. *History of the Arabs*, 9th ed. (New York: St. Martin's Press, 1967).

Hodgson, Marshall G. S. *The Venture of Islam: Conscience and History in a World Civilization*, 3 vols. (Chicago: University of Chicago Press, 1974).

Hourani, Albert. *Arabic Thought in the Liberal Age, 1798–1939* (London: Oxford University Press, 1962).

Hunter, Shireen. *The Politics of Islamic Revivalism: Diversity and Unity* (Bloomington, Ind.: Indiana University Press, 1988).

Hussain, Jassim M. *The Occultation of the Twelfth Imam* (London: The Muhammadi Trust, 1982).

Ibn Ishaq. *The Life of Muhammad,* Alfred Guillaume, trans. (London: Oxford University Press, 1967).

Iqbal, Sir Muhammad. *The Reconstruction of Religious Thought in Islam* (Lahore, Pakistan: Sh. Muhammad Ashraf, 1951).

Izutsu, Toshihiko. *God and Man in the Koran: Semantics of the Koranic Weltanschauung* (Tokyo: Keio Institute of Cultural and Linguistic Studies, 1964).

_____. *Ethico-Religious Concepts in the Quran* (Montreal: McGill University Press, 1966).

Jafri, S. H. M. *The Origins and Early Development of Shia Islam* (London and New York: Longman, 1979).

Jansen, J. J. G. *The Interpretation of the Koran in Modern Egypt* (Leiden: E. J. Brill, 1974).

Jeffrey, Arthur. *The Qur'an as Scripture* (New York: Russell F. Moore, 1957).

_____, ed. *Islam: Muhammad and His Religion* (New York: Liberal Arts Press, 1958).

_____. *A Reader on Islam: Passages from Standard Arabic Writings Illustrative of the Beliefs and Practices of Muslims* (The Hague: Mouton, 1962).

Jomier, Jacques. *The Bible and the Koran* (Chicago: Henry Regnery, 1967).

Juynboll, G. H. A. *The Authenticity of the Tradition Literature* (Leiden: E. J. Brill, 1969).

Kamal, Ahmad. *The Sacred Journey, Being a Pilgrimage to Mecca* (New York: Duell, Sloan and Pearce, 1961).

Kateregga, Badru David, and W. Shenk. *Islam and Christianity* (Grand Rapids, Mich.: William B. Eerdmans, 1980).

Kepel, Giles. *Muslim Extremism in Egypt: The Prophet and the Pharaoh* (Berkeley: University of California Press, 1986).

Kerr, Malcolm H. *Islamic Reform: The Political and Legal Theories of Muhammad Abduh and Rashid Rida* (Berkeley: University of California Press, 1966).

Khadduri, Majid. *War and Peace in the Law of Islam* (Baltimore: Johns Hopkins University Press, 1955).

Lapidus, Ira. *A History of Islamic Societies* (Cambridge and New York: Cambridge University Press, 1988).

Levy, Reuben. *The Social Structure of Islam* (Cambridge: Cambridge University Press, 1957).

Lings, Martin. *A Sufi Saint of the Twentieth Century* (Berkeley: University of California Press, 1973).

_____. *What is Sufism?* (Berkeley: University of California Press, 1977; New York: Oxford University Press, 1973).

_____. *Muhammad* (New York: Inner Traditions International, 1983).

MacDonald, Duncan Black. *The Religious Attitude and Life in Islam* (New York: AMS Press, 1970).

Martin, Richard C. *Islam: A Cultural Perspective* (Englewood Cliffs, N.J.: Prentice-Hall, 1982).

Massignon, Louis. *The Passion of al-Hallaj: Mystical Martyr of Islam*, 4 vols., H. Mason, trans. (Princeton, N.J.: Princeton University Press, 1983).

Mawdudi, Abul Ala. *The Meaning of the Qur'an* (Lahore, Pakistan: Sh. Muhammad Ashraf, 1967).

_____. *Let Us Be Muslims*, Khurram Murad, ed. (Leicester, England: The Islamic Foundation, 1985).

McNeil, William H., and Marilyn R. Waldman, eds. *The Islamic World* (Chicago: University of Chicago Press, 1983).

Minai, Naila. *Women in Islam* (New York: Seaview Books, 1981).

Momen, Moojan. *An Introduction to Shii Islam* (New Haven, Conn.: Yale University Press, 1985).

Mottahedeh, Roy. *The Mantle of the Prophet: Religion and Politics in Iran* (New York: Simon and Schuster, 1985).

Munson, Henry, Jr. *Islam and Revolution in the Middle East* (New Haven, Conn.: Yale University Press, 1988).

Nagata, Judith. *The Reflowering of Malaysian Islam* (Vancouver: University of British Columbia Press, 1984).

Nanji, Azim. *The Nizari Ismaili Tradition in the Indo-Pakistan Subcontinent* (New York: Caravan Books, 1978).

Nasr, Seyyed Hossein. *Three Muslim Sages: Avicenna, Suhrawardi, Ibn 'Arabi* (Cambridge, Mass.: Harvard University Press, 1964).

_____. *Ideals and Realities of Islam* (Boston: Beacon Press, 1972).

_____. *Sufi Essays* (London: Allen & Unwin, 1972).

_____. *Islamic Life and Thought* (Albany: State University of New York Press, 1981).

_____, ed. *Islamic Spirituality* (New York: Crossroads, 1987).

Nicholson, Reynold A. *Rumi: Poet and Mystic* (London: Allen & Unwin, 1950).

_____. *The Mystics of Islam* (London: Routledge and Kegan Paul, 1966).

_____. *Studies in Islamic Mysticism* (Cambridge: Cambridge University Press, 1973).

Padwick, Constance E. *Muslim Devotions: A Study of Prayer Manuals in Common Use* (London: S.P.C.K., 1961).

Parrinder, Geoffrey. *Jesus in the Qur'an* (New York: Oxford University Press, 1977).

Peters, F. E. *Allah's Commonwealth: A History of the Near East 600–1100 A.D.* (New York: Simon and Schuster, 1973).

_____. *Children of Abraham* (Princeton, N.J.: Princeton University Press, 1982).

Qaradawi, Yusuf al-. *The Lawful and the Prohibited in Islam* (Indianapolis: American Trust Publications, n.d.).

Rahman, Fazlur. *Islam*, 2nd ed. (Chicago: University of Chicago Press, 1979).

_____. *Major Themes of the Qur'an* (Minneapolis and Chicago: Bibliotheca Islamica, 1980).

_____. *Islam and Modernity: The Transformation of an Intellectual Tradition* (Chicago: University of Chicago Press, 1982).

Rauf, Muhammad Abdul. *Islam: Creed and Worship* (Washington, D.C.: The Islamic Center, 1974).

_____. *The Islamic View of Women and the Family* (New York: Robert Speller, 1977).

Rippin, Andrew and Jan Knappert. *Textual Sources for the Study of Islam* (Totowa, N.J.: Barnes & Noble, 1987).

Rodinson, Maxime. *Mohammed*, Anne Carter, trans. (New York: Vintage Books, 1974).

Ruthven, Malise. *Islam and the World* (London: Penguin, 1984).

Sachedina, Abdulaziz. Islamic Messianism (Albany: State University of New York Press, 1981).

Savory, R.M., ed. *Introduction to Islamic Civilization* (Cambridge: Cambridge University Press, 1976).

Schacht, Joseph. *An Introduction to Islamic Law* (Oxford: Clarendon Press, 1964).

Schacht, Joseph, with C. E. Bosworth, eds. *The Legacy of Islam*, 2nd ed. (Oxford: Clarendon Press, 1974).

Schimmel, Annemarie. *Mystical Dimensions of Islam* (Chapel Hill: University of North Carolina Press, 1975).

_____. *The Triumphal Sun: A Study of the Works of Jalaluddin Rumi*, rev. ed. (London and the Hague: East-West Publications, 1980).

_____. *And Muhammad Is His Messenger* (Chapel Hill: University of North Carolina Press, 1985).

Schimmel, Annemarie, and Abdoldjavad Falsturi, eds. *We Believe in One God* (New York: Seabury Press, 1979).

Al-Shafii, Muhammad ibn Idris. *Islamic Jurisprudence: Shafii's Risala*, Majid Khadduri, trans. (Baltimore: Johns Hopkins University Press, 1961).

Smith, Jane I. *An Historical and Semantic Study of the Term "Islam" as Seen in a Sequence of Qur'an Commentaries* (Missoula, Mont.: Scholars Press, 1975).

Smith, Jane Idleman, and Yvonne Yazbeck Haddad. *The Islamic Understanding of Death and Resurrection* (Albany: State University of New York Press, 1981).

Smith, Margaret. *Rabia the Mystic and Her Fellow Saints in Islam* (Cambridge: Cambridge University Press, 1928).

Smith, Wilfred Cantwell. *Islam in Modern History* (Princeton, N.J.: Princeton University Press, 1957).

Stowasser, Barbara Freyer, ed. *The Islamic Impulse* (Washington, D.C.: Georgetown University CCAS, 1987).

Tabatabai, Allamah Sayyid Muhammad Husayn. *Shiite Islam*, Sayyid Husayn Nasr, trans. (Houston: Free Islamic Literatures, n.d.).

Tabatabai, Hossein Moderressi. *An Introduction to Shii Law* (London: Ithaca Press, 1984).

Trimingham, J. Spencer. *The Sufi Orders in Islam* (Oxford: Oxford University Press, 1971).

Voll, John Obert. *Islam: Continuity and Change in the Modern World* (Boulder, Col.: Westview Press, 1982).

Von Grunebaum, Gustave E. *Medieval Islam* (Chicago: University of Chicago Press, 1953).

_____. *Muhammadan Festivals* (New York: Henry Schuman, 1958).

Watt, W. Montgomery. *Free Will and Predestination in Early Islam* (London: Luzac, 1948).

_____. *The Faith and Practice of al-Ghazali* (London: Allen & Unwin, 1953).

_____. *Muhammad: Prophet and Statesman* (London: Oxford University Press, 1961).

_____. *Islamic Philosophy and Theology* (Edinburgh: Edinburgh University Press, 1962).

_____. *The Formative Period of Islamic Thought* (Edinburgh: Edinburgh University Press, 1973).

_____. *Islam and Christianity Today* (London: Routledge and Kegan Paul, 1983).

Williams, John Alden, ed. *Islam* (New York: George Braziller, 1961).

_____. *Themes of Islamic Civilization* (Berkeley: University of California Press, 1971).

Wolfson, Harry Austryn. *The Philosophy of the Kalam* (Cambridge, Mass.: Harvard University Press, 1976).

Index